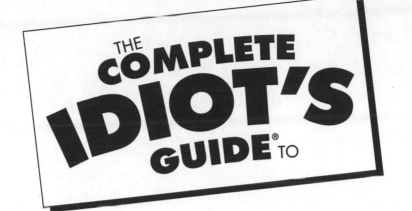

THE COMPLETE IDIOT'S GUIDE® TO

Learning Spanish

Fourth Edition

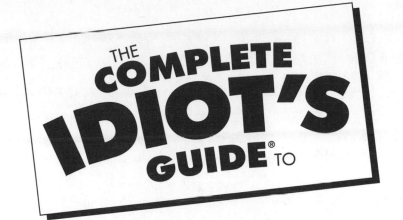

THE COMPLETE IDIOT'S GUIDE® TO

Learning Spanish

Fourth Edition

by Gail Stein

ALPHA

A member of Penguin Group (USA) Inc.

ALPHA BOOKS

Published by the Penguin Group

Penguin Group (USA) Inc., 375 Hudson Street, New York, New York 10014, USA

Penguin Group (Canada), 90 Eglinton Avenue East, Suite 700, Toronto, Ontario M4P 2Y3, Canada (a division of Pearson Penguin Canada Inc.)

Penguin Books Ltd., 80 Strand, London WC2R 0RL, England

Penguin Ireland, 25 St. Stephen's Green, Dublin 2, Ireland (a division of Penguin Books Ltd.)

Penguin Group (Australia), 250 Camberwell Road, Camberwell, Victoria 3124, Australia (a division of Pearson Australia Group Pty. Ltd.)

Penguin Books India Pvt. Ltd., 11 Community Centre, Panchsheel Park, New Delhi—110 017, India

Penguin Group (NZ), 67 Apollo Drive, Rosedale, North Shore, Auckland 1311, New Zealand (a division of Pearson New Zealand Ltd.)

Penguin Books (South Africa) (Pty.) Ltd., 24 Sturdee Avenue, Rosebank, Johannesburg 2196, South Africa

Penguin Books Ltd., Registered Offices: 80 Strand, London WC2R 0RL, England

Copyright © 2006 by Gail Stein

International Standard Book Number: 978-1-59257-485-8
Library of Congress Catalog Card Number: 2005938261

09 08 07   8 7 6 5 4 3

Interpretation of the printing code: The rightmost number of the first series of numbers is the year of the book's printing; the rightmost number of the second series of numbers is the number of the book's printing. For example, a printing code of 06-1 shows that the first printing occurred in 2006.

Printed in the United States of America

Note: This publication contains the opinions and ideas of its author. It is intended to provide helpful and informative material on the subject matter covered. It is sold with the understanding that the author and publisher are not engaged in rendering professional services in the book. If the reader requires personal assistance or advice, a competent professional should be consulted.

The author and publisher specifically disclaim any responsibility for any liability, loss, or risk, personal or otherwise, which is incurred as a consequence, directly or indirectly, of the use and application of any of the contents of this book.

Most Alpha books are available at special quantity discounts for bulk purchases for sales promotions, premiums, fund-raising, or educational use. Special books, or book excerpts, can also be created to fit specific needs.

For details, write: Special Markets, Alpha Books, 375 Hudson Street, New York, NY 10014.

Publisher: *Marie Butler-Knight*
Editorial Director: *Mike Sanders*
Senior Managing Editor: *Jennifer Bowles*
Senior Acquisitions Editor: *Paul Dinas*
Development Editor: *Christy Wagner*
Senior Production Editor: *Billy Fields*
Copy Editor: *Keith Cline*

Cartoonist: *Shannon Wheeler*
Cover Designer: *Bill Thomas*
Book Designer: *Trina Wurst*
Indexer: *Brad Herriman*
Layout: *Becky Harmon*
Proofreading: *Donna Martin*

This book is dedicated to:
My tremendously patient and supportive husband, Douglas
My incredibly loving and understanding children: Eric, Michael, and Katherine
My proud parents, Jack and Sara Bernstein

Contents at a Glance

Contents

Appendixes

Foreword

The Complete Idiot's Guide to Learning Spanish [now in its fourth edition] is an easy-going, self-teaching guide that provides the student of Spanish with the necessary tools to learn and assimilate information that will enable the student to interact effectively in a Spanish-speaking context.

Each chapter deals dynamically with practical grammatical aspects that help build one's vocabulary and language structures. In addition, this book focuses on the cultural nuances that are often neglected when learning a foreign language. Thus, the student not only learns the linguistic system of Spanish but also the cultural subtleties, namely, common idiomatic expressions and body language pertinent to Spanish. All these elements are essential to avoid being misunderstood or frustrated when visiting a Spanish-speaking country and communicating with native speakers.

Gregory D. Lagos-Montoya

Gregory D. Lagos-Montoya is a visiting professor of Spanish linguistics at Rutgers University and professor of contrastive linguistics at Universidad de Los Lagos, Osorno-Chile.

Introduction

Today, more than ever, knowledge of at least one foreign language is essential for both business-related and pleasurable pursuits. Sophisticated improvements in travel and communication have made the world our neighborhood. The world is now accessible to everyone: to you, to me, and to the generations that will follow.

Learn Spanish, and you enter a world that can provide you with endless opportunities, intriguing experiences, and exciting challenges. Learn Spanish, and you have the key to open the door to a different lifestyle, a distinctive culture, and a unique outlook on life. Learn Spanish, and you possess a valuable tool that will serve you well when you least expect it. Open your mind and immerse yourself in the beauty of the language and the culture. Study Spanish purposefully, with patience and love. You will be rewarded again and again.

Right from the start, you'll feel that this book was written with *you* in mind. It is extremely user-friendly and will make your language learning experience pleasant, satisfying, and entertaining. You'll find the approach easygoing and clear-cut, enabling you to start communicating almost instantly with a reasonable amount of skill and an encouraging sense of achievement.

In addition, in this revised and updated fourth edition, I've included a state-of-the-art, up-to-the-minute interactive CD to supplement the text in the book. The CD's cutting-edge digital technology enables you to learn the language in a fun way: more quickly and more efficiently.

How This Book Is Organized

This book takes you from basic material to a deeper understanding of the patterns of the Spanish language and finally to a higher level of expertise and accomplishment. This book is unique—it is a phrase book, a grammar book, a cultural guide, and a dictionary all wrapped up in one. Its goal is to enable you to handle common, everyday situations proficiently and competently. Whether you're a student, a traveler, a businessperson, or simply a lover of languages, this book provides you with the knowledge and skills you need in a format that is simple to understand and easy to use. Thematically linked vocabulary, useful expressions, grammar, and practical activities for mastery and enrichment are presented in every chapter. Authentic materials immerse you in the Spanish culture and give you a thorough understanding of the people. Here's what you can expect to find in this book.

Part 1, "The Basics," shows you why Spanish is a language you should learn. The simple, phonetic pronunciation guides will have you pronouncing the language properly almost immediately. You'll also see how much Spanish you already know based on your knowledge of English. Don't fret over grammar—basic, elementary terms and rules are painlessly presented along with high-frequency idioms, slang, and gestures indigenous to the culture. Right from the start, you'll be asking and answering simple questions and even engaging in basic conversations.

Part 2, "Traveling Around," enables you to plan and take a trip to a Spanish-speaking country. When it's time to introduce yourself, you'll be able to use greetings and salutations, describe yourself and others traveling with you, and talk about your job. If you're the curious type, asking questions will prove easy. The chapters in Part 2 can help you find your way to the airport, obtain necessary ground transportation, and even rent a car. Don't worry about giving or receiving directions; I explain that. Finally, Part 2 helps you acquire a room with the creature comforts you prefer.

Part 3, "Having Fun," enables you to go out and have a great time in any Spanish-speaking country. Everything that makes for a superb experience is covered in this part: food, sports, museums, tourist attractions, musical events, and leisure activities. You learn to plan your daily activities around the weather, offer suggestions, and make your opinions and preferences known. The food chapters can help you stick to your diet or go all out. If you love to shop, one of the chapters can help you buy anything from typical native handicrafts to a tropical Guayabera shirt. Conversion charts for sizing clothes are provided to help you make correct selections.

Part 4, "Problem-Solving," prepares you not only for simple, minor inconveniences, but also for problems that are more serious in nature. Consult this part when you need a haircut, a stain removed, your camera fixed, a replacement contact lens, new heels on your shoes, prescription drugs, or a package sent.

I wrote **Part 5, "Taking Care of Business,"** to meet the needs of people who want to conduct business transactions: making deposits and withdrawals, opening a checking account, and taking out a loan. A mini-dictionary of bank terms is included. There's also a section of computer terms and phrases, as well as a section to help you rent or buy property and discuss your present and future needs.

What's on the CD

You can listen to this book, too! Get your pronunciation right.

As an addition to the fourth edition, I've included a supplemental CD in the back of the book to make your Spanish-learning experience more complete and satisfying by providing you with a wealth of additional information and exercises.

Actually, I've discovered new software that will make the book live for you. Download the CD on your computer (the software is included free), and you will have an AV Book® of the book. You will hear Spanish spoken as native Spanish speak so you can work on your pronunciation and learn to understand the language as it is spoken.

You can scan chapters, flip through them with ease, and search for the information or explanations you need. Anything in the book will be at your fingertips in a flash. You can highlight passages and save your personal margin notes on the computer.

Here's some of what you can expect to find on the CD:

- An unabridged MP3 AV Book® of this book.

- The full text of the book.

- "Supplemental Exercises": a section full of supplemental, interactive exercises to help you master and perfect your knowledge of Spanish in an enjoyable yet challenging way.

- "Cultural Tidbits": a culture section that explains what makes the Spanish-speaking world tick.

If you persevere and study this book from cover to cover—and the CD—you will learn and practice skills that will enable you to be confident in both social and business situations where Spanish is required. If you have the time and the patience and are willing to make the effort, you can successfully communicate in a new and beautiful language in a relatively short period of time.

Extras

In addition to grammatical explanations, useful phrases and expressions, and vocabulary lists, this book provides a wealth of interesting and informative facts formatted throughout the text as sidebars. Look for the following icons that set these tidbits apart:

In a Flash

These notes feature tips for learning and perfecting your Spanish in a fast, fun way.

Memory Master

These boxes help you quickly understand grammar or refresh your memory with rules from previous chapters.

¡Atención!

Read these warnings to avoid making unnecessary or embarrassing mistakes.

How to Use This Book and CD

This book and its accompanying CD are tailor-made for you, whether you're a beginner or a more seasoned Spanish student; whether you're learning for business or for pleasure; or whether you're trying to perfect oral, reading, or writing skills. Let's take a quick look at the various sections in each chapter:

- The conversational introductory paragraphs help you understand—by means of personal, funny, anecdotal examples—why you may need the upcoming information.

- The extensive vocabulary lists offer a wide choice of words you may need in any given particular situation. These lists are ideal for reference: they are *not* meant to be memorized in their entirety. Choose only the words you think you'll need, and concentrate on learning them. The others will be at your fingertips just in case you have to rely on them. You never know when they might come in handy.

- The grammar is presented with concise, clear-cut explanations and examples. Your goal should be to develop an understanding of the rules that make Spanish work, so you can apply them automatically without agonizing over awkward, oftentimes incomprehensible literal translations that don't make the grade. You only need a basic knowledge of grammar before you can communicate on a level where you can be understood and can understand what is said to you. The more you listen to and speak Spanish, the quicker the grammar rules will fall into place and become an internalized part of the communicative process, in much the same way as they did when you were learning your native language as a child.

◆ Authentic reading materials give you an idea of what you might encounter in a variety of situations in a Spanish-speaking country: from general information contained in a tourist brochure, to directions to a monument, to instructions on how to get things to work properly, to newspaper ads and weather reports. Use these selections to perfect your comprehension skills. While reading, remember that it's unreasonable to expect to recognize and understand each and every word. A more reasonable goal is to be able to get the gist of what you've read and to be able to use it to your advantage.

◆ Writing exercises, many based upon authentic materials, are provided to reinforce grammar rules and allow you to use what you've internalized to the fullest. As your listening, speaking, and reading skills improve, so will your ability to write. Bear in mind that, as in any language, the more you read, the better you will write.

How should you use this book? The simple answer is: in any way that will help you achieve the goals you've set for yourself.

Acknowledgments

The author would like to acknowledge the contributions, input, support, and interest of the following people: John Aliano; Trecia Ashman; Charles Bowles; Héctor Cardwood, head pastry chef of the San Juan Marriott; María Chin and Brenda D'vila of the San Juan Marriott; Nancy Chu; Micqual Coaxum; Gabriel Cruz; Trudy and Richard Edelman; Marc Einsohn; Raymond C. Elias; Angela Felipe; Barbara Gilson; Michelle and Stephen Gordon; Robert Grandt; Martin S. Hyman; Martin Leder; Christina Levy; Anne Marie Loffredo; Justin Mark; Marion Meitner; Robby Menke; Jennifer Nicholson; Violetta Ostafin; Liseth Prado; Catherine Ramai; Max Rechtman; Cynthia Reyes; Dr. Angel Rueda; Mary Russell; Barbara Shevrin; Maritza Trujillo; Herbert Waldren; Tywonne Wesley.

About the Author

Gail Stein, M.A., is a retired language instructor who taught in New York City public junior and senior high schools for more than 33 years. She has authored several books about French and Spanish, including *The Complete Idiot's Guide to Spanish; The Pocket Idiot's Guide to French; The Pocket Idiot's Guide to Spanish Phrases; The Complete Idiot's Guide to French Verbs; The Complete Idiot's Guide to Spanish Verbs;* the *French Is Fun* series; the *French Practice and Testing* series; French first-, second-, and third-year review books; the *Spanish Practice and Testing* series; and *French at a Glance*. She helped write *Salon Stories: The Best Kept Secrets*, a book for the beauty industry, and is currently co-authoring a medical book. Gail has also assisted in a revision project of the French curriculum for the New York City Board of Education and has served as an adjunct professor to St. John's University in its Early Admission Extension Program. She has given presentations and demonstration lessons at numerous foreign-language conferences and has had her lessons videotaped by the New York City Board of Education for national distribution. Gail Stein's name appears in *Who's Who Among America's Teachers* for the years 2000, 2002, and 2004.

Special Thanks to the Technical Reviewer

The Complete Idiot's Guide to Learning Spanish, Fourth Edition, was reviewed by an expert who double-checked the accuracy of what you'll learn here, to help us ensure that this book gives you everything you need to know about learning Spanish. Special thanks are extended to Clark M. Zlotchew.

Clark M. Zlotchew, Ph.D. in romance languages and literatures, teaches Spanish language, linguistics, and Hispanic literature at SUNY College at Fredonia, New York. He has had a dozen published works, ranging from literary criticism to translations from Spanish and interviews with Latin American writers. His latest books are the second edition of *Alpha Teach Yourself Spanish in 24 Hours* (2004) and a military/action novel under a pen name.

Trademarks

All terms mentioned in this book that are known to be or are suspected of being trademarks or service marks have been appropriately capitalized. Alpha Books and Penguin Group (USA) Inc. cannot attest to the accuracy of this information. Use of a term in this book should not be regarded as affecting the validity of any trademark or service mark.

Part 1

The Basics

Truth be told, the fastest, easiest, most efficient way to pick up Spanish is to start with basic grammar. Just learn a few simple rules—that's all it takes!

The thought of learning grammar probably sounds like an immediate turn-off. Nonsense! Don't let it be! The rules are quite simple, and I won't overtax your memorization skills. You'll also learn how to speak idiomatically so you don't sound like an inexperienced *gringo* (American speaker). Take the plunge—you'll soon be able to understand and to communicate in Spanish with confidence and ease.

Why You Should Study Spanish

In This Chapter

◆ What Spanish has to offer

◆ Tips for learning Spanish

◆ Ways to study and succeed

◆ Twenty important phrases

If you haven't already purchased this book, you're probably leafing through it wondering, *Can I* really *do this?* No doubt you're deciding whether you'll have the time, whether you have what it takes to stick with it, and whether, indeed, it'll pay off in the end. Just like David Letterman on late-night television, I'm going to give my top 10 reasons why you should study Spanish:

10. You want to impress your date at a Spanish restaurant by ordering in Spanish.

9. You loved the movie *Man of La Mancha* so much you want to read *Don Quijote* in its original language.

8. When you meet Paloma Picasso on the street, you want to be able to ask her questions she'll understand.

7. You want to buy time-share property on the beach in Puerto Rico.

6. When you get pulled over for speeding in Tijuana, you don't want to wind up in jail.

5. You want to study flamenco dancing in Madrid.

4. You can get a discount on Cuban cigars if you order them *en español*.

3. You want to sing along with Richie Valens when they play "La Bamba" on the oldies station.

2. You want to run with the bulls in Pamplona, but they don't understand English.

1. One word: *Cancún*.

Seriously Speaking

Now that we've had a little fun, it's time to seriously consider why you should study Spanish. Let's take a look at some more credible reasons:

10. You love music, especially music with a Latin beat.

9. You love to dance, especially salsa!

8. You're an aficionado of Spanish movies, and you really would enjoy watching them without having to read the distracting, poorly translated, and sometimes invisible subtitles.

7. You're an artist at heart.

6. You definitely are not money-hungry, but you'd like to improve your chances in the job market.

5. You want to live in a warm climate, and the countries in Spanish America have a lot to offer: beautiful landscape, friendly people, delicious food—and you won't need an expensive winter wardrobe.

4. Speaking of food, you love to cook.

3. You hate to cook but you love to eat, and you like everything hot and spicy.

2. You want to prove to yourself that you are smart enough to learn a new language.

1. You're a traveler.

Tips for the Beginner

For beginners, learning a foreign language must seem like an intimidating task. There is so much to learn: proper pronunciation, vocabulary, grammar. How and where does one begin? Here are a few do's and don'ts to get you started:

Do …

♦ Start by concentrating on the pronunciation guide. Practicing and mastering the sounds of the language first will make the chapters that follow easier to master.

♦ Examine your immediate language goals, and focus on them. If you plan on traveling, learn the vocabulary and expressions you'll use on your trip. If you're a student, pay more attention to grammatical structures and verb conjugations. If you're a businessperson, familiarize yourself with the words and phrases that will lead to a successful deal.

♦ Learn the basics first, especially the idiosyncrasies of the language that make it different from English: the fact that nouns have a masculine or feminine gender, the fact that adjectives must agree in number and gender with the nouns and pronouns they modify and that they are generally placed after these words, and the differing irregular verbs.

♦ Enjoy your learning experience. Take your time. Study one small segment at a time until you've mastered it.

Don't …

♦ Be intimidated by the amount of material in a chapter. You certainly aren't expected to learn or retain it all even after you've made significant progress. Use this book and CD as resources and reference guides, and visit and revisit the most personally challenging and useful material repeatedly until you feel comfortable with it. Over time, you'll find that the chapters become easier and easier as you build upon what you've already mastered.

♦ Feel compelled to be in a rush. This is a book that needs to be studied and restudied. Keep it handy for easy reference.

♦ Be afraid to skip the parts you won't use or you find too difficult at the beginning. You can always pick up the book again at a later date.

♦ Be too hasty to lend this book to a friend, to give it away, or to put it up for sale on your favorite online auction. Even if you feel you've mastered Spanish, you never know when you'll have a simple question to which you can find the answer within these pages.

Tips for Those Who Know Some Spanish

If you've already had the opportunity to study Spanish, you may feel familiar and confident enough with your speaking and linguistic skills to quickly pass over the beginning chapters that cover the bare basics. For you, parts of this book will be a refresher course that will enable you to fine-tune your skills. Here are a few do's and don'ts for those with more intermediate abilities:

Do …

◆ Briefly review what you already know and then spend time perfecting the language skills you'll need the most.

◆ Understand that there's more than one way to express most ideas, and this book provides choices. Select the phrases and expressions that are easiest for you to remember. Concentrate on learning them while keeping in mind that other alternatives exist, should you need them.

◆ Strive to develop your oral and written communication skills as much as possible, for these are most important if you travel or are part of the business world. To speak well, you must listen carefully. To write well, you must concentrate on reading everything you can get your hands on.

◆ Focus on your long-range goals. Ask yourself what you feel you'd like to have accomplished after having read and studied the various chapters in this book.

Don't …

◆ Expect perfection. Native speakers of any language make mistakes without even realizing it.

◆ Worry about your accent and then shy away from communicating. Native speakers will respect and appreciate your attempts at speaking or writing their language, especially if it's foreign to you. And in most instances, native speakers will go out of their way to help you.

◆ Expect to translate word for word from language to language. In most cases, it doesn't work. In a best-case scenario, translating will make your Spanish sound very stilted and awkward. Use idioms and colloquial expressions to speak the way a native would.

◆ Expect to learn every vocabulary word and grammar rule in the book. That's unrealistic and, therefore, frustrating and self-defeating. Whatever you don't learn or can't remember, you can always look up. So just like the beginners, don't give away your copy of *The Complete Idiot's Guide to Learning Spanish*. Let it serve as a constant resource guide.

Go for It!

The best way to become proficient in a language is to plunge right in. Immerse yourself in anything and everything Spanish. Have a love affair with the language and culture. Follow these suggestions to ensure a long-lasting and fulfilling relationship with Spanish:

◆ Examine your goals honestly, evaluate your linguistic abilities, and pace yourself accordingly. Don't rush—take your time studying the language. Set aside a special time each day to devote only to learning Spanish.

◆ Invest in or borrow a good bilingual dictionary. Keep in mind that pocket varieties might be too skimpy and might be inappropriate for learning a new language. Carefully check what's available in your local bookstore or library before purchasing a dictionary. A number of companies publish current, popular, easy-to-use dictionaries that provide comprehensive listings of current, colloquial vocabulary words. (The best dictionaries include those by Simon & Schuster and Larousse.) Find them in any bookstore to fit any size pocketbook.

◆ Take advantage of any opportunities to listen to the language. Rent Spanish movies and try not to read the English subtitles. If they broadcast in your area, listen to public service radio or television stations that provide Spanish programs. In addition, search bookstores and public or college libraries for language tapes that will help you hear and master spoken Spanish. Then try to create your own tapes and use them to perfect your accent. You can also ask to use the language laboratories and computer programs available in many high schools and universities.

◆ Use the CD that accompanies this new edition to perfect your spoken Spanish. Listen to it while you're driving or just sitting home alone with nothing to do, and imitate the speaker to the best of your ability. Immersion is the best way to plunge right in and learn the language in the same manner that native speakers do.

◆ Read everything you can get your hands on, including fairy tales, children's books, and comic books. Try to read Spanish newspapers such as *El Diario*, *El Nuevo Herald*, *La Opinión*, or *Hoy*. If you're not too bashful, read aloud to practice your pronunciation and comprehension at the same time.

◆ Set up *un rincón español* (a Spanish corner) in a convenient place in your home. Decorate it with posters or articles. Label any items whose names you want to learn and display them for easy viewing. Keep all your materials together and organized in this special Spanish spot.

Fear Not!

Some people are truly afraid to study a foreign language. They think it will be too much work, too hard, and too time-consuming. In reality, however, if you take it slowly and don't allow yourself to become overly concerned with the grammar and pronunciation, you'll manage very well. To help you feel more at ease as you begin your task, remember the following points:

In a Flash

Buy a Spanish newspaper. Every day, choose one article that interests you. Underline and make a list of all the words whose meanings you don't recognize. Spend a few minutes each day studying these words. In a week's time, you'll develop an extensive Spanish vocabulary.

◆ Don't be intimidated by grammar. Everyone makes mistakes, even in his or her native language. Besides, only one or two correctly used words (especially verbs) will often enable people to understand you.

◆ Don't be intimidated by pronunciation. Don't be shy: put on your best Spanish accent, and speak, speak, speak. All countries have different regional accents. Certainly yours will fit in somehow.

◆ Don't be intimidated by native speakers. They are usually helpful to anyone who makes a sincere attempt to communicate in their language.

◆ Don't be intimidated by the reputation foreign languages have for being difficult. As you will see right from the start, Spanish is fun and easy.

How to Study

As a more than 33-year veteran New York City public junior high and high school French and Spanish teacher, I have seen and dealt with every type of student imaginable—from those who've gone on to graduate with honors from the finest Ivy League schools to those who have dropped out. Except for the extraordinarily rare individual who defies all odds and excels at a second language without opening a book, the rest of us have to study. Over the years, I compiled a list of suggestions to help students acquire better study habits and to make the task of learning a foreign language more enjoyable. I'll share them with you here because I want you to succeed. Here's my list.

How to Succeed in a Foreign Language Without Really Trying

Let's face it: the overwhelming majority of us don't and can't intuitively learn a foreign language. First things first, understand that you have to study to succeed; there's no getting around it. That said, the more effort you exert, the more rewards you will reap.

♦ You should commit certain key phrases to memory because they will be useful in a tremendous number of situations. For example, *Quisiera* (I would like) can be used to say the following: *Quisiera comer.* (I'd like to eat.) *Quisiera ir a Colombia.* (I'd like to go to Colombia.) *Quisiera comprar esto.* (I'd like to buy this.) *Quisiera una habitación.* (I'd like a room.) Learn the expressions and then plug in the vocabulary word or phrase that fits the circumstances. You'll only need a few key phrases before you'll be able to comfortably communicate in Spanish.

♦ Psychological studies have proven that, for the maximal retention of facts, the optimal times to study are first thing in the morning or right before you go to bed. So keep your *Complete Idiot's Guide* on your night table or the supplemental CD in your laptop next to your bed.

♦ While studying, use as many of your senses as you can. This helps reinforce the new material you've learned in as many ways as possible. Remember, language is acquired in four steps: listening, speaking, reading, and then writing.

♦ Think in Spanish as often as possible. Don't stop to translate. See if you can make yourself formulate your ideas in your second language.

♦ Practice a little every day. Short practice and study periods are much more effective than one long, drawn-out cramming session.

♦ Use what you already know in English to help you communicate and understand Spanish. Many Spanish and English words have the same Latin roots. So if you hear or see words that seem familiar, there's a good chance you'll be able to correctly guess their meaning. Learn and use as many cognates (words that are the same or almost the same in both languages) as you can.

- Be organized. Keep all your language materials together in one place.

- If you can, find a partner who wants to learn the language with you. You'll see rapid results if you work together closely. Practice and test each other regularly.

- The absolute best way to learn and master a foreign language is to teach it to another person. You cannot teach something you don't understand or you don't know well, so if you can teach it, you know it.

Learning Specifics

Pronunciation: If one of your goals is to sound like a native, here are some tips you should follow:

- Listen to everything you can find in Spanish: television and radio shows, films, CDs. The more you listen, the sooner you'll be able to speak the language.

- Speak as much as you can with whomever you can. Don't be shy. If you're alone, record yourself on tape and play it back. Keep your very first tape. Study and practice some more and then re-record yourself. Compare the two tapes to see how much progress you've made.

Vocabulary: Knowing the proper vocabulary words to use in various situations is the key to perfecting good communication skills. Here are some ideas for acquiring the words and phrases you'll use the most:

- Make flashcards for various groups of words (vegetables, hotel words, business terms, and so on). Write the English on one side and the Spanish on the other side of the card. Start with the easier of the two tasks: look at the Spanish word and see if you can give its English meaning. Now for the hard part: look at the English word and see if you can give its Spanish equivalent. Set aside a specific amount of time every day for vocabulary practice.

- Label things in your house (furniture, rooms, food) or your car. This way, you immerse yourself as much as possible in the language and learn as you go through the motions of doing your daily chores.

♦ Fold a sheet of loose-leaf paper into four long columns. Write down in the first column all the English words you want to learn the Spanish equivalents of. Put away your book and CD. Try saying and also writing the Spanish words in the second column. When you've completed the second column, fold back the first column to see if you can write the English words in column 3. Now check your work. All the correct words can be considered words you've mastered. All the words you got wrong or didn't know have to be studied more carefully before you fold back the first two columns to try again to complete the fourth column with the correct Spanish word. Continue in this manner using both sides of the paper until you've mastered all the words you deem important. Remember, writing down what you've studied helps reinforce what you've learned.

Column 1	Column 2	Column 3	Column 4
pear	pera	pear	(mastered word)
apple	**mansana**	apple	(incorrect, needs more work)
	manzana (correct)		

Verb conjugations: You'll want to be sure your verbs agree with the subjects you use so your Spanish sounds impeccable. Here are two good study guidelines:

♦ Use flashcards to practice learning how to give the proper oral conjugation of verbs.

♦ Practice saying the verbs as you write them on a piece of paper. Write the verb several times until you have it memorized.

Twenty Phrases You Should Know

No matter what your reason for studying Spanish, the 20 phrases in the following table are an absolute must for you to master.

¡Atención!

Perdóneme is used to asked for forgiveness, whereas *con permiso* is used when passing another person.

Phrase	Spanish	Pronunciation
Please	Por favor	*pohr fah-bohr*
Thank you very much	Muchas gracias	*moo-chahs grah-see-yahs*
You're welcome	De nada	*deh nah-dah*
Excuse me	Perdóneme	*pehr-doh-neh-meh*
	Con permiso	*kohn pehr-mee-soh*
My name is …	Me llamo …	*meh yah-moh*
I would like …	Quisiera …	*kee-see-yeh-rah*
	Me gustaría	*meh goos-tah-ree-yah*
I need …	Necesito …	*neh-seh-see-toh*
	Me falta(n) …	*meh fahl-tah(n)*
Do you have …	¿Tiene Ud. …?	*tee-yeh-neh oo-stehd*
Please give me …	Déme, por favor	*deh-meh pohr fah-bohr*
Could you help me please?	¿Podría ayudarme por favor?	*poh-dree-yah ah-yoo-dahr-meh pohr fah-bohr*
Do you speak English?	¿Habla Ud. inglés?	*ah-blah oo-stehd een-glehs*
I speak a little Spanish.	Hablo un poco de español.	*ah-bloh oon poh-koh deh ehs-pah-nyohl*
I don't understand.	No comprendo.	*noh kohm-prehn-doh*
Please repeat.	Repita, por favor.	*rreh-pee-tah pohr fah-bohr*
What did you say?	¿Qué dijo Ud.?	*keh dee-hoh oo-stehd*
I'm lost.	Estoy perdido (a) (perdida).	*ehs-toy pehr-dee-doh (pehr-dee-dah)*
I'm looking for …	Busco …	*boos-koh*
	Estoy buscando …	*ehs-toy boos-kahn-doh*
Where is the bathroom?	¿Dónde está el baño?	*dohn-deh ehs-tah ehl bah-nyoh*
Where is the police station?	¿Dónde está la comisaría de policía?	*dohn-deh ehs-tah lah koh-mee-sah-ree-yah deh poh-lee-see-yah*
Where is the American embassy?	¿Dónde está la embajada americana?	*dohn-deh ehs-tah lah ehm-bah-hah-dah ah-meh-ree-kah-nah*

Note that Ud. *is the abbreviation for* usted *(you).*

¡Buena suerte! (*bweh-nah swehr-teh;* good luck!)

Chapter

Say It Right!

In This Chapter

- The stress of it all
- Find fluidity
- Get a native accent
- Phonetically yours

You want to learn how to roll your *r*'s and purr like a wild *tigre*. You also want to learn how to make your *v*'s sound like *b*'s and how to silence some letters while emphasizing others. Lose your inhibitions, put on your best Spanish accent, and repeat and practice the sounds of the language. Remember, although Spanish is a foreign language to you, it is very phonetic; therefore, it is very easy to pronounce. That's right, just read what you see and pronounce it the way you think it should be pronounced. Chances are you've got it right.

Think of this lesson as a verbal workout. Like any other skill you might want to perfect, proper Spanish pronunciation requires a certain amount of practice and dedication. Don't hesitate to sit down and talk to yourself, read aloud, or sing along with your favorite Spanish singer. If you want to be successful, begin slowly at first and then gradually increase your efforts until you find yourself working at a comfortable pace. Avoid burning out by trying to accomplish too much too soon. Remember, practice makes perfect.

Let's take a look at a few rules that will help you sound like a true Spanish speaker. You'll be purrrrring away in no time!

When There's Stress Involved

The rules for stress in Spanish are rather straightforward, but they do require your concentration at first. Follow these simple guidelines:

- ◆ If a word ends in a vowel, *n*, or *s*, place the stress on the next-to-last syllable, for example: *escuela, excelente, apartamento, examen, insectos*.

- ◆ If the word ends in any other letters besides a vowel, *n*, or *s*, stress the last syllable, for example: *hotel, explicar, salud*.

- ◆ All exceptions to the preceding two rules have an accent over the vowel of the stressed syllable, for example: se**gún**, **lá**piz, fran**cés**, **mé**dico.

The only exceptions to these rules are for words of foreign origin, usually words taken from English, that retain their original spelling and pronunciation (for example: **san**dwich, **In**ternet).

Unlike English, in which words are often phonetically confusing, difficult to sound out, and contain syllables with varying amounts of stress, Spanish words are pronounced exactly as they are written. The songlike flow of Spanish is one of the reasons it's considered a Romance language.

In a Flash

Remember the Spanish newspaper you got in Chapter 1? Read aloud one paragraph from any article while sitting in front of a mirror. If possible, record yourself and then listen to the playback. Spend a few minutes each day watching your face and the movement of your lips and tongue. Move on to another article when you are pleased with how you sound.

Acceptable Accents

Don't worry that you'll have trouble sounding great. Spanish is a relatively simple language to pronounce. Sure, there are accent marks, but don't let them trouble or confuse you. Luckily, there are only three accents in the language:

- ◆ The most common accent (´) only requires that you put more stress on the syllable containing that letter. Examples include *mamá* (*mah-mah*), *interés* (*een-teh-rehs*), *terrífico* (*teh-rree-fee-koh*), *avión* (*ah-bee-yohn*), and *único* (*oo-nee-koh*).

◆ The tilde (~) only appears over an *n* (*ñ*, which is considered a separate letter). It produces the *ny* sound, as in the *ni* in onion. An example is *mañana* (*mah-nyah-nah*), which means "tomorrow" or "morning."

◆ The two dots over a letter (dieresis) (̈) are used in diphthongs (combinations of two vowels). This accent is very rarely seen and only occurs on the letter *u* after the letter g and before an e or an i to indicate that the u is actually pronounced (rather than silent as in guitarra). An example is *vergüenza* (*behr-goo-wehn-sah*), which means "shame."

As you can see, accents in Spanish really create no problems at all. You'll get more practice with them later in the chapter.

¡Atención!

Remember, if an accent is placed on a vowel, you must stress that syllable for correct pronunciation. Keep in mind that sometimes accent marks are not placed on capital letters and sometimes, rather than indicating stress, they are placed on words to distinguish their meanings, as in *el* (the) and *él* (he), *que* (that), and *qué* (what?).

Perfecting Your Accent

Did you ever notice how some people can pick up another language and sound authentic with very little effort at all, but other people just can't seem to lose their native, hometown accent? If you're lucky, you can sound great by simply imitating the Spanish speakers you've heard on TV, in the movies, on the radio, or in your neighborhood. Right from the start, you'll be able to reproduce accentuation and pronunciation with minimal effort. Positive feedback will be immediate, and a feeling of accomplishment will be yours with little practice.

How lucky for you. You probably have a "good ear" and also are somewhat musically talented. You probably could skip a large part of this chapter and maybe even ignore some of the phonetic spellings yet still manage quite well. Some people, however, view foreign pronunciation with trepidation. If you were born with a "tin ear," chances are the words and phrases you speak just won't sound right at first. You'll need to spend a bit more time practicing your pronunciation. If you keep at it, however, you'll eventually get the hang of it.

Memory Master

The Spanish *r* is always rolled. At the beginning of a word or after the consonants *l* (*alrededor*; around), *n* (*honra*; honor), or *s* (*Israel*; Israel), the *r* requires two or three trills, just like the double *r* (*rr*).

Remember, no matter how you sound, you'll be understood if you use the correct words. That should be your goal. Nobody is going to laugh at you. In the end, your level of competence in pronunciation is no big deal. Relax, try your best, and above all, don't be discouraged.

Vowels and Consonants

Unlike the English alphabet, the Spanish alphabet contains 28 letters, and 5 of those 28 letters are vowels—*a*, *e*, *i*, *o*, and *u*. The following table gives the pronunciation of these vowels.

Pronouncing Vowels Properly

Vowel	Sound	Example	Pronunciation
a	ah	artista	*ahr-tees-tah*
e	eh	egoísta	*eh-goh-ees-tah*
i	ee	isla	*ees-lah*
o	oh	objeto	*ohb-heh-toh*
u	oo	uno	*oo-noh*

The other 23 letters of the Spanish alphabet are consonants. Three letters in the Spanish alphabet not in the English alphabet are *ch*, *ll*, and *ñ*. (*Ch* and *ll* are no longer considered separate letters in the Spanish alphabet, but some Spanish dictionaries have not yet noted this change.) The letter *w* is not considered part of the Spanish alphabet because it's only used in words of foreign origin, such as *water closet*, *weekend*, *western*, *wharf*, *whiskey*, and *wintergreen*.

The following table illustrates the Spanish consonants. Note the sounds and the sample words with their phonetic spellings. After studying the table, repeat the sample words aloud to practice your pronunciation.

Pronouncing Consonants Properly

Letter	Sound	Example	Pronunciation
b	same as English	bebé	*beh-beh*
c	soft c (s) before e and i; hard c (k) elsewhere	centro catedral	*sehn-troh* *kah-teh-drahl*

Letter	Sound	Example	Pronunciation
ch	ch	cheque	*cheh-keh*
d	d	dama	*dah-mah*
f	f	fiesta	*fee-yehs-tah*
g	soft h before e and i; hard g elsewhere	general gala	*heh-neh-rahl* *gah-lah*
h	silent	hispano	*ees-pah-noh*
j	h	julio	*hoo-lee-yoh*
k	k	kilo	*kee-loh*
l	l	libre	*lee-breh*
ll	y	llama	*yah-mah*
m	m	mamá	*mah-mah*
n	n	necesario	*neh-seh-sah-ree-yoh*
ñ	ny	nino	*nee-nyoh*
p	p	papá	*pah-pah*
q	k	Quito	*kee-toh*
r	r (slightly rolled); rr (r rolled two or three times)	libro carro	*lee-broh* *kah-rroh*
s	s	salsa	*sahl-sah*
t	t	toro	*toh-roh*
v	less-explosive English b	vigor	*bee-gohr*
x	English ks (sinks)	exacto	*ehk-sahk-toh*
y	y	yoga	*yoh-gah*
z	s	zoo	*soh*

The Diphthong Dilemma

The Spanish language contains many diphthongs. A *diphthong* is a combination of two vowels—one weak and one strong—that appear in the same syllable. The strong vowels are *a*, *e*, and *o*; pronounce them with a lot of emphasis. The weak vowels, *i* and *u*, should be said more softly. Use the following table to practice pronouncing diphthongs.

Spanish Diphthongs to Practice Aloud

Diphthong	Sound	Example	Pronunciation	Meaning
ai	*ah-yee*	aire	*ah-yee-reh*	air
au	*ow*	autor	*ow-tohr*	author
ay	*ah-yee*	hay	*ah-yee*	there is, there are
ei	*eh-yee*	seis	*seh-yees*	six
eu	*eh-yoo*	Europa	*eh-yoo-roh-pah*	Europe
ia	*ee-yah*	serio	*seh-ree-yoh*	serious
ie	*ee-yeh*	siesta	*see-yehs-tah*	nap
io	*ee-yoh*	avión	*ah-bee-yohn*	airplane
iu	*ee-yoo*	ciudad	*see-yoo-dahd*	city
oi	*oy*	oigo	*oy-goh*	I hear
ua	*wah*	lengua	*lehn-gwah*	tongue, language
ue	*weh*	cuenta	*kwehn-tah*	check (bill)
ui	*wee*	cuidado	*kwee-dah-doh*	be careful
uo	*oo-oh*	continúo	*kohn-tee-noo-oh*	continuous

Don't Sound Like a *Gringo!*

Now that you're an expert on the Spanish alphabet and Spanish diphthongs, read each of the following sentences aloud to practice and improve your pronunciation (you don't want to sound like a gringo—slang for an American speaker):

El país es grande.
ehl pah-yees ehs grahn-deh
The country is big.

Oiga, hay seis respuestas.
oy-gah, ah-yee seh-yees rrehs-pwehs-tahs
Listen, there are six answers.

Mi abuelo es viejo.
mee ah-bweh-loh ehs bee-yeh-hoh
My grandfather is old.

Paula va al cine.
pow-lah bah ahl see-neh
Paula goes to the movies.

El anciano tiene
cien años.
ehl ahn-see-yah-noh tee-yeh-neh
see-yehn ahn-yohs
The old man is 100 years old.

Chapter 3

The Spanish You Know

In This Chapter

◆ Cognates and comprehension

◆ Use what you already know

◆ False friends

Do you love *chocolate?* What about *potatoes* and *tomatoes?* Do you take a *taxi* often? When the weather is nice, do you sit on your *patio?* Can you play the *piano?* Perhaps you have a sweater made from *alpaca* wool. And you've probably been stung by a *mosquito* more than once in your life. Well, look at that—you know some Spanish already!

You're probably unaware that your vocabulary is filled with words and phrases borrowed from Spanish. Many other Spanish words and expressions are so similar to ours that you'll be able to use and understand them with very little trouble. By the time you finish this chapter, you'll be well on your way to creating simple, correct Spanish sentences that will enable you to express your ideas and opinions.

You Know This!

My husband makes frequent trips to the video store, especially in the summer when all the television stations show reruns. He takes his time and often spends an hour or more trying to pick out the perfect film for the evening.

His taste is very eclectic: one night we'll watch a Japanese samurai warrior film, and the next night we'll watch a French romantic comedy. More often than not, he picks out foreign films. He thinks they're interesting and different from what we're used to. Although he only speaks English, he enjoys the experience of listening to native speakers.

One night he rented *Like Water for Chocolate*, a wonderful but sad Mexican love story. We sat in front of the TV for about 2 hours, totally involved in the tale being told. At one point, to my great astonishment, I noticed my husband wasn't reading the titles. I thought perhaps he was bored by the romance, but that wasn't the case. When I asked him why he wasn't reading, he said he understood what the people were saying. How could that be? He had never even studied Spanish. He replied that the words sounded just like English to him. I gave it some thought, and I understood his point. There is a logical explanation.

That explanation is *cognates*. Simply put, a cognate is a word spelled the same, or almost the same, in two different languages and has the same definition. In many cases, we've borrowed a word from Spanish and incorporated it into our vocabulary without giving much thought to the word's origin. Naturally, cognates are pronounced somewhat differently in each language, but the meaning of the Spanish word will be perfectly clear to an English speaker.

Let's take a closer look and see how much Spanish you already know.

A Perfect Match

The following table lists cognates with the same meaning in both Spanish and English. The left column contains adjectives you can use to describe the nouns in the middle and right columns. Using the skills you've learned, pronounce the Spanish words and compare them to their English equivalents. Your goal is to sound Spanish.

> **Memory Master**
>
> Although a noun's gender is often easily identifiable in Spanish, it is best to learn the noun with its corresponding article. See Chapter 6 for more details. For now, just remember that *el* is the article for masculine singular nouns and *la* is for feminine singular nouns.

When you look at the list of cognates, notice that the Spanish nouns are listed under a specific definite article, *el* or *la*. These articles both mean "the," and each indicates the gender of the noun (masculine or feminine, respectively). All Spanish nouns (people, places, things, ideas) have a gender. This might seem strange to you at first because we do not have anything similar in English. For now, just remember that if you want to express that Spanish is easy, you must say, *"El español es fácil."*

Perfect Cognates

Adjectives	Masculine Nouns El *(ehl)*	Feminine Nouns La *(lah)*
horrible *(oh-rree-bleh)*	color *(koh-lohr)*	banana *(bah-nah-nah)*
natural *(nah-too-rahl)*	chocolate *(choh-koh-lah-teh)*	fiesta *(fee-yehs-tah)*
popular *(poh-poo-lahr)*	doctor *(dohk-tohr)*	alpaca *(ahl-pah-kah)*
sociable *(soh-see-yah-bleh)*	hotel *(oh-tehl)*	plaza *(plah-sah)*
terrible *(teh-rree-bleh)*	soda *(soh-dah)*	radio *(rrah-dee-yoh)*
tropical *(troh-pee-kahl)*	motor *(moh-tohr)*	taxi *(tahk-see)*

Almost Perfect Partners

Near cognates are words that look so similar in both languages that their meanings are unmistakable. Perhaps a letter or two is different, or there might be an accent mark on the Spanish word; essentially, however, the words are the same. Look at the words in the following table and see whether you can figure out the meanings of all the words.

Near Cognates

Adjectives	Masculine Nouns El *(ehl)*	Feminine Nouns La *(lah)*
americano *(ah-meh-ree-kah-noh)*	aniversario *(ah-nee-behr-sah-ree-yoh)*	aspirina *(ahs-pee-ree-nah)*
confortable *(kohn-fohr-tah-bleh)*	automóvil *(ow-toh-moh-beel)*	bicicleta *(bee-see-kleh-tah)*
curioso *(koo-ree-yoh-soh)*	banco *(bahn-koh)*	blusa *(bloo-sah)*
delicioso *(deh-lee-see-yoh-soh)*	ciclismo *(see-klees-moh)*	catedral *(kah-teh-drahl)*
diferente *(dee-feh-rehn-teh)*	diccionario *(deek-see-yoh-nah-ree-yoh)*	computadora *(kohm-poo-tah-doh-rah)*

continues

Near Cognates (continued)

Adjectives	Masculine Nouns El (*ehl*)	Feminine Nouns La (*lah*)
difícil (*dee-fee-seel*)	grupo (*groo-poh*)	dieta (*dee-yeh-tah*)
elegante (*eh-leh-gahn-teh*)	jardín (*har-deen*)	familia (*fah-mee-lee-yah*)
excelente (*ehk-seh-lehn-teh*)	limón (*lee-mohn*)	hamburguesa (*ahm-boor-geh-sah*)
famoso (*fah-moh-soh*)	mecánico (*meh-kah-nee-koh*)	lámpara (*lahm-pah-rah*)
grande (*grahn-deh*)	parque (*pahr-keh*)	medicina (*meh-dee-see-nah*)
importante (*eem-pohr-tahn-teh*)	plato (*plah-toh*)	guitarra (*gee-tah-rrah*)
imposible (*eem-poh-see-bleh*)	presidente (*preh-see-dehn-teh*)	mansión (*mahn-see-yohn*)
interesante (*een-teh-reh-sahn-teh*)	programa (*proh-grah-mah*)	música (*moo-see-kah*)
magnífico (*mahg-nee-fee-koh*)	menú (*meh-noo*)	nacionalidad (*nah-see-yoh-nah-lee-dahd*)
moderno (*moh-dehr-noh*)	restaurante (*rrehs-tow-rahn-teh*)	opinión (*oh-pee-nee-yohn*)
necesario (*neh-seh-sah-ree-yoh*)	salario (*sah-lah-ree-yoh*)	persona (*pehr-soh-nah*)
ordinario (*ohr-dee-nah-ree-yoh*)	supermercado (*soo-pehr-mehr-kah-doh*)	región (*rreh-hee-yohn*)
posible (*poh-see-bleh*)	teatro (*teh-yah-troh*)	rosa (*rroh-sah*)
probable (*proh-bah-bleh*)	teléfono (*teh-leh-foh-noh*)	turista (*too-rees-tah*)

Spanish words that begin with *es-* are often near cognates. You can guess the meaning of many Spanish words beginning with *es-* by simply dropping the initial *e-*.

Spanish	Pronunciation	English
escarlata	*ehs-kahr-lah-tah*	scarlet
escéptico	*ehs-sehp-tee-koh*	skeptical
escultor	*ehs-kool-tohr*	sculptor
espacio	*ehs-pah-see-yoh*	space
España	*ehs-pah-nyah*	Spain
especial	*ehs-peh-see-yahl*	special
espectáculo	*ehs-pehk-tah-koo-loh*	spectacle, show
espía	*ehs-pee-yah*	spy
espiral	*ehs-pee-rahl*	spiral
espléndido	*ehs-plehn-dee-doh*	splendid
esquí	*ehs-kee*	ski
estudiar	*ehs-too-dee-yahr*	to study
estupendo	*ehs-too-pehn-doh*	stupendous

Versatile Verbs

Many Spanish verbs (words that show action or a state of being) are so similar to their English counterparts you should have no difficulty recognizing their meanings.

Spanish verbs are governed by certain rules that are explained in Chapter 7. For now, look at the three major verb families—verbs ending in -*ar*, -*er*, and -*ir*. Any verbs belonging to a family are considered regular; those that do not belong to a family are irregular. Each family has its own set of rules that are also explained in Chapter 7. (Irregular verbs don't follow the family rules. Think of them as the black sheep. More information about irregular verbs is available in later chapters.) Check out the following members of the three major families, and see whether you can determine their meanings.

> **Memory Master**
>
> In Spanish, adjectives must agree in number and gender with the nouns they describe. I cover this in detail in Chapter 9, but for now, just remember to use adjectives ending with -*o* to describe masculine nouns and adjectives ending with -*a* to describe feminine nouns. Adjectives ending in -*e* can describe either one.

-ar Verbs			
acompañar	entrar	negar	reservar
adorar	explicar	observar	respirar
celebrar	ignorar	pasar	telefonear
comenzar	invitar	practicar	terminar
declarar	marchar	preparar	usar
eliminar	modificar	reparar	verificar

-er Verbs		
comprender	responder	vender

-ir Verbs		
aplaudir	dividir	omitir
decidir	persuadir	recibir
describir	preferir	sufrir

You've Got the Swing of It!

The preceding section showed that you know a lot more Spanish than you realized. As a matter of fact, I'll bet you can easily read and understand the following sentences without any problems:

1. Juan prepara el menú.
2. El mecánico repara el carro.
3. El turista usa la información.
4. El programa termina.
5. Marta celebra su aniversario.
6. José adora el programa.

False Amigos

Don't assume every Spanish word that looks like an English word is a cognate. Nothing is ever that simple. Although you might think you've mastered cognates, every rule has exceptions. In the case of cognates, exceptions are called *false friends*. False friends are words spelled exactly or almost the same in both Spanish and English, but they have different meanings in each language. They might even be different parts of speech. Beware of the false friends listed in the following table. You want to use them correctly.

False Friends

Spanish	English	Spanish	English
asistir	to attend	hay	there is (are)
caro	expensive	librería	bookstore
comer	to eat	joya	jewel
fábrica	factory	pan	bread
flor	flower	sopa	soup

Now You're a Pro!

A complimentary copy of a Spanish newspaper was delivered to your hotel room. Curiosity has gotten the best of you, and you've decided to see how much Spanish you already know. Identify the sections of the newspaper shown in the following figure, and determine the contents of the articles.

DEPORTES
Bogotá, defiende su título

ECONOMICAS
**Informe confirma vitalidad
de la economía**

INTERNACIONAL
China pone interés en restaurantes de comida rápida

INFORMACION
ARTERIOESCLEROSIS TIENE UNA SOLUCION

Answer Key

You've Got the Swing of It!

1. Juan prepares the menu.

2. The mechanic repairs the car.

3. The tourist uses the information.

4. The program ends.

5. Marta celebrates her anniversary.

6. José adores the program.

Now You're a Pro!

Sports: Bogotá defends its title.

Economy: A report confirms the vitality of the economy.

International: China shows an interest in fast-food restaurants.

Information: There is a solution to arteriosclerosis.

4

Grappling With Grammar

In This Chapter

- ◆ An overview of basic grammar
- ◆ Tips on using a bilingual dictionary

There's more to speaking a foreign language than merely translating words from one language to another—despite what you might remember from high school. To communicate effectively, you cannot simply walk around with a dictionary and read from it. You must learn to use the language and its patterns the way native speakers do.

For any student of a foreign language, one of the most difficult concepts to grasp is that different languages follow different grammatical patterns. Trying to translate word for word from one language to the next often produces awkward results and, in many instances, becomes an exercise in futility. To truly sound like a native, a student must have not only a grammatical understanding of the language but also a colloquial, idiomatic command of it.

Grammar? Good Grief!

Does the word *grammar* send chills up your spine? Does it bring back bad memories of the days when you sat in school learning the parts of speech, conjugating verbs, and diagramming sentences?

Well, that was then and this is now. To learn a foreign language, you don't have to become an expert grammarian. All you need is to know some of the simple parts of speech: nouns, verbs, adjectives, and adverbs. Don't panic—just follow along and see how simple it is.

Nouns

Nouns refer to people, places, things, or ideas. Unlike in English, in Spanish all nouns have a gender (masculine or feminine). As in English, however, they also have a quantity or number (singular or plural). Articles that serve as noun identifiers often help indicate gender and number. (You will learn more about this in Chapter 6.) In Spanish, as in English, nouns can be replaced by pronouns.

Verbs

Verbs are words that show action or a state of being. In both English and Spanish, verbs are generally conjugated. In English, this is so automatic (because we've been doing it practically since birth) that we don't even realize we are doing it. *Conjugating* means using the correct form of the verb so it agrees with the subject. In English, for example, we say "I am," "you are," "he is," and so on; "I look," but "she looks."

It's improper to mix and match the subjects and verb forms, whether you're speaking in English or in Spanish. Imagine how strange it would sound to you if a Spanish speaker said, "I is from Cuba." You would understand the meaning, of course, which is what the person is striving for—to be understood.

Never lose hope; you'll always be able to get your message across. The language, however, does have a much better ring to it when the subjects and verbs correspond. (Verb conjugation is explained in greater depth in Chapter 7.)

Adjectives

Adjectives are words that describe nouns. Unlike in English, in Spanish all adjectives agree in number and gender with the nouns they modify. If a noun is singular, you must describe it with a singular adjective. If the noun is feminine, be sure to use the correct feminine form of the adjective.

Another difference is that, in English, adjectives generally precede the nouns they modify, as in "the blue house." In Spanish, most adjectives come after the nouns they describe. Translated into Spanish, "the blue house" becomes *la casa azul,* in which *casa* means "house" and *azul* means "blue." (You find out more about adjectives in Chapter 9.)

Adverbs

Adverbs are words that describe verbs, adjectives, or other adverbs. Adverbs are used about the same way in both languages. In English, most adverbs end in *-ly*, such as *slowly*. In Spanish, most adverbs end in *-mente*, such as *lentamente* (slowly). (I discuss adverbs in greater detail in Chapter 18.)

Just Look It Up: A Bilingual Dictionary Crash Course

Using a bilingual dictionary requires a little more knowledge than using an English dictionary. That's right, I'm talking grammar again. To use a bilingual dictionary effectively and correctly, you must know and be aware of the differences among the various parts of speech.

Before looking up your first word, take time to study the abbreviations at the front of your dictionary. You probably will find a long, comprehensive list. Don't get discouraged. Only a handful of the abbreviations really require your attention, as the following table shows.

Abbreviation	Meaning
adj	Adjective.
adv	Adverb.
f	Feminine noun. (Gender will be explained further in Chapter 6.)
m	Masculine noun.
n	Noun. Sometimes *s.* is used. The *n.* designation generally is used only if the noun can be either masculine or feminine.
pl	Plural noun. (More information about plural nouns is in Chapter 6.)
vi (or *v. intr.*)	Intransitive verb. An intransitive verb can stand alone as a sentence, as in "I run."
vt (or *v tr*)	Transitive verb. A transitive verb can be followed by a direct object, as in "He puts on his coat." Unlike "run" in the preceding example, however, "puts on" cannot stand alone. A transitive verb also can be used in the passive tense, in which the subject is acted upon, as in "I was helped."
vr	Reflexive verb. When using a reflexive verb, the subject acts upon itself, as in "I comb my hair." (Reflexive verbs are discussed in Chapter 20.)

In a Flash _____

Think quickly of the many different ways you can use *record*, *fire*, *place*, *stand*, and *well*. Now look them up in the dictionary and see what you find.

Ready for an exercise in using a bilingual dictionary? Let's use the English word *mean* as an example. Consider the following sentences and how the meaning of the word *mean* changes:

That boy is *mean*. (adjective)

What can that *mean?* (verb)

What is the *mean* (average)? (noun)

If we change *mean* to its plural form, the meaning changes again:

What is the *means* of transportation? (noun)

Now look up the word *mean* in a bilingual dictionary. You might see the following:

mean [min] *vt* significar; *adj* (miserly) tacaño(-a), (unkind) mezquino(na), malo(a); *n* (average) promedio *m*, media *f;* see also *means*.

means [minz] *n* (method, way) medio *m;* *npl* (money) recursos.

Based on the Spanish definitions of *mean* provided here, look at the following English sentences, determine which part of speech *mean* is in each, and complete the translated sentences in Spanish using the correct translation of *mean:*

♦ That boy is mean.

Figure out the part of speech and complete the following Spanish sentence:

Ese muchacho es _____.

The correct answer is *mezquino*, an adjective.

♦ What can that mean?

The Spanish sentence would be:

¿Qué puede _____ eso?

Did you use *significar*, a verb? Great!

♦ What is the mean?

This term refers to the average of two numbers. Because the correct word can be either masculine or feminine, you have to use *el* in front of the masculine word and *la* in front of the feminine word. (Articles are discussed in more detail in Chapter 6.) The Spanish translation would be:

¿Cuál es _____?

Did you choose *el promedio* or *la media?*
Both are correct.

◆ What is the means of transportation?

Means is plural in English but is masculine
and singular in Spanish. Use *el* before the
noun you choose.

Your Spanish sentence should be:

¿Cuál es _____ de transporte?

The answer is *el medio.*

Memory Master

In Spanish, an inverted question
mark (¿) or exclamation point (¡)
is placed at the beginning of a
sentence to prepare you for what
will follow. It's really a very
clever idea.

As you can see, to successfully look up the meaning of a word you want to use, you
must do three things:

1. Verify the part of speech—noun, verb, adjective, or adverb—you want to use.

2. Verify that you have found the right word by looking up the Spanish word you
   have chosen to see whether the English meaning is the one you want.

3. Be sure you're using the correct form of the word in number (singular or plural)
   and in gender (masculine or feminine).

Dictionary Exercise

Use your bilingual dictionary to find the correct word to complete each of the
following Spanish sentences:

1. That boy dances *well.*
   Ese muchacho baila _____.

2. Where is the *well?*
   ¿Dónde está _____?

3. I heard *the cry* of the animal.
   Oí _____ del animal.

4. The child is going *to cry.*
   El niño va a _____.

5. I have *just* ten dollars.
   Tengo _____ diez dólares.

6. The punishment is *just.*
   El castigo es _____.

7. The mechanic is going *to check*
   the motor.
   El mecánico va a _____ el
   motor.

8. I am going to cash my *check.*
   Voy a cobrar mi _____.

Answer Key

Dictionary Exercise

1. bien
2. el pozo
3. el grito
4. llorar
5. solamente
6. justo
7. verificar
8. cheque

Idioms Aren't for Idiots

In This Chapter

◆ What are idioms?

◆ What is slang?

◆ How do I use them?

A knowledge of idioms is important for a complete understanding of a language. Imagine you're shopping in one of Madrid's finest jewelry stores. You overhear a conversation between a couple as they examine the diamond necklaces. The woman selects one she likes, but her husband replies "*Este collar cuesta un ojo de la cara*." You interpret this to mean that the necklace costs an eye taken from your face. Sounds like a pretty drastic measure, wouldn't you say? In reality, the expression *costar un ojo de la cara* means "to cost a small fortune," although you'd never figure that out from the vocabulary and grammar in the sentence.

What's Appropriate? Idioms and Slang

In any language, an *idiom* is a particular word or expression whose meaning cannot be readily understood by analyzing its component words. It is, however, still considered an acceptable part of the standard vocabulary of the language. You might be familiar with the following common English idioms:

- Look on the bright side
- Fall head over heels
- On the other hand
- To be down and out

What's the difference between an idiom and slang? *Slang* refers to colorful, popular, informal words or phrases that are *not* part of the standard vocabulary of a language. Slang is considered unconventional and has evolved to describe particular items or situations in street language. Slang vocabulary is composed of coinages; arbitrarily changed words; and extravagant, forced, or facetious figures of speech. The following are some examples of English slang:

- Give me a break!
- Get real!
- Tough luck!
- Get a life!

Idioms are acceptable in oral and written phrases; slang, although freely used in informal conversations, is generally considered substandard in formal writing or speaking. Some slang is, at best, X-rated.

Is It an Idiom, or Is It Slang?

When you speak a foreign language, it's important to know what phrases you can use politely and which will be offensive. Take a look at the following popular expressions. Are they idioms or slang? Certainly, these expressions couldn't be translated word for word. Read them carefully and decide whether they are idioms (acceptable terms) or slang (street language):

- You drive me crazy.
- Keep your shirt on.

Did you recognize that these sentences contain idiomatic expressions used in English all the time? Now compare the preceding sentences with the following:

- She just flipped out.
- That's tacky!

Did you notice that the slang sentences used substandard English and were more offensive than those containing idiomatic expressions? Excellent! You probably won't use much Spanish slang, but the idioms will come in handy.

Spanish has many idioms. This chapter looks at six categories of idioms you might find helpful:

- Travel and transportation
- Time
- Location and direction
- Expressing opinions
- Physical conditions
- Weather conditions

Other idiomatic expressions appear in the appropriate chapters.

Taking Off

Let's say you're taking a trip. You might be asked, "Are you going on a plane or on a boat?" In Spanish, the word for "on" is *sobre*. If you say *"Voy sobre el avión,"* you are saying you're going to ride on the exterior of the plane. To avoid putting yourself in such an awkward position, you should learn the idiomatic expressions covered in the following table.

> **Memory Master**
>
> The preposition *en* is usually used when one travels *inside* a means of ground transportation, such as a subway. Use *a* when traveling *on* something that allows you to safely feel the wind blowing in your hair.

Travel and Transportation

Idiom	Pronunciation	Meaning
en bicicleta	*ehn bee-see-kleh-tah*	by bicycle
a caballo	*ah kah-bah-yoh*	by horseback
a pie	*ah pee-yeh*	by foot
en automóvil	*ehn ow-toh-moh-beel*	by car
en avión	*ehn ah-bee-yohn*	by plane
en barco	*ehn bahr-koh*	by boat

continues

Travel and Transportation (continued)

Idiom	Pronunciation	Meaning
en autobús	*ehn ow-toh-boos*	by bus
en metro	*ehn meh-troh*	by subway
en taxi	*ehn tahk-see*	by taxi
en tren	*ehn trehn*	by train
en carro	*ehn kah-rroh*	by car

Memory Master

Use *hasta* + time when you want to tell someone when you'll be seeing each other again:

Hasta el lunes.
ahs-tah ehl loo-nehs
Until Monday.

Time Is on My Mind

How time-conscious are you? Do you always wear your watch because time is of the essence? Are you up and at 'em at the crack of dawn so you get a head-start on your day? Or are you the laid-back type who doesn't give time a second thought? Whatever your personality, the idioms in the following table will serve you well whenever time is on your mind.

Time Expressions

Idiom	Pronunciation	Meaning
hasta la noche	*ah-stah lah noh-cheh*	see you this evening
hasta mañana	*ah-stah mah-nyah-nah*	see you tomorrow
a tiempo	*ah tee-yehm-poh*	on time
hasta el sábado	*ah-stah ehl sah-bah-doh*	until Saturday
hasta luego	*ah-stah loo-weh-goh*	see you later
adiós	*ah-dee-yohs*	good-bye
temprano	*tehm-prah-noh*	early
a veces	*ah beh-sehs*	from time to time
tarde	*tahr-deh*	late
hace (+ time) que	*ah-seh keh*	(time) + ago
por semana, día, mes	*pohr seh-mah-nah, dee-yah, mehs*	by week, day, month
inmediatamente	*een-meh-dee-yah-tah-mehn-teh*	immediately

Follow the Leader

Among the most useful idioms are those that tell you how to get where you want to go. For example, I always have to know where the nearest restroom can be found—just in case. Is it upstairs, downstairs, next to someplace important, near, or far (heaven forbid)? If you haven't learned the proper terms, you could wind up at the baggage claim instead of the *baño* or, worse yet, at the wrong gender's *baño*. This is why the idioms of location and direction in the following table are worth studying.

Idioms Showing Location and Direction

Idiom	Pronunciation	Meaning
al lado de	*ahl lah-doh deh*	next to
a la derecha de	*ah lah deh-reh-chah deh*	to the right of
a la izquierda de	*ah lah ees-kee-yehr-dah deh*	to the left of
en casa	*ehn kah-sah*	at home
al otro lado (de)	*ahl oh-troh lah-doh (deh)*	on the other side
dar a	*dahr ah*	to face
enfrente de	*ehn-frehn-teh deh*	in front of opposite
hacia	*ah-see-yah*	toward
frente a	*frehn-teh ah*	facing, opposite
al centro	*ahl sehn-troh*	downtown
por aquí	*pohr ah-kee*	this way
por allá	*pohr ah-yah*	that way

Following Directions

You've just checked into your hotel and you're eager to get your bearings. You go to the *recepción* to ask where you can find certain places. Someone gives you a map, but unfortunately, some of the buildings are not identified. The following figure is a map of a city street. Use the following Spanish directions to label the missing buildings:

continues

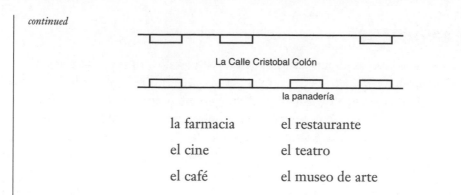

continued

La Calle Cristobal Colón

la panadería

la farmacia   el restaurante

el cine   el teatro

el café   el museo de arte

A la izquierda de la panadería hay un teatro. Al lado del teatro hay un café.
Frente al café hay un restaurante. A la derecha de la panadería hay una farmacia.
Al otro lado de la calle, frente a la farmacia, hay un cine. A la izquierda del cine,
enfrente del teatro, hay un museo de arte moderno.

What's Your Opinion?

Everyone has opinions. Whether you're talking about your flight, the food you ate,
the movie you watched, the people you met, or your life in general, you need to know
how to properly express your feelings. The following table should help.

Expressing Opinions with Idioms

Idiom	Pronunciation	Meaning
en mi opinión	*ehn mee oh-pee-nee-yohn*	in my opinion
a decir verdad	*ah deh-seer behr-dahd*	to tell the truth
al contrario	*ahl kohn-trah-ree-yoh*	on the contrary
en vez de	*ehn behs deh*	instead of
por supuesto	*pohr soo-pwehs-toh*	of course
claro	*klah-roh*	of course
está bien	*eh-stah bee-yehn*	all right
no importa	*noh eem-pohr-tah*	it doesn't matter
de acuerdo	*deh ah-kwehr-doh*	agreed
sin duda	*seen doo-dah*	without a doubt
es evidente	*ehs eh-bee-dehn-teh*	it is evident

How Are You?

If you've ever been to the Dominican Republic, you know it can get extremely hot, especially in the summertime. Suppose you're visiting a friend there in August. To express your discomfort, you say *"Estoy calor."* Your host, a very polite person, looks at you and has to refrain from laughing. Why? In English, we use adjectives to describe how we feel; thus, you've chosen (so you think) "I am hot." In Spanish, however, you must say, "I have heat" (which doesn't mean you are sick and have a fever). Saying "I am hot" tells your Spanish host you are hot to the touch. This sounds very strange to us, but *tengo calor* is the expression you need. Remember, our idioms don't always make sense either.

You'll notice that all the idioms in the following table begin with the verb *tener,* which means "to have." Remember that the form of the verb changes as the subject of the sentence changes and that it is used to describe physical conditions, whereas in English we use the verb "to be." (Conjugating verbs is covered in detail in Chapter 7.)

Idiomatic Physical Conditions

Idiom	Pronunciation	Meaning
tener calor	*teh-nehr kah-lohr*	to be hot
tener hambre	*teh-nehr ahm-breh*	to be hungry
tener frío	*teh-nehr free-yoh*	to be cold
tener vergüenza	*teh-nehr behr-goo-wehn-sah*	to be ashamed
tener dolor de	*teh-nehr doh-lohr deh*	to have an ache in
tener miedo de	*teh-nehr mee-yeh-doh deh*	to be afraid of
tener razón	*teh-nehr rrah-sohn*	to be right
tener sed	*teh-nehr sehd*	to be thirsty
tener sueño	*teh-nehr sweh-nyoh*	to be sleepy
tener XX años	*teh-nehr ____ ah-nyohs*	to be XX years old

How's the Weather?

It's always a good idea to stay on top of the weather when you travel because most of your plans are probably contingent upon it. Discussing weather in Spanish requires

In a Flash

Look at the weather section of your newspaper. Give the weather reports for as many different cities as you can. Look out your window and give a report for your town.

using a different verb from the one we use in English. If you said to your host, "*Está frío*," he or she would think you were talking about something you had touched. The Spanish use the verb *hacer* (to do or to make) to describe most weather conditions, as in "It makes cold." Study the common weather expressions in the following table.

Idiomatic Weather Expressions

Idiom	Pronunciation	Meaning
hace buen tiempo	*ah-seh bwehn tee-yehm-poh*	It's nice weather.
hace calor	*ah-seh kah-lohr*	It's hot.
hace fresco	*ah-seh frehs-koh*	It's cool.
hace sol	*ah-seh sohl*	It's sunny.
hace viento	*ah-seh bee-yehn-toh*	It's windy.
hace frío	*ah-seh free-yoh*	It's cold.
hace mal tiempo	*ah-seh mahl tee-yehm-poh*	It's bad weather.
¿Qué tiempo hace?	*keh tee-yehm-poh ah-seh*	What is the weather?

Never use *hacer* when discussing snow or rain. Use *nieva* (*nee-yeh-bah*), which means "It's snowing," and *llueve* (*yoo-weh-beh*), which means "It's raining."

Idiomatically Speaking

Which Spanish idioms would you use in the following situations?

1. You want to tell a friend that the weather is beautiful …

2. You want to tell a friend that you'll see him tomorrow …

3. A friend asks how you're traveling to Puerto Rico. Express that you are going by boat: *Voy* …

4. A stranger asks you for directions to the museum. Express that it is to the left: *Está* …

5. You want to tell a friend that she is right: *Tienes* …

6. A friend asks if you want to go to the movies. Express that it doesn't matter.

Answer Key

Following Directions

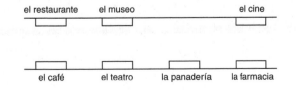

| el restaurante | el museo | | el cine |
| el café | el teatro | la panadería | la farmacia |

Idiomatically Speaking

1. Hace buen tiempo.

2. Hasta mañana.

3. en barco

4. a la izquierda

5. razón

6. No importa.

Chapter 6

Sexually Speaking

In This Chapter

- ◆ Tips on determining gender
- ◆ Masculine and feminine nouns
- ◆ Ways to change from singular to plural

In this chapter, I help you better understand how the Spanish view gender. Unlike in English, in Spanish every single noun (person, place, thing, or idea) is designated as either masculine or feminine and either singular or plural. That's right—the taco you're consuming, the ball you're throwing, and the museum you're visiting all have a specific gender. How is the determination made? Sometimes it's obvious, sometimes there are clues, and sometimes it's just downright tricky. This chapter will teach you to make the right connections.

The Battle of the Sexes

Deciding which gender to use is obvious when you're speaking about a man or a woman. But what if you want to talk about a lovely store you passed the other day? Which gender do you use with *tienda* (store)? You don't know the rules yet, so do you assume it's feminine because women like to shop more than men? Better not (although *tienda* is feminine)—you could get into big trouble with that kind of sexist presumption.

Suppose you want to purchase a tie you saw in a store. You might assume that *corbata* is masculine because men wear ties more than women. But you would be wrong—*corbata* is a feminine word. How about a dress? It must be feminine; after all, dresses are not for men. Wrong again! The word for dress, *vestido*, is masculine.

By now you're probably saying, "How can that be? It doesn't make sense!" You're absolutely correct. For the most part, it makes no sense. Fortunately, there are clues to help you with these words and others like them. Should you come across a noun whose gender is a mystery to you, you can always resort to your trusty Spanish dictionary. Remember, even if you make a mistake in gender, as long as you have the correct vocabulary word, you'll be understood.

Noun Markers

All nouns in Spanish have a gender, either masculine (*m.*) or feminine (*f.*). They also are singular (*sing.*) or plural (*pl.*). Noun markers can help you identify these characteristics for any noun. The most common markers, shown in the following table, are definite articles (*the*) and indefinite articles (*a*, *an*, or *one*).

Singular Noun Markers

Article	Masculine	Feminine
the	el (*ehl*)	la (*lah*)
a, an, one	un (*oon*)	una (*oo-nah*)

Some nouns in Spanish, such as those shown in the following table, are easy to categorize because they obviously refer to masculine or feminine people.

Gender-Obvious Nouns

Noun	Pronunciation	Meaning
Masculine		
el padre	*ehl pah-dreh*	the father
el abuelo	*ehl ah-bweh-loh*	the grandfather
el chico	*ehl chee-koh*	the boy

Noun	Pronunciation	Meaning
Masculine		
el amigo	*ehl ah-mee-goh*	the friend
el tío	*ehl tee-yoh*	the uncle
el primo	*ehl pree-moh*	the cousin
el hombre	*ehl ohm-breh*	the man
Feminine		
la madre	*lah mah-dreh*	the mother
la abuela	*lah ah-bweh-lah*	the grandmother
la chica	*lah chee-kah*	the girl
la amiga	*lah ah-mee-gah*	the friend
la tía	*lah tee-yah*	the aunt
la prima	*lah pree-mah*	the cousin
la mujer	*lah moo-hehr*	the woman

A few nouns can be either masculine or feminine. Just change the article to refer to either gender. The following table identifies some high-frequency nouns for which this rule applies.

Either-Gender Nouns

Noun	Pronunciation	Meaning
artista	*ahr-tees-tah*	artist
dentista	*dehn-tees-tah*	dentist
estudiante	*ehs-too-dee-yahn-teh*	student
joven	*hoh-behn*	youth
modelo	*moh-deh-loh*	model

Some nouns are always masculine or always feminine, despite the gender of the person to whom they refer. Observe the nouns in the following table.

Always Masculine	Always Feminine
bebé (baby)	persona (person)
bombero (firefighter)	víctima (victim)

Some endings help determine the gender of the noun and make marking easier. You might have noticed in the preceding list that the masculine nouns ended in -*o* and -*e*, and the feminine nouns ended in -*a* (although feminine nouns also can end in -*e*). If you don't know the gender of a Spanish word, you usually can make an accurate guess by looking at the vowel the word ends with. The following table shows you the gender-identifying endings.

Gender-Identifying Endings

Masculine Endings	Example	Feminine Endings	Example
-*o*	abrigo	-*a*	pluma
-*ema*	tema	-*ión*	lección
consonants (usually)	reloj	-*dad*	ciudad
		-*tad*	libertad
		-*tud*	juventud
		-*umbre*	costumbre
		-*ie*	serie

Gender-Benders

Of course, there are always some exceptions to the rule, just to be sure you don't get overconfident. Keep the following in mind for future use.

Masculine Nouns That End in -*a*

Masculine Noun	Pronunciation	Meaning
el clima	*ehl klee-mah*	the climate
el día	*ehl dee-yah*	the day
el drama	*ehl drah-mah*	the drama
el problema	*ehl proh-bleh-mah*	the problem
el programa	*ehl proh-grah-mah*	the program
el telegrama	*ehl teh-leh-grah-mah*	the telegram

Feminine Nouns That End in -o

Feminine Noun	Pronunciation	Meaning
la mano	*lah mah-noh*	the hand
la foto (short for fotografía)	*lah foh-toh*	the photo
la moto (short for motocicleta)	*lah moh-toh*	the motorcycle

Gender Changes

Masculine nouns that end in *-és*, *-r*, or *-n* add *-a* at the end to form the feminine equivalent, as in the following examples:

el francés the Frenchman	la francesa the French woman
el autor the author	la autora the authoress
el alemán the German	la alemana the German woman

In the following two cases, none of these rules apply:

el actor the actor	la actriz the actress
el emperador the emperor	la emperatriz the empress

Note that any accent marks over the masculine nouns in the preceding examples are dropped for the feminine equivalent.

When There's More Than One

When a Spanish noun refers to more than one of something, it becomes plural. Just like in English, right? Not quite. As shown in the following table, it's not enough to simply change the noun to its plural form in Spanish. The article must be made plural as well.

Plural Noun Markers

| | Spanish | |
English	Masculine	Feminine
the	los	las
some	unos	unas

Plural Nouns

Forming plural nouns in Spanish is not difficult. Most Spanish nouns can be made plural by adding -*s* to the singular form, as shown in the following table.

Singular	Plural	Meaning
el libro	los libros	the books
un libro	unos libros	some books
la mesa	las mesas	the tables
una mesa	unas mesas	some tables

For Spanish nouns that end in a consonant (including -*y*), add -*es* to the noun to form the plural.

Singular	Plural	Meaning
el rey	los reyes	the kings
el mes	los meses	the months
un mes	unos meses	some months
la explicación	las explicaciones	the explanations
una explicación	unas explicaciones	some explanations

For Spanish nouns that end in -*z*, change the *z* to a *c* and then add -*es* to form the plural.

Singular	Plural	Meaning
el pez	los peces	the fish
un pez	unos peces	some fish
la actriz	las actrices	the actresses
una actriz	unas actrices	some actresses

It might be necessary to add or delete an accent mark to maintain the original stress.

Singular	Plural	Meaning
el joven	los jóvenes	the young people
el examen	los exámenes	the tests
el francés	los franceses	the French (people)
la reunión	las reuniones	the meetings

Except for nouns ending in *-és*, no ending is added for nouns ending in *-s*.

Singular	Plural	Meaning
el martes	los martes	Tuesdays
el paréntesis	los paréntesis	parentheses

Mixed Doubles

In a mixed group of males and females, the masculine plural form always prevails. *Los amigos,* for example, can refer to male friends or a group of male and female friends. If there are only females present, use *las amigas. Los hijos* can refer to sons or to children of both genders. If there are only daughters, however, use *las hijas.*

Some nouns are always plural, as shown in the following table.

In a Flash

Set up *un rincón español* (a Spanish corner) in your home where you study Spanish. Label the items you keep there: photos, stationery items, books, and so on. Practice identifying them using *el, la, los,* and *las.* Then switch to *un, una, unos,* and *unas.* Then change all the singular nouns to plural and vice versa.

Always-Plural Nouns

Noun	Pronunciation	Meaning
las gafas	*lahs gah-fahs*	eyeglasses
las vacaciones	*lahs bah-kah-see-yoh-nehs*	vacation
las tijeras	*lahs tee-heh-rahs*	scissors

More Than One

Imagine you're describing what you saw on vacation to your friends back home. Although you try not to, you tend to exaggerate a little. Tell everyone you saw more than one of the following.

Example: almacén (*ahl-mah-sehn*) department store

Ví los almacenes.
I saw the department stores.

1. tienda (*tee-yehn-dah*) store

2. actriz (*ahk-trees*) actress

3. restaurante (*rrehs-tow-rahn-teh*) restaurant

4. palacio (*pah-lah-see-yoh*) palace

5. automóvil (*ow-toh-moh-beel*) automobile

6. flor (*flohr*) flower

7. rey (*rreh*) king

8. francés (*frahn-sehs*) Frenchman

Practice with Plurals

You've misplaced some items in your hotel room. You know how messy these places can get, especially when you're living out of a suitcase. You've found most of your missing items. Now you're looking for one more of each of the following.

Example: llaves (*yah-behs*) keys

Busco la llave.
I am looking for the key.

1. lápices (*lah-pee-sehs*) pencils
2. regalos (*rreh-gah-lohs*) gifts
3. collares (*koh-yah-rehs*) necklaces
4. paquetes (*pah-keh-tehs*) packages
5. revistas (*rreh-bees-tahs*) magazines
6. lociones (*loh-see-yoh-nehs*) lotions

Answer Key

More Than One

1. las tiendas
2. las actrices
3. los restaurantes
4. los palacios
5. los automóviles
6. las flores
7. los reyes
8. los franceses

Practice with Plurals

1. el lápiz
2. el regalo
3. el collar
4. el paquete
5. la revista
6. la loción

Chapter 7

Going Places

In This Chapter

- ◆ Subject pronouns
- ◆ Ways to conjugate verbs
- ◆ Tips on asking questions
- ◆ Common regular verbs

In Chapter 6, you learned how easy it is to determine whether a Spanish noun is masculine or feminine and how simple it is to form plurals. In this chapter, I show you how to replace a noun with a pronoun and also how to construct simple Spanish sentences by using verbs to talk about a variety of activities.

Using the language in everyday situations is an excellent way to practice your Spanish. Imagine you're on a trip in a Spanish-speaking country. What will you do there? There's probably something for everyone: cosmopolitan cities, ancient ruins, sandy beaches. What will you see? The choices are endless: cathedrals, museums, parks, bullfights. Who will you meet? What about the Spanish-speaking communities of South and Central America and Spain? You'll have countless opportunities to use your newfound skills. Let's go!

What's the Subject?

Verbs are words that express an action, occurrence, or a state of being. To form a complete sentence, you also need to know who or what is the subject of the verb. The subject can be stated (as in "*I* would like to go to the Prado" or "*The tour bus* has just arrived"), or it can be understood in a command (as in "Visit the Alhambra," where the subject is understood to be *you*). The subject can be a noun or a pronoun that replaces the noun. In the sentence "The toreador is entering the arena," for example, *the toreador* can be replaced with the pronoun *he* to form the new sentence "He is entering the arena."

Subject Pronouns

Just as in English, subject pronouns in Spanish, shown in the following table, are given a person (first, second, or third) and a number (singular or plural). In Spanish, however, subject pronouns are used far less frequently than in English. This is because verbs have different endings depending on who is performing the action. If you listen carefully, you can usually determine the subject, even when it's not specified in the sentence. In general, Spanish only uses subject pronouns for the following:

◆ *Clarity*, to differentiate who is doing the action for cases in which verb forms are the same:

Él (or Ella or Ud.) habla bien.
He (or she or you) speak(s) well.

Él descansa mientras Ud. trabaja.
He rests while you work.

¡Atención!

Although subject pronouns usually are omitted, you'll notice that Spanish speakers regularly use the pronouns *usted* and *ustedes* in conversation. In writing, *usted* is usually abbreviated as *Ud.* and *ustedes* as *Uds:*

Ud. es muy inteligente.
You (sing.) are very intelligent.

Uds. son amables.
You (pl.) are very nice.

◆ *Emphasis*, to clearly underline the fact that the subject will be performing the action:

Voy a España.
I'm going to Spain.

Yo voy a España.
I'm going to Spain.

◆ *Politeness*, to be extremely formal and to show impeccable manners and deference to an individual:

¡Pase **Ud.**!
Enter!

Subject Pronouns

Person	Singular	Plural
first	yo (*yoh*) I	nosotros (*noh-soh-trohs*) we
second	tú (*too*) you	vosotros (*boh-soh-trohs*) you
third	él (*ehl*) he	ellos (*eh-yohs*) they
	ella (*eh-yah*) she	ellas (*eh-yahs*) they
	usted (*oo-stehd*) you	ustedes (*oo-steh-dehs*) you

Note that, in Spanish, distinctions are made to accommodate groups containing only females: *nosotros* becomes *nosotras*, *vosotros* becomes *vosotras*, and *ellos* becomes *ellas*. What happens when you want to refer to a mixed group? *Nosotros*, *vosotros*, and *ellos* are used, regardless of the number of males and females in the group.

Says You!

If you studied the preceding "Subject Pronouns" table carefully, you probably noticed that there are two singular and two plural forms for the English word *you*. *Tú* (singular) and *vosotros* (plural) are used when speaking to a friend, relative, child, or pet. *Tú* and *vosotros* are called familiar forms. *Usted* (singular) and *ustedes* (plural) are used to show respect to an older person or when speaking to someone you don't know very well. These are referred to as polite forms and generally are abbreviated as *Ud*. and *Uds*. The abbreviations are always capitalized.

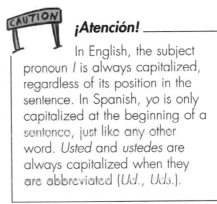

¡Atención!

In English, the subject pronoun *I* is always capitalized, regardless of its position in the sentence. In Spanish, *yo* is only capitalized at the beginning of a sentence, just like any other word. *Usted* and *ustedes* are always capitalized when they are abbreviated (*Ud.*, *Uds.*).

Pronouns are useful because they enable you to speak fluidly without having to constantly repeat the noun. Imagine how tedious it would be to hear "Jorge is Spanish. Jorge is from Madrid. Jorge really knows Jorge's way around the country." Subject pronouns can replace proper nouns as shown in the following table.

Noun	Pronoun
Ricardo	él
Marta	ella
Pedro y Carlos	ellos
Ana y Susana	ellas
Pablo y Carlota	ellos

Just Keep Moving

You routinely use verbs to express action, motion, or a state of being. In Spanish, there are two types of verbs: regular and irregular. All regular verbs follow a set pattern of rules particular to the family to which the verb belongs (-*ar*, -*er*, or -*ir* family). These verbs are easy to use after you've learned the pattern. Irregular verbs, on the other hand, do not have a specific pattern; you must memorize their conjugations individually. Fortunately, regular verbs far outnumber irregular verbs. To get you off to a fast start, this chapter only covers regular verbs.

Regular Verbs

The basic "to" form of a verb is referred to as the *infinitive* (to live, to laugh, to love). In dictionaries (of any language), verbs are presented in the infinitive form, the form of the verb before it has been conjugated.

Memory Master

Sometimes a subject is followed by two verbs. In these instances, only conjugate the first verb. The second should remain in the infinitive:

Quiero salir.
I want to go out.

Sabemos jugar al tenis.
We know how to play tennis.

Deben ir al centro.
They have to go downtown.

Most people are totally unaware that, when they speak in English, they conjugate verbs without giving this grammatical process a second thought. It just comes naturally as the result of copying speech patterns when you first learn to talk. *Conjugation*, quite simply, refers to changing the ending of a regular verb or, perhaps, changing the entire form of an irregular verb so it agrees with its subject. The following shows the infinitive verb "to sing" (a regular verb in English), for example, conjugated into three of its forms:

I sing, You sing, He sings

The verb "to be" is an irregular verb. Here it is conjugated the same way:

I am, You are, He is

In Spanish, there are three large families of regular verbs—verbs whose infinitives end in *-ar*, *-er*, or *-ir*. All verbs within a family are conjugated in exactly the same manner. After you learn the pattern for a family, you know how to conjugate all the verbs in that family.

The *-ar* Verb Family

Let's start by looking at the -ar verb family, which is by far the largest. Notice that the endings are really quite simple. To conjugate -ar verbs, drop -ar from the infinitive and add the endings shown in the following table.

Hablar—to Speak

Singular Forms	Plural Forms
Yo habl**o**	Nosotros habl**amos**
I speak	We speak
Tú habl**as**	Vosotros habl**áis**
You (*sing.*) speak	You (*pl.*) speak
Él, Ella, Ud. habl**a**	Ellos, Ellas, Uds. habl**an**
He, she, you (*sing.*) speak(s)	They, you (*pl.*) speak

If you want to increase your vocabulary quickly, you need to have as many verbs as possible on the tip of your tongue. The cognates in Chapter 3 and the lists of regular verbs in the following tables should get you off to a flying start and can help you in many everyday situations.

Common *-ar* Verbs

Verb	Pronunciation	Meaning
anunciar	*ah-noon-see-yahr*	to announce
ayudar	*ah-yoo-dahr*	to help
buscar	*boos-kahr*	to look for

continues

Common -*ar* Verbs (continued)

Verb	Pronunciation	Meaning
caminar	*kah-mee-nahr*	to walk
charlar	*chahr-lahr*	to chat
comprar	*kohm-prahr*	to buy
desear	*deh-seh-yahr*	to desire
enviar	*ehn-bee-yahr*	to send
escuchar	*ehs-koo-chahr*	to listen (to)
estudiar	*ehs-too-dee-yahr*	to study
expresar	*ehks-preh-sahr*	to express
firmar	*feer-mahr*	to sign
funcionar	*foonk-see-yoh-nahr*	to function
gastar	*gahs-tahr*	to spend (money)
hablar	*ah-blahr*	to speak, to talk
hallar	*ah-yahr*	to find
lavar	*lah-bahr*	to wash
llegar	*yeh-gahr*	to arrive
mandar	*mahn-dahr*	to order
mirar	*mee-rahr*	to look at
necesitar	*neh-seh-see-tahr*	to need
olvidar	*ohl-bee-dar*	to forget
organizar	*ohr-gah-nee-sahr*	to organize
pagar	*pah-gahr*	to pay
preguntar	*preh-goon-tahr*	to ask
quitar	*kee-tahr*	to remove
regresar	*rreh-greh-sahr*	to return
reservar	*rreh-sehr-bahr*	to reserve
telefonear	*teh-leh-foh-neh-yahr*	to phone
tomar	*toh-mahr*	to take
viajar	*bee-yah-hahr*	to travel
visitar	*bee-see-tahr*	to visit

Conjugation 101

Imagine you're traveling with a tour group to various countries in Central America. Practice the conjugation of *-ar* verbs to describe what everyone is doing.

Example: mirar (to look at)
Yo *miro* el programa.

1. anunciar (to announce)
   Él _____ la partida del avión.

2. buscar (to look for)
   Ellos _____ la oficina.

3. observar (to observe)
   Nosotros _____ mucho.

4. andar (to walk)
   Yo _____ por el parque.

5. nadar (to swim)
   Vosotros _____.

6. hablar (to speak)
   Tú _____ del viaje.

The -*er* Verb Family

Now let's look at another family that will also prove easy to manage. To conjugate *-er* verbs, drop *-er* from the infinitive.

Leer—to Read

Singular Forms	Plural Forms
Yo le**o** I read	Nosotros le**emos** We read
Tú le**es** You *(sing.)* read	Vosotros le**éis** You *(pl.)* read
Él, Ella, Ud. le**e** He, she, you *(sing.)* read(s)	Ellos, Ellas, Uds. le**en** They, you *(pl.)* read

Common -*er* Verbs

Verb	Pronunciation	Meaning
aprender	*ah-prehn-dehr*	to learn
beber	*beh-behr*	to drink
comer	*koh-mehr*	to eat
correr	*koh-rrehr*	to run
creer	*kreh-yehr*	to believe
deber	*deh-behr*	to have to, to owe
leer	*leh-yehr*	to read
prometer	*proh-meh-tehr*	to promise

Conjugation 102

In the summer, when lots of people take vacations all over, you'll see many people doing all kinds of things. Practice -*er* verb conjugation by choosing the verb that best completes the following sentences and then putting it in its correct form:

comer (to eat)   aprender (to learn)
correr (to run)   deber (to have to)
beber (to drink)   responder (to answer)

1. Tú _____ al centro.

2. Ellos _____ en el restaurante.

3. Nosotros _____ soda.

4. Ud. _____ a las preguntas.

5. Él _____ frases españolas.

6. Yo _____ firmar (to sign) muchos documentos.

The -*ir* Verb Family

If you've mastered the -*er* verb family, you'll find the -*ir* family to be a snap. When you study the following table, you'll understand why. To conjugate -*ir* verbs, drop -*ir* from the infinitive and add the appropriate endings, as shown in the table.

Decidir—to Decide

Singular Forms	Plural Forms
Yo decid**o** I decide	Nosotros decid**imos** We decide
Tú decid**es** You *(sing.)* decide	Vosotros decid**ís** You *(pl.)* decide
Él, Ella, Ud. decid**e** He, she, you *(sing.)* decide(s)	Ellos, Ellas, Uds. decid**en** They, you *(pl.)* decide

Common *-ir* Verbs

Verb	Pronunciation	Meaning
abrir	*ah-breer*	to open
asistir	*ah-sees-teer*	to attend
cubrir	*koo-breer*	to cover
decidir	*deh-see-deer*	to decide
escribir	*ehs-kree-beer*	to write
omitir	*oh-mee-teer*	to omit
partir	*pahr-teer*	to leave, to divide
subir	*soo-beer*	to go up, to climb
vivir	*bee-beer*	to live

Verbs whose infinitives end in *-er* or *-ir* have the same endings except for the *nosotros* and *vosotros* forms. In these forms, *-er* verbs use *-e* and *-ir* verbs use *-i* as the ending.

Conjugation 103

When traveling in a group, some people want to break away and do their own thing. It's important to them to spend their time the way they want. Using the following *-ir* verbs, tell what each tourist does.

1. vivir (to live)

    Vosotros _____ rápidamente.

continues

continued

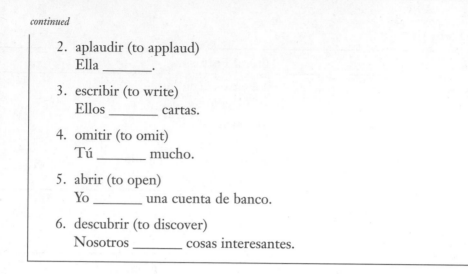

2. aplaudir (to applaud)
   Ella _____.

3. escribir (to write)
   Ellos _____ cartas.

4. omitir (to omit)
   Tú _____ mucho.

5. abrir (to open)
   Yo _____ una cuenta de banco.

6. descubrir (to discover)
   Nosotros _____ cosas interesantes.

Go Ahead! Ask Me!

If you're planning a trip, you surely have loads of questions to ask. This section starts with the quick and easy ones—those that require a simple "yes" or "no" answer. In Spanish, you have three ways to ask a "yes" or "no" question: by intonation, by using the *¿verdad?* tag, and by inversion.

Memory Master
When writing, Spanish speakers use two question marks: an upside-down one (¿) at the beginning of the question and a standard one (?) at the end.
¿Quieres hacer un viaje conmigo?
Would you like to take a trip with me?

When to Raise Your Voice

The easiest way to signify that you're asking a question is simply to change your intonation and to raise your voice at the end of the sentence, just as you do in English. To do this, speak with a rising inflection.

> ¿(Tú) quieres ir a México?
> Do you want to go to Mexico?

Notice how your intonation starts out lower and gradually keeps rising until the end of the sentence.

The Tags *¿Verdad?*, *¿No?*, and *¿Está Bien?*

Another way to ask a "yes" or "no" question is to simply add one of these tags: *¿verdad?* (*behr-dahd*), *¿no?* (*noh*), or *¿está bien?* (*ehs-tah bee-yehn*). These can mean "really?"

"isn't that so?" "is it?" "isn't it?" "are you?" "aren't you?" "do you?" "don't you?" or "all right?" at the end of the phrase.

Tú quieres ir a México, ¿ verdad? (¿*no?*) (¿*está bien?*)
You want to go to Mexico, right? (isn't that so?) (no?) (don't you?)

About Face

The third way to form a question is by inversion, in which the order of the subject (noun or pronoun) and the verb is simply reversed. Once again, you need to raise your voice at the end of the phrase to indicate that you are, in fact, asking a question.

¿Quieres (tú) ir a México?
Do you want to go to Mexico?

¿Son Uds. españoles?
Are you Spanish?

¿Es Juanita de Puerto Rico?
Is Juanita from Puerto Rico?

Remember, whether you're using intonation or inversion, you're asking for exactly the same information: a "*sí*" or "*no*" answer.

And the Answer Is ...

To answer a question affirmatively, use *sí* (pronounced *see*) and give your response, as in the following examples:

¿Fuma Ud.?   Sí, fumo.
Do you smoke?   Yes, I smoke.

To answer negatively, first say "*no*" and then repeat it before the conjugated verb. (Remember, if there are two verbs, only the first is conjugated.)

¿Fuma Ud.?   No, no fumo.
Do you smoke?   No, I don't smoke.
Or:
No, no quiero fumar. No, I don't want to smoke.

You can vary your negative responses by using one of the following negative expressions:

nunca (*noon-kah*)	nada (*nah-dah*)	nadie (*nah-dee-yeh*)
never	nothing	no one

Sentences can be made negative in Spanish in one of two ways:

◆ Put the negative word before the conjugated verb:

Nunca fumo.	Nada puedo ver.	Nadie llega.
I never smoke.	I can't see anything.	No one is arriving.

◆ Put *no* before the conjugated verb, and place the negative expression after the entire verb phrase. Notice how this creates a double negative, which is perfectly acceptable in Spanish.

No fumo nunca.	No puedo ver nada.	No llega nadie.
I never smoke.	I can't see anything.	No one is arriving.

When answering a question, you might even use a triple negative:

¿Quieres comer algo?
Do you want to eat something?

No, no quiero comer nada.
No, I don't want to eat anything.

Answer Key

Conjugation 101

1. anuncia	3. observamos	5. nadáis
2. buscan	4. ando	6. hablas

Conjugation 102

1. corres	3. bebemos	5. aprende
2. comen	4. responde	6. debo

Conjugation 103

1. vivís	3. escriben	5. abro
2. aplaude	4. omites	6. descubrimos

Part 2
Traveling Around

At some point in your life, no doubt, your travels will take you to a Spanish-speaking country. In a fast-paced world where people come and go at an ever-increasing rate, it's inevitable that one day your Spanish will come in handy and prove to be a useful tool.

You'll want to be able to introduce yourself and your traveling companions, perhaps to glean some useful travel tips on the plane. Of no small significance will be the capability to maneuver your way around the airport so you can get to your destination in a timely fashion. Your comfort will also surely be of paramount importance to you.

The highlights of Part 2 include how to get where you're going with style and grace and how to get what you need after you've arrived.

LET'S GO!

Chapter 8

Meetings and Greetings

In This Chapter

- Hellos and good-byes
- *Ser* and *estar*
- The present progressive tense
- Professions
- Ways to obtain information

By now you should feel confident in your ability to combine nouns or pronouns with regular verbs to create simple sentences and ask basic questions in Spanish. It's time to put your knowledge to work by engaging in a short conversation.

Imagine you're flying to Spain for the eagerly anticipated, well-deserved vacation about which you've always dreamed. You find yourself seated next to a Spanish-speaking person. Don't waste this golden opportunity. Introduce yourself. Get some pointers about places to visit, sights to see, and restaurants to sample. It's the perfect way to get your trip off to a great start.

Ask Your Friends

When you travel, do you get last-minute jitters? Are you nervous about how you'll manage after you've arrived in a country where not everyone speaks your language? To relieve this anxiety, consult your travel agent and your friends. They'll be happy to share their experiences and to give you tips, hints, and recommendations on where to stay, eat, and go sightseeing. If at all possible, speak to someone who has lived or spent considerable time in the country you plan to visit. If you find that person sitting next to you on the plane, don't be shy. Take the initiative and strike up a conversation.

Because your fellow traveler is still a stranger to you, good manners dictate that you employ a formal approach. Use some or all of the phrases in the following table as an opening to your conversation.

Phrase	Pronunciation	Meaning
Buenos días	*bweh-nohs dee-yahs*	Hello/Good morning
Buenas tardes	*bweh-nahs tahr-dehs*	Good afternoon
Buenas noches	*bweh-nahs noh-chehs*	Good evening
Señor	*seh-nyohr*	Mr., sir
Señorita	*seh-nyoh-ree-tah*	Miss, young woman
Señora	*seh-nyoh-rah*	Mrs., madam, woman
Me llamo	*meh yah-moh*	My name is
¿Cómo se llama?	*koh-moh seh yah-mah*	What is your name?
¿Cómo está Ud.?	*koh-moh ehs-tah oo-stehd*	How are you?
Muy bien	*mwee bee-yehn*	Very well
Regular	*rreh-goo-lahr*	So-so

An informal opening conversation (between young people or friends) might use the phrases in the following table.

Phrase	Pronunciation	Meaning
¡Hola!	*oh-lah*	Hi!
Me llamo	*meh yah-moh*	My name is
¿Cómo te llamas?	*koh-moh teh yah-mahs*	What's your name?
¿Cómo estás?	*koh-moh ehs-tahs*	How are you?

Phrase	Pronunciation	Meaning
¿Cómo te va?	*koh-moh teh bah*	How are you?
¿Qué tal?	*keh tahl*	How are things?
¿Qué pasa?	*keh pah-sah*	What's happening?
Nada de particular	*nah-dah deh pahr-tee-koo-lahr*	Nothing much

To Be or—to Be!

Many people respond favorably when asked questions about themselves. They like to be the center of attention and enjoy engaging in friendly conversation. If you'd like to get to know the person sitting next to you, ask him or her a few questions. What country or city is he from? How does she feel at the moment? Use the verbs *ser* (to be) and *estar* (to be) to ask these questions.

No, you didn't misread that. In Spanish, there are two ways to express the verb "to be." Let's say your teenage son was born with blond hair. If someone asked about him, you'd use the verb *ser* to say "*Es rubio.*" ("He's blond.") If he's anything like my son's friend who has green hair one day and pink the next, you might be tempted to respond with the verb *estar* (even though it's not really correct), "*Está rubio,*" to denote the impermanence of the hair-color situation. Sound strange? Don't worry. The differences between the two verbs will be clear by the end of this section.

First, let's take a closer look at the conjugations of these two verbs. Just like the English verb "to be," *ser* and *estar* are irregular; you must memorize all their forms. Because both verbs are used so frequently, learning them should be a top priority. Compare the conjugations in the following table. As you will see, Spanish has more irregular forms than English.

The Verbs *Ser* and *Estar* (to Be)

Ser	*Estar*
yo soy (*soy*)	yo estoy (*ehs-toy*)
tú eres (*eh-rehs*)	tú estás (*ehs-tahs*)
él, ella, Ud. es (*ehs*)	él, ella, Ud. está (*ehs-tah*)
nosotros somos (*soh-mohs*)	nosotros estamos (*ehs-tah-mohs*)
vosotros sois (*soy-ees*)	vosotros estáis (*ehs-tah-yees*)
ellos, ellas, Uds. son (*sohn*)	ellos, ellas, Uds. están (*ehs-tahn*)

Determining the Difference

You should have little trouble distinguishing between the two verbs. What happens if you inadvertently use the wrong one? Nothing much. You'll still be understood.

Use *ser* in the following situations:

- To express origin, nationality, or an inherent characteristic or quality:

  Ana es de Cuba.
  Ana is from Cuba.

  Mi hijo es rubio.
  My son is blond.

  Es cubana.
  She's Cuban.

  Es un anillo de oro.
  It's a gold ring.

- To describe the subject of a sentence and any traits that will probably remain unchanged for an extended period of time:

  Ricardo es alto.
  Ricardo is tall.

  El coche es nuevo.
  The car is new.

  Mi madre es profesora.
  My mother is a teacher.

  ¿Quién es? Soy yo.
  Who is it? It's me.

- To express time and dates:

  Son las dos.
  It's two o'clock.

  Es el once de julio.
  It's July 11.

- To express possession:

  Es mi libro.
  It's my book.

  Esta cartera es de Juan.
  This is Juan's wallet.

- Before the preposition *de* to express an inherent quality or characteristic:

  Somos de México.
  We are from Mexico.

  La casa es de madera.
  The house is made of wood.

- With certain impersonal expressions:

  Es necesario practicar.
  It's necessary to practice.

  Es importante estudiar.
  It's important to study.

Use *estar* in the following situations:

- To describe a state or condition of the subject:

  Yo estoy triste.
  I am sad.

  Las puertas están cerradas.
  The doors are closed.

  La casa está sucia.
  The house is dirty.

♦ To express location:

El hotel está en la ciudad.   ¿Dónde está el aeropuerto?
The hotel is in the city.   Where's the airport?

♦ To form the progressive tenses (explained later in this chapter):

Estoy cantando.   Está lloviendo.
I'm singing.   It's raining.

Idioms with *Estar*

Imagine you're having a phone conversation with a Spanish friend who says *"Estoy a punto de salir."* Your Spanish is not quite up to snuff yet, so you get insulted. You hear

the cognate *punto* (point), and you immediately jump to the conclusion that your friend is making a point of leaving because the phone call is boring. In fact, your friend was simply explaining to you that he or she was just about to leave when you called. If something doesn't sound right, it's probably because the speaker is using an idiomatic expression. The following table contains some idioms using *estar*.

> **Memory Master**
>
> To explain that you're from the United States, you could say the following:
>
> Soy de los Estados Unidos.
> (*soy deh lohs ehs-tah-dohs oo-nee-dohs*)

Idioms with *Estar*

Idiomatic Expression	Pronunciation	Meaning
estar a punto de + infinitive	*ehs-tahr ah poon-toh deh*	to be just about + infinitive
estar por	*ehs-tahr pohr*	to be in favor
estar por + infinitive	*ehs-tahr pohr*	to be inclined + infinitive
estar de acuerdo (con)	*ehs-tahr deh ah-kwehr-doh (kohn)*	to agree (with)
estar de vuelta	*ehs-tahr deh bwehl-tah*	to be back
No estoy de acuerdo con Ud.	*noh ehs-toy deh ah-kwehr-doh kohn oo-stehd*	I don't agree with you.
¿Cuándo estarán de vuelta?	*kwahn-doh ehs-tah-rahn deh bwehl-tah*	When will they be back?

You're now ready for a more extensive conversation with the person sitting next to you on the plane. Begin with one of the following phrases asking "Where are you from?":

¿De dónde es Ud.?   ¿De dónde eres?

Ser vs. Estar

Imagine you're sitting on a plane having an informal conversation with your traveling companion. The verb "to be" seems to be repeated over and over again. Should you use *ser* or *estar?* Complete the following sentences with the correct form of the necessary verb:

1. Nosotros _____ de países diferentes.

2. Este vuelo _____ muy interesante.

3. Sus maletas (suitcases) _____ aquí (here).

4. Los pilotos _____ responsables.

5. El aeropuerto _____ cerca de (near) la ciudad.

What Are You Up To?

You're on a plane going to Costa Rica. What are you doing right now? Are you thinking about your jealous friends back home? Maybe you took my advice and are speaking to the person seated next to you. Are you watching a movie or listening to the music being piped through the airline headphones? Perhaps you're just relaxing and tuning out the world. To describe whatever you are doing at this moment (an action in progress), you must use the present progressive tense. Here's an English example to which we all can relate:

> Right now, I'm soaking in the sun on Condado Beach in Puerto Rico.

Memory Master

In Spanish, the present tense expresses what generally happens in the present: *Miro la televisión.* (I [generally] watch television.) The present progressive, on the other hand, expresses what the subject is doing at this moment in time: *Estoy mirando la televisión.* (I'm watching television [right now].)

To form the present progressive in Spanish, use the present tense form of the verb *estar* that corresponds to the subject. *Estar* says that the subject is doing something. Next, choose the verb that expresses the action. You will need the gerund (the *-ing* form) of this verb. To form the gerund, do the following:

- ◆ For verbs whose infinitives end in *-ar*, drop *-ar* and add *-ando*.

Infinitive	Present Progressive	English
cant**ar**	cant*ando*	singing

- ◆ For verbs whose infinitives end in *-er* or *-ir*, drop *-er* or *-ir* and add *-iendo*.

Infinitive	Present Progressive	English
com**er**	com*iendo*	eating
escrib**ir**	escrib*iendo*	writing

- ◆ If a verb whose infinitive ends in *-er* or *-ir* has a stem ending in a vowel, add *-yendo* instead of *-iendo*.

Infinitive	Present Progressive	English
le**er**	le*yendo*	reading
o**ír**	o*yendo*	hearing

Some common irregular gerunds you might find useful include those in the following table.

Infinitive	Present Progressive	English
decir	diciendo	saying, telling
dormir	durmiendo	sleeping
ir	yendo	going
pedir	pidiendo	asking
seguir	siguiendo	following
venir	viniendo	coming

Now you can follow the simple formula for the formation of the present progressive tense—*estar* (conjugated) + gerund:

¿Qué estás haciendo?
keh ehs-tahs ah-see-yehn-doh
What are you doing?

Estoy escuchando música.
ehs-toy ehs-koo-chahn-doh moo-see-kah
I'm listening to music.

What's Happening?

Use the present progressive tense to express what these people are doing right now on a flight to Costa Rica.

1. I am reading a book.
2. He is listening to music.
3. We are eating.
4. You (fam.) are watching a film.
5. They are sleeping.

What's Your Line?

If you want to ask about someone's line of work or to talk about your own, you'll need the proper question and answer format. Use the following in a formal situation:

¿Cuál es su profesión?
What is your profession?

In an informal setting, use the following:

¿Cuál es tu profesión?
What is your profession?

Do not use the indefinite article *un* (*una*) when talking about someone's profession unless it is qualified by an adjective. Simply place the profession after the conjugated form of the verb *ser* (to be). The response to either of the preceding questions might be the following:

Soy sastre.   Ella es una buena camarera.
I am a tailor.   She is a good waitress.

Use *ser* to talk about the professions in the following table. Unless otherwise indicated, change -*o* to -*a* or add -*a* to the final consonant to get the female counterpart for the jobs listed.

La señora Rueda es profesora.   Mi tía es jueza.
Mrs. Rueda is a teacher.   My aunt is a judge.

Professions

Profession	Spanish	Pronunciation
dentist	dentista (*m.* or *f.*)	*dehn-tees-tah*
doctor	doctor (*m.*)	*dohk-tohr*
	médico (*m.*)	*meh-dee-koh*
firefighter	bombero	*bohm-beh-roh*
hairdresser	barbero	*bahr-beh-roh*
jeweler	joyero	*hoh-yeh-roh*
judge	juez	*hwehs*
lawyer	abogado	*ah-boh-gah-doh*
manager	gerente (*m.* or *f.*)	*heh-rehn-teh*
mechanic	mecánico	*meh-kah-nee-koh*
nurse	enfermero	*ehn-fehr-meh-roh*
police officer	policía (*m.* or *f.*)	*poh-lee-see-yah*
postal worker	cartero	*kahr-teh-roh*
secretary	secretario	*seh-kreh-tah-ree-yoh*
student	estudiante (*m.* or *f.*)	*ehs-too-dee-yahn-teh*
teacher	profesor	*proh-feh-sohr*
waiter	camarero	*kah-mah-reh-roh*
waitress	camarera	*kah-mah-reh-rah*

Tell Me All About It

The person next to you seems rather nice. Perhaps she can give you some pointers about what to see when you arrive. You'll need more than simple "yes" or "no" answers, though. What you really want is information. The words and phrases in the following table will see you through.

Gathering Information

Word/Phrase	Pronunciation	Meaning
adónde	*ah-dohn-deh*	to where
a qué hora	*ah keh oh-rah*	at what time
a quién	*ah kee-yehn*	to whom
a qué	*ah keh*	to what
cuál	*kwahl*	which
de quién	*deh kee-yehn*	of, about, from whom
cuánto	*kwahn-toh*	how much, how many
cómo	*koh-moh*	how
dónde	*dohn-deh*	where
de dónde	*deh dohn-deh*	from where
por qué	*pohr keh*	why
cuándo	*kwahn-doh*	when
quién*	*kee-yehn*	who, whom
qué	*keh*	what

Note that Spanish does not have separate words to distinguish between who (subject) and whom (object). The word quién *serves as both.*

Memory Master

All *interrogatives* (words that ask questions) in Spanish have accent marks. This distinguishes them from words that are spelled the same but state a fact rather than ask for information.

Getting Information

The easiest way to get information is to ask for it. The easiest way to ask for information is to put the question word (or words) immediately before the verb. If you're using a subject pronoun or noun, put that pronoun or noun after the verb. The following questions are some you might want to ask a traveling companion. Try them with the familiar *tú* form (in parentheses) as well:

¿Con quién viaja Ud.? (viajas)
With whom are you traveling?

¿Por qué viaja Ud.? (viajas)
Why are you traveling?

¿De dónde es Ud.? (eres)
Where are you from?

Qué mira Ud.? (miras)
What are you looking at?

Tell Me More

Ask as many questions as you can based on the information given to you in the following selection. You must ask Ana questions about herself and her friend, María.

Me llamo Ana. Soy de Quito. Mi amiga, María, es de San Juan. Deseamos amigas americanas para mantener correspondencia porque deseamos practicar el inglés. Hablamos inglés sólamente cuando estamos en clase. El inglés es una lengua muy interesante. Somos estudiantes muy serias.

Answer Key

Ser vs. Estar

1. somos   2. es   3. están   4. son   5. está

What's Happening?

1. Yo estoy leyendo un libro.
2. Él está escuchando música.
3. Nosotros estamos comiendo.
4. Tú estás mirando una película.
5. Ellos están durmiendo.

Tell Me More

¿Cómo te llamas? ¿De dónde eres? ¿Quién es su amiga? ¿De dónde es? ¿Qué desean? ¿Por qué? ¿Qué desean Uds. practicar? ¿Cuándo hablan inglés? ¿Cómo es el inglés? ¿Cómo son Uds?

Chapter **9**

Getting to Know You

In This Chapter

◆ Members of the family

◆ Ways to show possession

◆ How to present family and friends

◆ All about *tener* (to have)

◆ Words to describe people and things

Your conversations in Chapter 8 enabled you to make new friends and introduce yourself. If you're traveling with family members, sometime you'll have to introduce them or help them jump in and join the discussion. Perhaps you'll be presented to family members of your newfound friend. Be prepared for any and all circumstances.

Meet the Clan!

While sitting on a tour bus to El Yunque (the rainforest in Puerto Rico), I struck up a conversation with a lovely older couple carrying an adorable young child. I went on and on, admiring and cootchie-cooing their grandson. In retrospect, I really didn't know when to stop. Imagine my overwhelming embarrassment when, at the end of the trip, the gentleman politely took me aside and explained that the child was their son. I learned some very important lessons that day: keep your mouth shut; give the other person an opportunity to talk; and never, ever make assumptions when you meet someone. If you want to prevent a potentially mortifying situation such as this, consult the following table.

Family Members

Spanish	Pronunciation	Meaning
Male		
abuelo	*ah-bweh-loh*	grandfather
padrino	*pah-dree-noh*	godfather
padre	*pah-dreh*	father
padrastro	*pah-drahs-troh*	stepfather
hijo	*ee-hoh*	son, child
hermano	*ehr-mah-noh*	brother
hermanastro	*ehr-mah-nahs-troh*	stepbrother
primo	*pree-moh*	cousin
sobrino	*soh-bree-noh*	nephew
tío	*tee-yoh*	uncle
nieto	*nee-yeh-toh*	grandson
suegro	*sweh-groh*	father-in-law
yerno	*yehr-noh*	son-in-law
cuñado	*koo-nyah-doh*	brother-in-law
novio	*noh-bee-yoh*	boyfriend
Female		
abuela	*ah-bweh-lah*	grandmother
madrina	*mah-dree-nah*	godmother
madre	*mah-dreh*	mother
madrastra	*mah-drahs-trah*	stepmother
hija	*ee-hah*	daughter
hermana	*ehr-mah-nah*	sister
hermanastra	*ehr-mah-nah-strah*	stepsister
prima	*pree-mah*	cousin
sobrina	*soh-bree-nah*	niece

Spanish	Pronunciation	Meaning
Female		
tía	*tee-yah*	aunt
nieta	*nee-yeh-tah*	granddaughter
suegra	*sweh-grah*	mother-in-law
nuera	*nweh-rah*	daughter-in-law
cuñada	*koo-nyah-dah*	sister-in-law
novia	*noh-bee-yah*	girlfriend

You Belong to Me

You're somebody's somebody: your parents' child, your friend's friend, your brother's sister, your sister's brother, and so on. You can show possession in Spanish in two ways: by using the preposition *de* or by using possessive adjectives.

In English, we use *-'s* or *-s'* after a noun to show possession. But apostrophes don't exist in Spanish. If you want to talk about Santiago's sister, you have to say *la hermana de Santiago*, which translates as "the sister of Santiago." To express possession or relationship, use the preposition *de* (of) and change the word order from what you're accustomed to in English:

> Es la madre de Enrique.
> She's Enrique's mother.

If the possessor is referred to by a common noun such as "the boy" (He is the boy's father), in Spanish, *de* contracts with the definite article *el* to become *del* (of the):

> Es el padre *del* muchacho.
> He's the boy's father.

Possessive Adjectives

Possessive adjectives (my, your, his, her, and so on) are used to show that something belongs to someone. In Spanish, possessive adjectives agree with the nouns they describe (the person or thing possessed) rather than with the subject (the person possessing them). See how this compares with English in the following table.

English	Spanish
He speaks with his parents.	Habla con sus padres.
He speaks with their parents.	Habla con sus padres.
She speaks with our uncle.	Habla con nuestro tío.

You'd use *sus padres* (his or their parents) because *sus* agrees with the word *padres*, which is plural. *Sus* can mean his, her, its, your, or their. *Nuestro tío* (our uncle) is used because *nuestro* agrees with the word *tío*, which is masculine. This difference can make Spanish somewhat tricky for English speakers. Just remember that it's important to know the gender (masculine or feminine) of the item possessed. When in doubt, look it up. The following table summarizes the use of possessive adjectives.

Possessive Adjectives

Used Before Masculine Nouns		Used Before Feminine Nouns		English
Singular	Plural	Singular	Plural	
mi	mis	mi	mis	my
tu	tus	tu	tus	your
su	sus	su	sus	his, her, your, its
nuestro	nuestros	nuestra	nuestras	our
vuestro	vuestros	vuestra	vuestras	your
su	sus	su	sus	their

Totally Possessed

Give the possessive adjective you would use to talk about these people:

1. (their) _____ padres

2. (his) _____ hermana

3. (your, sing. fam.) _____ hija

4. (my) _____ padre

5. (your, pol.) _____ primos

6. (our) _____ familia

I'll Introduce You

When I travel, I like to speak to as many new and different people as I can. It's amazing how many great tips you can get and how much money you can save by listening to the experiences and advice of others. If you want to introduce yourself, you would say:

> Buenos días. Me llamo _____.
> *bweh-nohs dee-yahs. meh yah-moh*
> Hello. My name is _____.

You might ask about a companion:

> ¿Conoce Ud. (Conoces tú) a mi primo, Paco?
> *koh-noh-seh oo-stehd (koh-noh-sehs too) ah mee pree-moh pah-koh*
> Do you know my cousin, Paco?

If the answer to this question is no, you then would say:

> Quiero presentarle (presentarte) a mi primo, Paco.
> *kee-yeh-roh preh-sehn-tahr-leh (preh-sehn-tahr-teh) ah mee pree-moh pah-koh*
> I'd like to introduce you to my cousin, Paco.

Or you might respond:

> Le (Te) presento a mi primo, Paco.
> *leh (teh) preh-sehn-toh ah mee pree-moh pah-koh*
> Let me present you to my cousin, Paco.

To express pleasure at having met someone in a formal situation, you might say:

> Mucho gusto en conocerle.
> *moo-choh goo-stoh ehn koh-noh-sehr-leh*
> It's nice to meet (know) you.

If you are introduced to someone less formally, it's all right to say:

> Encantado (masculine speaker; Encantada
> for a feminine speaker)
> *ehn-kahn-tah-doh/ehn-kahn-tah-dah*
> Delighted.

Memory Master

If *su* makes the meaning of the possessor unclear, you can clarify your thoughts by adding *de* + the name of the person, or *de* + *él, de* + *ella*, or *de* + *Ud:*

> Es su padre.
> Es el padre de Marta.
> Es el padre de ella.

The correct reply to an introduction is:

> El gusto es mío.
> *ehl goos-toh ehs mee-yoh*
> The pleasure is mine.

More and More

That wasn't so difficult, was it? Now your curiosity has gotten the best of you, and you'd like to take the conversation a little further. Maybe you want to discuss your marital situation or your age or to ramble on about your family and friends. If you want to strike up a friendship, you have to keep the conversation flowing. The verb you'll find most helpful is *tener* (to have). Like the verbs *ser* and *estar* (to be), *tener* is an irregular verb; you must memorize all its forms, as seen in the following table.

Conjugating *Tener* (to Have)

Conjugated Form of *Tener*	Pronunciation	Meaning
Yo tengo	*tehn-goh*	I have
Tú tienes	*tee-yeh-nehs*	You have
Él, ella, Ud. tiene	*tee-yeh-neh*	He, she, one has
Nosotros tenemos	*teh-neh-mohs*	We have
Vosotros tenéis	*teh-neh-ees*	You have
Ellos, ellas, Uds. tienen	*tee-yeh-nehn*	They have

In Chapter 5, I showed you idioms with *tener* that describe physical conditions. (To refresh your memory, take a quick look back.) Now let's look at some different idioms with *tener.*

Imagine you finally have arrived at your destination after a long flight. You're tired and hungry, and all you want to do is get to your hotel and start your vacation. You want to find the exit, and you want to find it *now.* Spanish is an easy language; just add the letter *-o* and whatever you say will sound okay—right? You approach a distinguished-looking couple and ask, "*¿Tiene éxito?*" They look at you strangely, reply "*Sí,*" and walk away somewhat confused. You just asked them if they were successful, and you are no closer to your exit than you were a minute ago. To avoid this type of mistake, study the *tener* idioms in the following table.

Idioms with *Tener*

Idiom	Pronunciation	Expression
tener cuidado	*teh-nehr kwee-dah-doh*	to be careful
tener éxito	*teh-nehr ehk-see-toh*	to be successful
tener ganas de	*teh-nehr gah-nahs deh*	to feel like
tener lugar	*teh-nehr loo-gahr*	to take place
tener prisa	*teh-nehr pree-sah*	to be in a hurry
tener que + infinitive	*teh-nehr keh*	to have to + infinitive
tener suerte	*teh-nehr swehr-teh*	to be lucky

Be sure to conjugate the verb when you use it in context, as in the following examples:

Yo siempre tengo cuidado.
I'm always careful.

Nosotros tenemos éxito.
We are successful.

¿Tú tienes ganas de salir?
Do you feel like going out?

¡Atención!

Tener que indicates necessity. Be sure to give a correct translation when using the infinitive: *Yo tengo que trabajar.* (I have to work.)

What's He/She Like?

Your conversation with the person sitting next to you is becoming more intimate as the flight continues. If you were asked to describe yourself, what would you want to say? Are you a romantic? Do you consider yourself patient? Do your friends consider you introverted or extroverted?

If you want to describe a person, place, thing, or idea in detail, you must use adjectives. Spanish adjectives always agree in gender (masculine or feminine) and number (singular or plural) with the nouns or pronouns they modify. In other words, all the words in a Spanish sentence must conform. Notice the difference between the adjectives in the following examples:

Su padre está contento.   Su madre está contenta.
Her father is happy.   Her mother is happy.

Fortunately, adjectives follow the same (or similar) rules for gender and number formation as the nouns you studied in Chapter 6.

Adjectives Have Gender

Most adjectives can be made feminine by simply replacing the -o ending of the masculine singular form with an -a, as shown in the following table. Remember that the sound changes as well; the final -o sound (oh) of the masculine changes to the -a sound (ah) of the feminine.

Forming Feminine Adjectives

Masculine	Pronunciation	Feminine	Meaning
alto	*ahl-toh*	alta	tall
atractivo	*ah-trahk-tee-boh*	atractiva	attractive
bajo	*bah-hoh*	baja	short
bonito	*boh-nee-toh*	bonita	pretty
divertido	*dee-behr-tee-doh*	divertida	fun
enfermo	*ehn-fehr-moh*	enferma	sick
extrovertido	*ehks-troh-behr-tee-doh*	extrovertida	extroverted
feo	*feh-yoh*	fea	ugly
guapo	*gwah-poh*	guapa	pretty
impulsivo	*eem-pool-see-boh*	impulsiva	impulsive
introvertido	*een-troh-behr-tee-doh*	introvertida	introverted
listo	*lees-toh*	lista	ready
malo	*mah-loh*	mala	bad
moreno	*moh-reh-noh*	morena	dark-haired, dark-skinned
nuevo	*nweh-boh*	nueva	new
pequeño	*peh-keh-nyoh*	pequeña	small
rico	*rree-koh*	rica	rich
rubio	*rroo-bee-yoh*	rubia	blond
simpático	*seem-pah-tee-koh*	simpática	nice
tímido	*tee-mee-doh*	tímida	shy
viejo	*bee-yeh-hoh*	vieja	old

If an adjective already ends in an -*e*, -*a*, or a consonant, it's not necessary to make any changes at all. Both the masculine and feminine forms are spelled and pronounced exactly the same, as shown in the following table.

Adjectives Ending in -*e*, -*a*, or a Consonant

Adjective	Pronunciation	Meaning
***Adjectives Ending in* -e**		
alegre	*ah-leh-greh*	happy
amable	*ah-mah-bleh*	nice
eficiente	*eh-fee-see-yehn-teh*	efficient
independiente	*een-deh-pehn-dee-yehn-teh*	independent
inteligente	*een-teh-lee-gehn-teh*	intelligent
paciente	*pah-see-yehn-tee*	patient
pobre	*poh-breh*	poor
responsable	*rrehs-pohn-sah-bleh*	responsible
triste	*trees-teh*	sad
valiente	*bah-lee-yehn-teh*	brave
***Adjectives Ending in* -a**		
egoísta	*eh-goh-ees-tah*	selfish
idealista	*ee-deh-yah-lees-tah*	idealistic
materialista	*mah-teh-ree-yah-lees-tah*	materialistic
optimista	*ohp-tee-mees-tah*	optimistic
pesimista	*peh-see-mees-tah*	pessimistic
realista	*rreh-yah-lees-tah*	realistic
Adjectives Ending in a Consonant		
cortés	*kohr-tehs*	courteous
cruel	*kroo-wehl*	cruel
emocional	*eh-moh-see-yoh-nahl*	emotional
fácil	*fah-seel*	easy
joven	*hoh-behn*	young
normal	*nohr-mahl*	normal
sentimental	*sehn-tee-mehn-tahl*	sentimental
tropical	*troh-pee-kahl*	tropical

Although they end in a consonant, adjectives describing nationality add -*a* to form the feminine:

español	española
francés	francesa
alemán	alemana

Adjectives that end in -*or* add -*a* to form the feminine:

trabajador	trabajadora
hablador	habladora
encantador	encantadora

When There's a Crowd

Adjectives are often made plural in the same way as nouns:

♦ When the singular form of the adjective ends in a vowel, simply add an -*s*.

Singular	Plural	Meaning
alto	altos	tall
alta	altas	tall
egoísta	egoístas	selfish
grande	grandes	big

♦ If an adjective ends in a consonant, add -*es*.

Singular	Plural	Meaning
fácil	fáciles	easy
emocional	emocionales	emotional
sentimental	sentimentales	sentimental
popular	populares	popular

◆ Some adjectives add or drop an accent mark to maintain the original stress.

Singular	Plural	Meaning
joven	jóvenes	young
francés	franceses	French
inglés	ingleses	English
alemán	alemanes	German
cortés	corteses	courteous

The Perfect Position

In Spanish, descriptive adjectives are generally placed after the nouns they modify. Compare this with English, in which the opposite is done:

> un hombre interesante
> an interesting man

Descriptive adjectives can be placed before the noun to emphasize the quality of the adjective or its intrinsic characteristic:

> ¿Tienes malos recuerdos?
> Do you have bad memories?

> Miré las hojas verdes.
> I saw the green leaves.

In a Flash

Make a list of all the adjectives you would use to describe yourself. Then describe as many of your acquaintances as you can.

When used before a masculine, singular noun, *bueno* becomes *buen*, *grande* becomes *gran*, and *malo* becomes *mal*. *Grande* is also shortened to *gran* before a feminine, singular noun:

> Esteban es un buen muchacho.
> Stephen is a good boy.

> La gran mayoría aceptó la decisión.
> The great majority accepted the decision.

Give Your Own Descriptions

Some people have an opinion about everything—and they're not at all shy about expressing it. Tell how you feel about the people and places in the following list. Remember that to use the verb *ser*, you must be describing a inherent characteristic.

1. El Prado es un museo _____.

2. Las películas españolas son _____.

3. El presidente de los Estados Unidos es un hombre _____.

4. Las tiendas de Madrid son _____.

5. Las corridas de toros son _____.

Answer Key

Totally Possessed

1. sus   2. su   3. tu   4. mi   5. sus   6. nuestra

Give Your Own Descriptions

Sample responses:

1. importante

2. buenas

3. inteligente

4. magníficas

5. divertidas

Chapter 10

The Plane Has Landed

In This Chapter

- Planes and airports: getting around
- The verb *ir* (to go)
- How to give and receive directions
- Ways to get help when you need it

Your dream vacation is off to a good start, and you're settled in for a long, smooth flight. You've really accomplished quite a bit already. You've planned your trip, introduced yourself to your seatmates, and struck up conversations with people about all kinds of topics. Perhaps you've been successful in obtaining the names of some fabulous restaurants, attractions you don't want to miss, or even the phone number of someone who would be thrilled to show off his or her hometown when you arrive.

After you're on the ground and have deplaned, you'll discover there are many things to do before you can catch a ride to wherever you're staying. Your first stop might be the passport check. Then it's off to retrieve your bags so you can pass uneventfully through customs. You'll certainly want to pick up some local currency before you choose a means of transportation to your destination. You will be able to achieve all this and more by the time you finish this chapter.

On the Plane

The person next to you on the plane is constantly coughing in your face, is carrying his pet lizard in his shirt pocket, and has his headset turned up to the max (and you don't like his taste in music). You *must* change your seat. While you have the stewardess's attention, you'd like to ask some questions about takeoff and landing. In this section, I give you the vocabulary you need to solve these problems and to get the information you need.

el avión

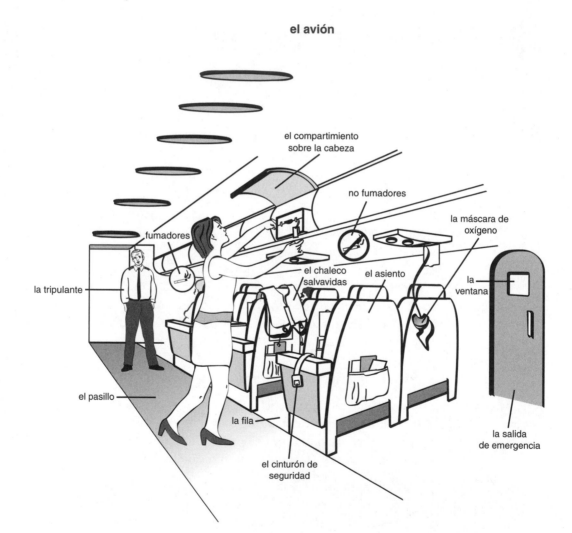

el compartimiento sobre la cabeza

no fumadores

la máscara de oxígeno

fumadores

el chaleco salvavidas

el asiento

la tripulante

la ventana

el pasillo

la fila

la salida de emergencia

el cinturón de seguridad

Once onboard the airplane, you will hear safety announcements that refer to items in and around the plane. If you have any questions or doubts, the words in the following table will help you figure things out.

Inside the Plane

Airport Term	Spanish	Pronunciation
airplane	el avión	*ehl ah-bee-yohn*
aisle	el pasillo	*ehl pah-see-yoh*
crew	la tripulación	*lah tree-poo-lah-see-yohn*
crew member	el/la tripulante	*ehl/lah tree-poo-lahn-teh*
emergency exit	la salida de emergencia	*lah sah-lee-dah deh eh-mehr-hehn-see-yah*
life vest	el chaleco salvavidas	*ehl chah-leh-koh sahl-bah-bee-dahs*
(no) smokers	(no) fumadores	*(noh) foo-mah-doh-rehs*
to smoke	fumar	*foo-mahr*
overhead compartment	el compartimiento sobre la cabeza	*ehl kohm-pahr-tee-mee-yehn-toh soh-breh lah kah-beh-sah*
oxygen mask	la máscara de oxígeno	*lah mahs-kah-rah deh ohk-see-heh-noh*
row	la fila	*lah fee-lah*
seat	el asiento	*ehl ah-see-yehn-toh*
seat belt	el cinturón de seguridad	*ehl seen-too-rohn deh seh-goo-ree-dahd*
tray	la bandeja	*lah bahn-deh-hah*
window	la ventana	*lah behn-tah-nah*

At the Airport

The plane has landed, and everyone rushes to collect his carry-on luggage and disembark. Once you're in the airport, expect to find signs everywhere pointing you in various directions. Where should you go first? You don't have much choice here. You need to proceed to passport control and customs, where it will be established that you're not an international jewel thief. Next, you might want to stop at a money exchange. If you're anything like me, you'll probably head for the nearest *baños* (bathrooms). The following table provides all the words you need to know to get through the airport and on your way to your first destination!

Inside the Airport

Airport Term	Spanish	Pronunciation
airline	la aerolínea	*lah ah-yee-roh-lee-neh-yah*
airline terminal	la terminal	*lah tehr-mee-nahl*
airport	el aeropuerto	*ehl ah-yee-roh-pwehr-toh*
arrival	la llegada	*lah yeh-gah-dah*
baggage claim area	el reclamo de equipaje	*ehl rreh-klah-moh deh eh-kee-pah-heh*
bathrooms	los baños	*lohs bah-nyohs*
bus stop	la parada de autobús	*lah pah-rah-dah deh ow-toh-boos*
car rental	el alquiler de carros	*ehl ahl-kee-lehr deh kah-rrohs*
carry-on luggage	el equipaje de mano	*ehl eh-kee-pah-heh deh mah-noh*
cart	el carrito	*ehl kah-rree-toh*
customs	la aduana	*lah ah-doo-wah-nah*
departure	la salida	*lah sah-lee-dah*
destination	el destino	*ehl dehs-tee-noh*
elevators	los ascensores	*lohs ah-sehn-soh-rehs*
entrance	la entrada	*lah ehn-trah-dah*
exit	la salida	*lah sah-lee-dah*
flight	el vuelo	*ehl bweh-loh*
gate	la puerta	*lah pwehr-tah*
information	la información	*lah een-fohr-mah-see-yohn*
landing	el aterrizaje	*ehl ah-teh-rree-sah-heh*
lost and found	la oficina de objetos perdidos	*lah oh-fee-see-nah deh ohb-heh-tohs pehr-dee-dohs*
to miss the flight	perder el vuelo	*pehr-dehr ehl bweh-loh*
money exchange	el cambio de dinero	*ehl kahm-bee-yoh deh dee-neh-roh*
passport control	el control de pasaportes	*ehl kohn-trohl deh pah-sah-pohr-tehs*

Airport Term	Spanish	Pronunciation
porter	el portero	*eh pohr-teh-roh*
security check	el control de seguridad	*ehl kohn-trohl deh seh-goo-ree-dahd*
stopover	la escala	*lah ehs-kah-lah*
suitcase	la maleta	*lah mah-leh-tah*
takeoff	el despegue	*ehl dehs-peh-geh*
taxis	los taxis	*lohs tahk-sees*
ticket	el boleto	*ehl boh-leh-toh*
trip	el viaje	*ehl bee-yah-heh*

Going Places

The irregular verb *ir* (to go) will come in handy if you need directions at the airport or anywhere else. When you want to tell someone exactly where you want to go, use the terms in the following table.

In a Flash

Make a list of all the places you and your friends are going this weekend.

Conjugating *Ir* (to Go)

Conjugated Form of *Ir*	Pronunciation	Meaning
yo voy	*yoh boy*	I go
tú vas	*too bahs*	you go
él, ella, Ud. va	*ehl (eh-yah, oo-stehd) bah*	he, she, you, one goes
nosotros vamos	*noh-soh-trohs bah-mohs*	we go
vosotros vais	*boh-soh-trohs bah-yees*	you go
ellos, ellas, Uds. van	*eh-yohs (eh-yahs, oo-steh-dehs) bahn*	they go

Ir is generally followed by the preposition *a* (to). If the location to which the subject is going is masculine, *a* contracts with *el* (the) to become *al* (to the), as in the following example:

> Yo voy al aeropuerto.
> I'm going to the airport.

No changes are necessary with *a la*, *a los*, or *a las*:

Vamos a la salida.   ¿Vas a las ventanas?
We're going to the exit.   Are you going to the windows?

Van a los ascensores.
They are going to the elevators.

Use *ir* + *a* to express going to a city, state, or country:

Voy a Nueva York.   ¿Van a México?
I'm going to New York.   Are they going to México?

Ana va a Florida.
Anna is going to Florida.

Use *ir* + *en* to express the many different ways to go someplace:

Yo voy a España en avión.
I'm going to Spain by plane.

An exception is when you decide to walk:

ir a pie   Vamos a casa a pie.
to go by foot   We walk home.

Where To?

It's been a long flight. After two piña coladas, people tend to become rather friendly and chatty. Everyone is discussing where he or she is going. Complete their sentences by filling in the correct form of *ir*:

1. Nosotros _____ a Barcelona.   4. Uds. _____ a Toledo.

2. Marta _____ a Madrid.   5. Yo _____ a Granada.

3. Tú _____ a Sevilla.   6. Vosotros _____ a Cádiz.

How Do I Get to ...?

It's easy to become disoriented in a large, bustling airport after a tiring journey. No doubt you will need to ask for directions at some point. Here are some easy phrases to help you on your way:

¿Dónde está la salida?
dohn-deh ehs-tah lah sah-lee-dah
Where is the exit?

La salida, por favor.
lah sah-lee-dah pohr fah-bohr
The exit, please.

¿Dónde están los taxis?
dohn-deh ehs-tahn lohs tahk-sees
Where are the taxis?

Los taxis, por favor.
los tahk-sees pohr fah-bohr
The taxis, please.

If you're not sure whether the airport has the facilities you're looking for, or if you just want to know if they're nearby, use the word *hay* (Is there?, Are there?, There is …, There are …). *Hay* probably is one of the most useful words in the Spanish language. Here is how it works to both ask and answer questions:

¿Hay baños por aquí?
ah-yee bah-nyohs pohr ah-kee
Are there bathrooms nearby?

Hay baños al lado de la entrada.
ah-yee bah-nyohs ahl lah-doh deh lah ehn-trah-dah
There are bathrooms next to the entrance.

Following Directions

Suppose the place you're looking for is out of pointing range. In this case, you'll need more specific directions. The verbs in the following table will help get you where you want to go.

Verbs Giving Directions

Verb	Pronunciation	Meaning
bajar	*bah-hahr*	to go down
caminar	*kah-mee-nahr*	to walk
continuar	*kohn-tee-noo-ahr*	to continue
cruzar	*kroo-sahr*	to cross
doblar	*doh-blahr*	to turn
ir	*eer*	to go
pasar	*pah-sahr*	to pass
seguir	*seh-geer*	to follow, to continue
subir	*soo-beer*	to go up
tomar	*toh-mahr*	to take

In a Flash

Pretend you have a Spanish-speaking visitor staying at your house. Give directions in Spanish to the nearest movie theater, museum, library, and supermarket.

To give you directions, a person in the know has to give you a command. Because you're being told where to go or what to do, the subject of the command is "you." In English, the subject "you" is understood and is not spoken. In Spanish, although often omitted, the subject pronoun for "you" can be used in the command.

You've already learned that there are four ways to say "you" in Spanish: the familiar *tú* and *vosotros* forms and the polite *Ud.* and *Uds.* forms. In this book, we concentrate only on the formal commands, the ones you'd give or get from someone you don't know well. (Chances are you'll be speaking to your loved ones in English.)

To form commands with regular verbs using *Ud.:*

1. Drop the *-o* ending from the *yo* form of the present tense of the verb you're using.

2. If the verb is an *-ar* infinitive verb, add an *-e.*

3. If the verb is an *-er* or *-ir* infinitive verb, add an *-a.*

To use *Uds.* as your subject, just add an *-n* to the *Ud.* form. The following table shows how it's done.

Infinitive	Present Tense *Yo* Form	Formal Commands Singular (*Ud.*)	Plural (*Uds.*)	Meaning
tomar	tomo	tome	tomen	take
leer	leo	lea	lean	read
abrir	abro	abra	abran	open

Memory Master

Spanish requires an upside-down exclamation mark (¡) at the beginning of an emphasized command and a regular exclamation mark (!) at the end.

Here are some examples:

¡Tome el autobús!
Take the bus!

¡Lea este folleto!
Read this brochure!

¡Abran sus maletas!
Open your suitcases!

Some Spanish verbs have an irregular *yo* form. You've already seen this with *tener*, and you'll come across others in later chapters. These verbs follow the same rules as regular verbs to form commands. The following table shows how it works with *tener*.

Infinitive	Present Tense *Yo* Form	Formal Commands Singular (*Ud.*)	Plural (*Uds.*)
tener	tengo	tenga	tengan

Here is an example of *tener* in a command:

¡Tengan cuidado!
Be careful!

The following three irregular verbs are useful in the command form.

Verb (Meaning)	Formal Commands Singular (*Ud.*)	Plural (*Uds.*)
dar (to give)	dé	den
ir (to go)	vaya	vayan
ser (to be)	sea	sean

Here is an example of using *ir* in a command:

¡Vaya al aeropuerto ahora!
Go to the airport now!

Giving Commands

Before you can receive or give commands, you'll need a little practice. Complete the following exercise by filling in the missing command forms as well as their meanings.

Verb	*Ud.*	*Uds.*	Meaning
ir	_____	_____	_____
continuar	_____	_____	_____

continues

continued

Verb	Ud.	Uds.	Meaning
bajar	_____	_____	_____
seguir*	siga	_____	_____
caminar	_____	_____	_____
subir	_____	_____	_____
pasar	_____	_____	_____
tomar	_____	_____	_____
doblar	_____	_____	_____
cruzar*	cruce	_____	_____

These verbs—and others ending in -car, -gar, -zar, and -guir—have special spelling changes that will be explained in Chapter 11. After you have learned the Ud. form, however, Uds. should be a snap for you.

Prepositions

Prepositions show the relation of a noun to another word in a sentence. Take a look back at the idiomatic expressions for direction and location in Chapter 5. These are, in fact, prepositional phrases. Study the simple prepositions in the following table. These also will be useful for giving or receiving directions.

Prepositions

Preposition	Pronunciation	Meaning
a	*ah*	to, at
alrededor (de)	*ahl-reh-deh-dohr (deh)*	around
antes (de)	*ahn-tehs (deh)*	before
cerca (de)	*sehr-kah (deh)*	near
contra	*kohn-trah*	against
de	*deh*	of, from, about
debajo (de)	*deh-bah-hoh (deh)*	under
delante (de)	*deh-lahn-teh (deh)*	in front (of)
después (de)	*dehs-pwehs (deh)*	after
detrás (de)	*deh-trahs (deh)*	behind, in back (of)
en	*ehn*	in

Preposition	Pronunciation	Meaning
encima (de)	*ehn-see-mah (deh)*	above
entre	*ehn-treh*	between, among
frente a	*frehn-teh ah*	opposite, facing
hacia	*ah-see-yah*	toward
lejos (de)	*leh-hohs (deh)*	far (from)
para	*pah-rah*	for, in order to
por	*pohr*	by, through
sin	*seen*	without
sobre	*soh-breh*	on, upon

Contractions

In certain cases, contractions form with the prepositions *a* and *de*, whether they're used alone or as part of a longer expression. *A* + *el* becomes *al*, and *de* + *el* becomes *del*, for example:

Voy al teatro.   Hablo del teatro.
I go to the theater.   I speak about the theater.

Hablo a la muchacha, a los hombres, y a las mujeres.
I speak to the girl, the men, and the women.

Por vs. Para

Because both *por* and *para* can mean "for," often there's confusion about when to use these prepositions. Study the following table to learn how to use them properly. Keep in mind, though, that even if you use the wrong word, you'll still be understood.

Por Indicates	*Para* Indicates
Motion:	*Destination to a place:*
Paso por el aeropuerto.	El avión sale para Madrid.
I pass by the airport.	The airplane leaves for Madrid.
Means, manner:	*Destination to a recipient:*
Viajo por tren.	Este regalo es para mi esposo.
I travel by train.	This gift is for my husband.

Por Indicates	*Para* Indicates
A period of time:	*A time limit:*
Trabajo por la noche.	La cita es para el lunes.
I work at night.	The appointment is for Monday.
Frequency; in exchange for:	*Purpose:*
Salgo una vez por semana.	Es un billete para entrar.
I go out once a week.	It's an admission ticket.
Son dos libros por $20.	
They are two books for $20.	

What Did You Say?

Have you ever gotten directions from someone and nodded as if you understood where to go, but with so many rights and lefts and so much pointing you actually lost track halfway through? The phrases in the following table will be an invaluable aid if you need something repeated or need more information.

Expressing Lack of Understanding and Confusion

Expression	Pronunciation	Meaning
Con permiso.	*kohn pehr-mee-soh*	Excuse me.
Yo no comprendo.	*yoh noh kohm-prehn-doh*	I don't understand.
Yo no le oigo.	*yoh noh leh oy-goh*	I don't hear you.
Repita por favor.	*rreh-pee-tah pohr fah-bohr*	Please repeat it.
Hable más despacio.	*hah-bleh mahs dehs-pah-see-yoh*	Speak more slowly.
¿Qué dijo?	*keh dee-hoh*	What did you say?

Always be polite. After getting directions from a Spanish-speaking person, you should say *Muchas gracias* (*moo-chahs grah-see-ahs;* Thank you). The answer you will probably receive is *De nada* (*deh nah-dah;* You're welcome).

Answer Key

Where To?

1. vamos   2. va   3. vas   4. van   5. voy   6. vais

Giving Commands

Verb	Ud.	Uds.	Meaning
ir	vaya	vayan	go
continuar	continué	continuén	continue
bajar	baje	bajen	go down
seguir*	siga	sigan	continue
caminar	camine	caminen	walk
subir	suba	suban	go up
pasar	pase	pasen	pass
tomar	tome	tomen	take
doblar	doble	doblen	turn
cruzar*	cruce	crucen	cross

Chapter 11

Getting There Is Half the Fun

In This Chapter

- Ways to get around town
- Go-go verbs
- How to ask questions
- Cardinal numbers
- Tips on telling time

Maneuvering your way through passport control, baggage claim, and customs can take a bit of time. Although you're probably tired and travel-worn, be patient. Despite your honest face and harried look, the people in charge have a job to do and really do need to unpack your suitcases. Really.

Maybe your travel agent has provided transfers (transportation to your final destination) as part of your travel package. If so, expect a bus, a car, or a taxi to be waiting to whisk you away. Look for a driver carrying a sign bearing your name or the name of your hotel. If not, it's up to you to find your own way. Some of your choices are presented in this chapter.

The Way to Go

You usually can find buses, subways, trains, taxis, and cars at the airport to get you where you want to go. Before making a choice, consider what is of foremost importance to you. If money is tight and you're traveling light, you might opt for a bus, subway, or train. If you're in a big hurry and money is no object, take a cab. If it's comfort you want and you're an experienced international driver, you might want to rent a car. Weigh all the pros and cons and make the decision that's best for you.

Method of Transportation	Pronunciation	Meaning
el coche	*ehl koh-cheh*	car
el automóvil	*ehl ow-toh-moh-beel*	car
el carro	*ehl kah-rroh*	car
el taxi	*ehl tahk-see*	taxi
el autobús	*ehl ow-toh-boos*	bus
el tren	*ehl trehn*	train
el metro	*ehl meh-troh*	subway

Go-Go Verbs

You might decide to *hacer una excursión* (*ah-sehr oo-nah ehks-koor-see-yohn;* go on an outing) by subway, bus, train, or car. Whatever means of transportation you choose, it's sure to be the right one for you. If you want to use the verbs in this paragraph (and other similar verbs) while planning a trip, you have to learn their idiosyncrasies and irregularities.

Go-go verbs are regular or irregular verbs whose *yo* form ends in -*go* instead of -*o*. Because these are all high-frequency verbs, it is best to spend a little time learning them. Let's start with verbs that are regular in all forms except *yo*.

Verb	Meaning	*Yo* Form	Remaining Conjugations
hacer	to make, to do	yo ha**go**	haces, hace, hacemos, hacéis, hacen
poner	to put	yo pon**go**	pones, pone, ponemos, ponéis, ponen
salir	to leave, to go out	yo sal**go**	sales, sale, salimos, salís, salen
traer	to bring	yo trai**go**	traes, trae, traemos, traéis, traen
valer	to be worth	yo val**go**	vales, vale, valemos, valéis, valen

Use *hacer* in the following phrases.

Phrase	Pronunciation	Meaning
hacer la maleta	*ah-sehr lah mah-leh-tah*	to pack
hacer una pregunta	*ah-sehr oo-nah preh-goon-tah*	to ask a question
hacer un viaje	*ah-sehr oon bee-yah-heh*	to take a trip
hacer una visita	*ah-sehr oo-nah bee-see-tah*	to pay a visit

For irregular go-go verbs, just concentrate on the *yo* form for the time being. You will see the complete conjugations of these verbs in later chapters.

Verb	Meaning	*Yo* Form
decir	to tell, to say	yo di**go**
oír	to hear	yo oi**go**
tener	to have	yo ten**go**
venir	to come	yo ven**go**

Other spelling changes occur in regular verbs to preserve the original sound of the verb. These changes occur before an *o* or an *a* and enable the consonant to be pro- nounced correctly. Because all the verbs you will be looking at end in *-er*, *-ir*, or *-uir*, the only subject affected in the present tense is *yo*, which ends in *-o*.

Why is that? Quite simply, it's because only *-ar* infinitives have verb forms that end in *-a*. All *yo* forms end in *-o*; therefore, all *yo* forms are affected.

Take a closer look at some of these verbs you might want to use with regularity:

◆ Verbs ending in *-cer* and *-cir* change *c* to *z* before *o* or *a*.

Verb	Affected Meaning	Unaffected Conjugation	Conjugations	Command
convencer	to convince	yo convenzo	convences convence convencemos convencéis convencen	Convenza Ud. Convenzan Uds.

◆ Verbs ending in *-ger* and *-gir* change *g* to *j* before *o* or *a*.

Verb	Affected Meaning	Unaffected Conjugation	Conjugations	Command
escoger	to choose	yo escojo	escoges escoge escogemos escogéis escogen	Escoja Ud. Escojan Uds.
dirigir	to direct	yo dirijo	diriges dirige dirigimos dirigís dirigen	Dirija Ud. Dirijan Uds.

◆ Verbs ending in *-guir* change *gu* to *g* before *o* or *a*.

Verb	Meaning	Affected Conjugation	Unaffected Conjugations	Command
seguir	to follow, continue	yo sigo	sigues sigue seguimos segues siguen	Siga Ud. Sigan Uds.

What's What?

When you're on a trip and you meet someone new, there are many questions you can ask, such as "What's your name? address? profession? What activities do you like?" The list is endless. In Spanish, two words can mean either which or what: *cuál* or *qué*. How do you know when to use each?

◆ *¿Qué?* asks "what" when referring to a description, a definition, or an explanation. It asks "which" when used before a noun.

¿Qué es esto?   ¿Qué libro lee Ud.?
What's this?   Which book are you reading?

¿Qué estás haciendo?
What are you doing?

◆ *¿Cuál? ¿Cuáles?* asks "what" before the verb *ser* (to be). It means "which (one[s])" before other verbs and the preposition de.

¿Cuál es su nombre?   ¿Cuáles deseas?
What's your name?   Which (ones) do you want?

¿Cuál de los dos prefieres?
Which (one) of the two do you prefer?

If you want to go off on your own, expect to ask questions using *¿qué?* and *¿cuál?* to get you where you want to go. Do you feel confident enough to ask what bus you need to take and what its number is? These are the questions you would need:

¿Qué autobús tomo?   ¿Cuál es su número?
keh ow-toh-boos toh-moh   *kwahl ehs soo noo-meh-roh*
Which bus do I take?   What is its number?

Using *¿Qué?* and *¿Cuál?*

Now that you've learned about *¿qué?* and *¿cuál?* you can ask the nosy questions you didn't know how to ask before. Imagine you're speaking to the passenger next to you in the customs line. Ask her for the following information:

1. Name   4. What her nationality is

2. Address   5. Which subway line to take to Mexico City

3. What she is reading

Fill 'Er Up

Do you feel daring enough to rent a car at *un alquiler de coches?* Be sure to compare the rates and models available at several rental agencies before making a final decision. Keep in mind that the cost of fuel in other countries is generally more than double the price in the United States. The following phrases will prove useful when renting a car:

Quiero alquilar un (make of car).
kee-yeh-roh ahl-kee-lahr oon
I'd like to rent a (make of car).

Prefiero el cambio automático.
preh-fee-yeh-roh ehl kahm-bee-yoh ow-toh-mah-tee-koh
I prefer automatic transmission.

¿Cuánto cuesta por día (por semana) (por kilómetro)?
kwahn-toh kwehs-tah pohr dee-yah (pohr seh-mah-nah) (por kee-loh-meh-troh)
How much does it cost per day (per week) (per kilometer)?

¿Cuánto cuesta el seguro?
kwahn-toh kwehs-tah ehl seh-goo-roh
How much is the insurance?

¿Está incluída la gasolina?
ehs-tah een-kloo-wee-dah lah gah-soh-lee-nah
Is the gas included?

¿Acepta Ud. tarjetas de crédito? ¿Cuáles?
ah-sehp-tah oo-stehd tahr-heh-tahs deh kreh-dee-toh? kwah-lehs
Do you accept credit cards? Which ones?

¡Atención!

Use *el semáforo* (*una luz de tráfico*) to refer to a traffic light. Don't forget to stop *al semáforo rojo* (at the red light) and to go *al semáforo verde* (at the green light).

So you've decided to rent a car. That's great, but take a tip from me—carefully inspect the car, inside and out. You never know what might go wrong once you're on the road. Be sure you have *un gato* (*oon gah-toh*; a jack) and *una goma de repuesto* (*oo-nah goh-mah deh rreh-pwehs-toh*; a spare tire) in the trunk. It's no fun to get stuck on a road in the middle of nowhere. The following tables list some other car parts you might need to know.

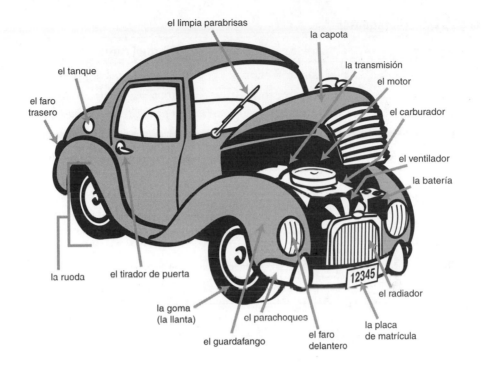

Car Parts

Car Part	Spanish	Pronunciation
battery	la batería	*lah bah-teh-ree-yah*
bumper	el parachoques	*ehl pah-rah-choh-kehs*
carburetor	el carburador	*ehl kahr-boo-rah-dohr*
door handle	el tirador de puerta	*ehl tee-rah-dohr deh pwehr-tah*
fan	el ventilador	*ehl behn-tee-lah-dohr*
fender	el guardafango	*ehl gwahr-dah-fahn-goh*
gas tank	el tanque	*ehl tahn-keh*
headlight	el faro delantero	*ehl fah-roh deh-lahn-teh-roh*
hood	la capota	*lah kah-poh-tah*
license plate	la placa de matrícula	*lah plah-kah deh mah-tree-koo-lah*
motor	el motor	*ehl moh-tohr*
radiator	el radiador	*ehl rah-dee-yah-dohr*
taillight	el faro trasero	*ehl fah-roh trah-seh-roh*

continues

Car Parts   (continued)

Car Part	Spanish	Pronunciation
tire	la goma, la llanta	*lah goh-mah, lah yahn-tah*
transmission	la transmisión	*lah trahns-mee-see-yohn*
trunk	el baúl	*ehl bah-ool*
wheel	la rueda	*lah roo-weh-dah*
windshield wiper	el limpia parabrisas	*ehl leem-pee-yah pah-rah-bree-sahs*

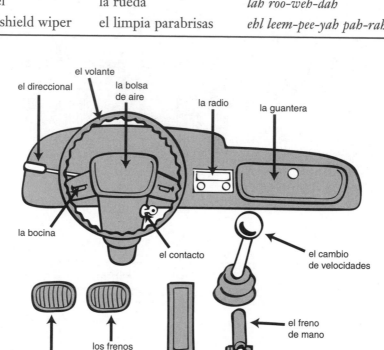

Interior Car Parts

Car Part	Spanish	Pronunciation
accelerator	el acelerador	*ehl ah-seh-leh-rah-dohr*
directional signal	el direccional	*ehl dee-rehk-see-yoh-nahl*
gear shift	el cambio de velocidades	*ehl kahm-bee-yoh deh beh-loh-see-dah-dehs*
horn	la bocina	*lah boh-see-nah*

Chapter 11: Getting There Is Half the Fun   113

Car Part	Spanish	Pronunciation
ignition	el contacto	*ehl kohn-tahk-toh*
radio	la radio	*lah rrah-dee-yoh*
steering wheel	el volante	*ehl boh-lahn-teh*
brakes	los frenos	*lohs freh-nohs*
clutch pedal	el embrague	*ehl ehm-brah-geh*
glove compartment	la guantera	*lah gwahn-teh-rah*
hand brake	el freno de mano	*ehl freh-noh deh mah-noh*
air bag	la bolsa de aire	*lah bohl-sah deh ah-yee-reh*
anti-lock brakes	los frenos anti-bloqueantes	*lohs freh-nohs ahn-tee bloh-keh-yahn-tehs*

In most parts of the world, distance is measured in kilometers. The following table shows the approximate equivalents.

Distance Measures (Approximate)

Miles	Kilometers
.62	1
3	5
6	10
12	20
31	50
62	100

Show Me the Way to Go Home

You've rented a car but have failed to learn to translate the road signs. Now you've received a traffic ticket while visiting a foreign country. Ouch. Take a moment to read the road signs in the following figure. Some of them are trickier than they first seem.

My husband and I, with kids in tow, were traveling from Santo Domingo to the lovely Casa de Campo resort at the other side of the Dominican Republic. When we got to a fork in the road, which crept up on us a little too quickly, I screamed, "Go this way!" He went that way. We got lost, of course. How much easier life would have been had I just said "Go north." Don't be like me; know your compass directions.

Direction	Pronunciation	Meaning
al norte	*ahl nohr-teh*	to the north
al este	*ahl ehs-teh*	to the east
al sur	*ahl soor*	to the south
al oeste	*ahl oh-wehs-teh*	to the west

How Much?

If you want to be able to say what number bus, subway, or flight you're taking or find out just how big a dent that rent-a-car is going to make in your pocket, you need to know the Spanish numbers in the following table. They also come in handy for other uses, such as asking what time the bank opens.

Cardinal Numbers

Number	Spanish	Pronunciation
0	cero	*seh-roh*
1	uno	*oo-noh*
2	dos	*dohs*
3	tres	*trehs*
4	cuatro	*kwah-troh*
5	cinco	*seen-koh*
6	seis	*seh-yees*
7	siete	*see-yeh-teh*
8	ocho	*oh-choh*
9	nueve	*noo-weh-beh*
10	diez	*dee-yehs*
11	once	*ohn-seh*
12	doce	*doh-seh*
13	trece	*treh-seh*
14	catorce	*kah-tohr-seh*
15	quince	*keen-seh*
16	dieciséis	*dee-yehs-ee-seh-yees*
17	diecisiete	*dee-yehs-ee-see-yeh-teh*
18	dieciocho	*dee-yehs-ee-oh-choh*
19	diecinueve	*dee-yehs-ee-noo-weh-beh*
20	veinte	*behn-teh*
21	veintiuno	*behn-tee-oo-noh*
22	veintidós	*behn-tee-dohs*
30	treinta	*treh-een-tah*
40	cuarenta	*kwah-rehn-tah*
50	cincuenta	*seen-kwehn-tah*
60	sesenta	*seh-sehn-tah*
70	setenta	*seh-tehn-tah*

continues

Cardinal Numbers (continued)

Number	Spanish	Pronunciation
80	ochenta	*oh-chehn-tah*
90	noventa	*noh-behn-tah*
100	cien	*see-yehn*
101	ciento uno	*see-yehn-toh oo-noh*
200	doscientos	*dohs see-yehn-tohs*
500	quinientos	*kee-nee-yehn-tohs*
700	setecientos	*seh-teh-see-yehn-tohs*
900	novecientos	*noh-beh-see-yehn-tohs*
1,000	mil	*meel*
2,000	dos mil	*dohs meel*
100,000	cien mil	*see-yehn meel*
1,000,000	un millón	*oon mee-yohn*
2,000,000	dos millones	*dohs mee-yoh-nehs*

Spanish numbers are not too tricky. Be aware of the following rules, however:

◆ The conjunction *y* (and) is used only for compound numbers between 30 and 99. Use of *y* with numbers between 16 and 29 is very rare:

dieciséis libros   veintiun días
16 books   21 days

But:

treinta y nueve dólares *$39*

◆ The numbers 16 through 19 and 21 through 29 are generally written as one word. The numbers 16, 22, 23, and 26 have accents on the last syllable:

16: dieciséis   *23:* veintitrés

22: veintidós   *26:* veintiséis

The numbers 16 through 19 and 21 through 29 may also be written as two words joined by *y*:

16: diez y seis   *23:* veinte y tres

◆ The Spanish, as do many other European cultures, write the number 1 with a little hook on top. To distinguish a 1 from the number 7, put a line through the 7 when you write it.

◆ In numerals and decimals, the Spanish use periods where we use commas, and vice versa. For example (English/Spanish): 1,000/1.000; .25/0,25; $9.95/$9,95.

◆ *Uno* (one) is used only when counting. *Uno* becomes *un* before masculine nouns and *una* before feminine nouns:

uno, dos, tres one, two, three	treinta y un muchachos thirty-one boys
un hombre y una mujer a man and a woman	veintiuna muchachas twenty-one girls

◆ In compounds of *cien* (*doscientos*, *trescientos*), there must be agreement with a feminine noun:

doscientos hombres two hundred men	trescientas mujeres three hundred women

◆ Use *cien* before nouns and the numbers *mil* and *millones*. Before all other numbers, use *ciento*:

cien libros one hundred books	cien mil personas one hundred thousand people
ciento veinte carros one hundred and twenty cars	cien millones de dólares one billion dollars

◆ *Un*, although not used before *ciento* or *mil*, is used before *millón*. If a noun follows *millón*, put *de* between *millón* and the noun:

mil quinientos años fifteen hundred years	un millón de habitants a million inhabitants

---

Your Number's Up

Phone numbers in Madrid consist of seven numbers—one group of three and two pairs. The regional code for Madrid is (91). Whenever you call from outside the city, you must dial this number before the phone number. In South American, Central American, and Caribbean countries, phone numbers are grouped in three pairs. How would you ask the operator for the following numbers:

45   67   89   _____   325   11   72   _____

What's the Time?

You will probably hear the following question often:

¿Qué hora es?
keh oh-rah ehs
What time is it?

The following table shows you how to answer it.

Telling Time

The Time	Spanish	Pronunciation
It is 1:00.	Es la una.	*ehs lah oo-nah*
It is 2:05.	Son las dos y cinco.	*sohn lahs dohs ee seen-koh*
It is 3:10.	Son las tres y diez.	*sohn lahs trehs y dee-yehs*
It is 4:15.	Son las cuatro y cuarto.	*sohn lahs kwah-troh ee kwahr-toh*
It is 5:20.	Son las cinco y veinte.	*sohn lahs seen-koh ee behn-teh*
It is 6:25.	Son las seis y veinticinco.	*sohn lahs seh-yees ee behn-tee-seen-koh*
It is 7:30.	Son las siete y media.	*sohn lahs see-yeh-teh ee meh-dee-yah*
It is 7:35. (25 min. to 8)	Son las ocho menos veinticinco.	*sohn lahs oh-choh meh-nohs behn-tee-seen-koh*
It is 8:40. (20 min. to 9)	Son las nueve menos veinte.	*sohn lahs noo-weh-beh meh-nohs behn-teh*
It is 9:45. (15 min. to 10)	Son las diez menos cuarto.	*sohn lahs dee-yehs meh-nohs kwahr-toh*
It is 10:50. (10 min. to 11)	Son las once menos diez.	*sohn lahs ohn-seh meh-nohs dee-yehs*
It is 11:55. (5 min. to noon)	Son las doce menos cinco.	*sohn lahs doh-seh meh-nohs seen-koh*
It is noon.	Es el mediodía.	*ehs ehl meh-dee-yoh-dee-yah*
It is midnight.	Es la medianoche.	*ehs lah meh-dee-yah-noh-cheh*

In schedules and timetables, the official 24-hour system is commonly used. Midnight is the 0 hour:

0 h 15 = 12:15 A.M.   21 h 50 = 9:50 P.M.

15 horas = 3:00 P.M.

All numbers are expressed in full in the 24-hour system:

22 h 45 = veintidós horas cuarenta y cinco

Keep the following in mind when you tell time:

- Use *es* for "it is" when it's 1 o'clock. For other numbers, because they are plural, use *son*.

- To express the time after the hour, use *y* and the number of minutes past the hour.

- To express time before the next hour (after half past), use the number of the following hour then *menos* + the number of minutes to the next hour:

Son las tres menos cuarto.
It's 2:45.

You also might hear the time expressed as follows:

Son las dos y cuarenta y cinco.
It's 2:45.

To schedule activities or find out when something is planned, you'll need to know more than how to tell time. Imagine you asked someone when a sporting event was taking place and the person responded "*Hace dos horas.*" You might take this to mean "At 2 o'clock" or maybe "There are two hours before the match." Wrong. In fact, you've missed the match because it started two hours ago. The expressions in the following table will help you get there next time.

Time Expressions

Time Expressions	Spanish	Pronunciation
a second	un segundo	*oon seh-goon-doh*
a minute	un minuto	*oon mee-noo-toh*
an hour	una hora	*oo-nah oh-rah*
in the morning	de la mañana	*deh lah mah-nyah-nah*
in the afternoon (P.M.)	de la tarde	*deh lah tahr-deh*
in the evening	de la noche	*deh lah noh-cheh*
at what time?	¿a qué hora?	*ah keh oh-rah*
at exactly 2 o'clock	a las dos en punto	*ah lahs dohs ehn poon-toh*

continues

Time Expressions   (continued)

Time Expressions	Spanish	Pronunciation
at about 2 o'clock	a eso de las dos	*ah eh-soh deh lahs dohs*
a quarter of an hour	un cuarto de hora	*oon kwahr-toh deh oh-rah*
a half hour	una media hora	*oo-nah meh-dee-yah oh-rah*
in an hour	en una hora	*ehn oo-nah oh-rah*
in a couple of hours	en un par de horas	*ehn oon pahr deh oh-rahs*
in a second (flash)	en un abrir y cerrar de ojos	*ehn oon ah-breer ee seh-rrahr deh oh-hohs*
in a while	dentro de un rato	*dehn-troh deh oon rrah-toh*
often	a menudo	*ah meh-noo-doh*
until 2 o'clock	hasta las dos	*ahs-tah lahs dohs*
before 3 o'clock	antes de las tres	*ahn-tehs deh lahs trehs*
after 3 o'clock	después de las tres	*dehs-pwehs deh lahs trehs*
from what time?	¿desde qué hora?	*dehs-deh keh oh-rah*
from 6 o'clock	desde las seis	*dehs-deh lahs seh-yees*
an hour ago	hace una hora	*ah-seh oo-nah oh-rah*
per hour	por hora	*pohr oh-rah*
early	temprano	*tehm-prah-noh*
late	tarde	*tahr-deh*
late (in arriving)	en retraso	*ehn rreh-trah-soh*
on time	a tiempo	*ah tee-yehm-poh*
good-bye	adiós	*ah-dee-yohs*

Answer Key

Using ¿Qué? and ¿Cuál?

1. ¿Cuál es su nombre?
2. ¿Cuál es su dirección?
3. ¿Qué lee Ud.?
4. ¿Cuál es su nacionalidad?
5. ¿Qué metro va a la Ciudad de México?

Your Number's Up

cuarenta y cinco

trescientos veinticinco

sesenta y siete

once

ochenta y nueve

setenta y dos

Chapter **12**

Settling In

In This Chapter

- ◆ Hotel facilities
- ◆ Ordinal numbers
- ◆ Shoe verbs

Your plane has landed, you've cleared customs, and you've found a mode of transportation that caters to your pocketbook and your needs. No matter how you've chosen to travel, remember to look out the window as you ride along. Taking in your surroundings right from the start will give you the lay of the land and help you get your bearings. Before you know it, you'll be at your hotel.

For some people, when it comes to travel accommodations, the bare necessities are acceptable. After all, why pay for luxurious décor when you plan to spend most of your time outside your room? You'd rather use the money for entertainment and souvenirs. Others prefer downright opulence. For them, vacation means being treated like royalty. Whatever your personal preferences might be, this chapter teaches you how to get the room and services you desire.

A Room with a View?

Before reserving a room anywhere, even here in the United States, be sure to verify with your travel agent or the hotel management that the facilities you need will be at your disposal. When you arrive, you want to be assured that your expectations will be met. Ask all important questions before you send a deposit. Use the following table to help you find out what hotel facilities are available.

Hotel Facilities

Facilities	Spanish	Pronunciation
bar	el bar	*ehl bahr*
business center	el centro de negocios	*ehl sehn-troh deh neh-goh-see-yohs*
cashier	el cajero	*ehl kah-heh-roh*
concierge (caretaker)	el conserje	*ehl kohn-sehr-heh*
doorman	el portero	*ehl pohr-teh-roh*
elevator	el ascensor	*ehl ah-sehn-sohr*
fitness center	el gimnasio	*ehl heem-nah-see-yoh*
gift shop	la tienda de regalos	*lah tee-yehn-dah deh rreh-gah-lohs*
laundry and dry-cleaning service	la lavandería	*lah lah-bahn-deh-ree-yah*
maid service	la gobernanta	*lah goh-behr-nahn-tah*
restaurant	el restaurante	*ehl rrehs-tow-rahn-teh*
swimming pool	la piscina	*lah pee-see-nah*
valet parking	la atendencia del garaje	*lah ah-tehn-dehn-see-yah dehl gah-rah-heh*

Do you want a great view when you book a hotel room? I never thought I did until I went to Dorado Beach in Puerto Rico. We booked a room facing the pool. What a mistake! Night and day all we heard were kids screaming and yelling. And we were trying to get away from ours! Next time I go, you can be sure I'll ask for *una habitación con vista al mar*. I'll expect a lot of other amenities, too. Use the following table to help you get exactly what you want.

Getting What You Want

Amenities	Spanish	Pronunciation
a single room	una habitación con una sola cama	*oo-nah ah-bee-tah-see-yohn kohn oo-nah soh-lah kah-mah*
a double room	una habitación con dos camas	*oo-nah ah-bee-tah-see-yohn kohn dohs kah-mahs*
air conditioning	el aire acondicionado	*ehl ah-yee-reh ah-kohn dee-see-yoh-nah-doh*
alarm clock	el despertador	*ehl dehs-pehr-tah-dohr*
balcony	el balcón	*ehl bahl-kohn*
bathroom (private)	el baño privado	*ehl bah-nyoh pree-bah-doh*
on the courtyard	con vista al patio	*kohn bees-tah ahl pah-tee-yoh*
on the garden	con vista al jardín	*kohn bees-tah ahl har-deen*
on the sea	con vista al mar	*kohn bees-tah ahl mahr*
safe (deposit box)	la caja fuerte	*lah kah-hah fwehr-teh*
shower	la ducha	*lah doo-chah*
telephone (dial-direct)	el teléfono (directo)	*ehl teh-leh-foh-noh (dee-rehk-toh)*
television (color)	la televisión (en color)	*lah teh-leh-bee-see-yohn (ehn koh-lohr)*
toilet facilities	el W.C. el baño los servicios	*ehl doh-bleh-beh seh ehl bah-nyoh lohs sehr-bee-see-yohs*

What Do You Need?

What if you need something for your room to make your stay more enjoyable? Any of the phrases in the following table may help you.

Phrase	Pronunciation	Meaning
Quisiera	*kee-see-yeh-rah*	I would like
Me falta(n)	*meh fahl-tah(n)*	I need
Necesito	*neh-seh-see-toh*	I need

I have to have enough towels. That's one of my pet peeves. Unfortunately, hotels never seem to give you enough. If something you need or want is missing from your room, don't be shy. Ask for it! Remember, the management wants to please you and to make your stay enjoyable. The following table lists a few things you might need.

Necessities

Necessity	Spanish	Pronunciation
an ashtray	un cenicero	*oon seh-nee-seh-roh*
a bar of soap	una barra de jabón	*oo-nah bah-rrah deh hah-bohn*
a beach towel	una toalla de baño	*oo-nah toh-wah-yah deh bah-nyoh*
a blanket	una manta	*oo-nah mahn-tah*
hangers	unas perchas	*oo-nahs pehr-chahs*
ice cubes	cubitos de hielo	*koo-bee-tohs deh yeh-loh*
mineral water	agua mineral	*ah-gwah mee-neh-rahl*
a pillow	una almohada	*oo-nah ahl-moh-ah-dah*
a roll of toilet paper	un rollo de papel higiénico	*oon rroh-yoh deh pah-pehl ee-hee-yeh-nee-koh*
tissues	pañuelos de papel	*pah-nyoo-weh-lohs deh pah-pehl*
a towel	una toalla	*oo-nah toh-wah-yah*
a transformer (an electric adapter, converter)	un transformador	*oon trahns-fohr-mah-dohr*

Remember that the verb *faltar* agrees with the number of items needed:

Me falta una toalla.   Me faltan seis perchas.
I need a towel.   I need six hangers.

Going Up

When you get on an elevator in a Spanish-speaking country, someone will probably ask you, "*¿Qué piso, por favor?*" (*keh pee-soh pohr fah-bohr*). In this situation, you will be happy you studied the ordinal numbers in the following table.

Ordinal Numbers

Ordinal Number	Spanish	Pronunciation
first	primero	*pree-meh-roh*
second	segundo	*seh-goon-doh*
third	tercero	*tehr-seh-roh*
fourth	cuarto	*kwahr-toh*
fifth	quinto	*keen-toh*
sixth	sexto	*sehks-toh*
seventh	séptimo	*sehp-tee-moh*
eighth	octavo	*ohk-tah-boh*
ninth	noveno	*noh-beh-noh*
tenth	décimo	*deh-see-moh*

The Spanish ordinal numbers can be abbreviated as shown below. A superscript ^{o} is used after an ordinal number referring to a masculine noun while a superscript $(^a)$ is used after an ordinal number referring to a feminine noun. Superscript ^{er} is used for primer and tercer when they are followed by a noun, when they stand alone, superscript ^{o} is used.

Used Before a Masculine Noun	Used Before a Feminine Noun
primer 1er	primera 1^a
segundo 2°	segunda 2^a
tercer 3er	tercera 3^a
cuarto 4°	cuarta 4^a

Es el 3er día.   Es el 1°.   Es la 4ª vez.
It's the third day.   It's the first.   It's the fourth time.

Keep the following in mind when using ordinal numbers:

◆ *Primero* and *tercero* drop their final -*o* before a masculine singular noun:

el primer día   el tercer hombre
the first day   the third man

But:

| la primera semana | el siglo tercero | la tercera mujer |
| the first week | the third century | the third woman |

◆ Ordinal numbers can be made feminine by changing the final *-o* of the masculine form to *-a*, as in the following:

| el segundo acto | la segunda escena |
| the second act | the second scene |

¡Atención! _____

The only cardinal number that has a masculine and feminine form is *un, una*. All ordinal numbers from 1 to 10 are masculine singular forms.

◆ The Spanish usually use ordinal numbers through the tenth. After that, cardinal numbers are used.

| la cuarta cuadra | la Sexta Avenida |
| the fourth block | Sixth Avenue |

la página veinte
page 20

Using Ordinal Numbers

The Hotel Escobar is a luxury high-rise establishment. Express on which floors the families are staying:

1. (5th) Los Cabrera están en el _____ piso.

2. (9th) Los Pérez están en el _____ piso.

3. (4th) Los Nuñez están en el _____ piso.

4. (3th) Los Hidalgo están en el _____ piso.

5. (1st) Los Ruiz están en el _____ piso.

6. (7th) Los Rivera están en el _____ piso.

It's Time for a Change

Verbs are perhaps the most useful tool in any language because they help you express actions. You couldn't have a conversation without them. A few categories of regular *-ar*, *-er*, and *-ir* verbs in Spanish require spelling changes within the stem of the verb. Only the beginning of the verb is affected; the regular endings remain the same.

I like to call these verbs "shoe verbs" because the rules for the spelling changes work as if we put the subject pronouns that follow one set of rules within the shoe and the others outside the shoe. To make this more clear, let's look at the pronouns that go inside and outside the shoe.

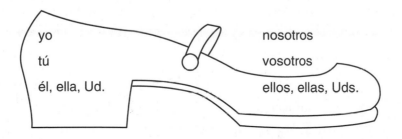

In other words, the verb forms for *yo, tú, él, ella, Ud., ellos, ellas,* and *Uds.* follow one set of rules. *Nosotros* and *vosotros* follow a different set of rules. Now let's look at the different categories.

Memory Master
Shoe verb infinitives are often shown with their appropriate change in parentheses: *pensar* (ie); *mostrar* (ue).

Verbs Ending in *-ar* and *-er*

For verbs ending in *-ar* or *-er*, the stem vowel change takes place in the present tense. The *e* changes to *ie* and *o* changes to *ue* in all forms of the shoe except *nosotros* and *vosotros*.

pensar *(to think)*

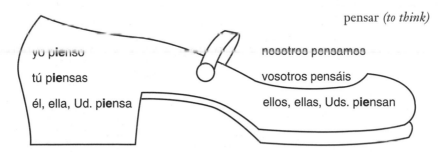

Other verbs that can be conjugated just like *pensar* include the following.

Verb	Pronunciation	Meaning
atravesar	*ah-trah-beh-sahr*	to cross
cerrar	*seh-rrahr*	to close

continues

continued

Verb	Pronunciation	Meaning
comenzar	*koh-mehn-sahr*	to begin
empezar	*ehm-peh-sahr*	to begin
quebrar	*keh-brahr*	to break

querer *(to want)*

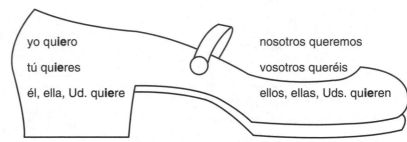

yo qu**ie**ro   nosotros queremos

tú qu**ie**res   vosotros queréis

él, ella, Ud. qu**ie**re   ellos, ellas, Uds. qu**ie**ren

Other verbs that can be conjugated just like *querer* include the following.

Verb	Pronunciation	Meaning
descender	*deh-sehn-dehr*	to descend
entender	*ehn-tehn-dehr*	to understand
perder	*pehr-dehr*	to lose

mostrar *(to show)*

yo m**ue**stro   nosotros mostramos

tú m**ue**stras   vosotros mostráis

él, ella, Ud. m**ue**stra   ellos, ellas, Uds. m**ue**stran

Other verbs that can be conjugated just like *mostrar* include the following.

Verb	Pronunciation	Meaning
almorzar	*ahl-mohr-sahr*	to eat lunch
contar	*kohn-tahr*	to tell
costar	*kohs-tahr*	to cost
encontrar	*ehn-kohn-trahr*	to meet, find
jugar (u to ue)	*hoo-gahr*	to play games, sports
recordar	*rreh-kohr-dahr*	to remember

As you probably noticed in the list of verbs similar to *mostrar*, the *o* in the stem changes to *ue* in all the verbs except one—*jugar* (to play). There is no *o* in *jugar*; instead, the *u* changes to *ue*. It is a high-frequency verb, so pay special attention to this distinction.

The verb *jugar* changes *u* to *ue* as follows:

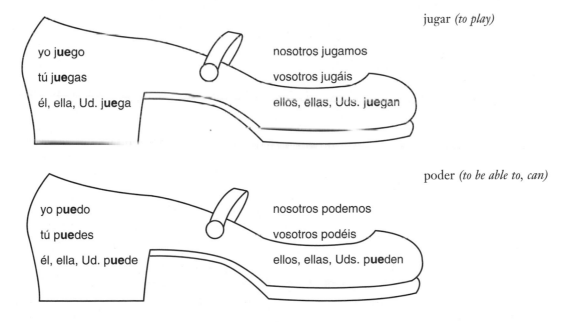

jugar *(to play)*

yo j**ue**go   nosotros jugamos

tú j**ue**gas   vosotros jugáis

él, ella, Ud. j**ue**ga   ellos, ellas, Uds. j**ue**gan

poder *(to be able to, can)*

yo p**ue**do   nosotros podemos

tú p**ue**des   vosotros podéis

él, ella, Ud. p**ue**de   ellos, ellas, Uds. p**ue**den

Other verbs that can be conjugated just like *poder* include the following.

Verb	Pronunciation	Meaning
doler	*doh-lehr*	to ache, pain
resolver	*rreh-sohl-behr*	to resolve
volver	*bohl-behr*	to return

Verbs Ending in *-ir*

For verbs ending in *-ir*, the stem vowel change also takes place in the present tense. The *e* changes to *ie*, *o* changes to *ue*, and *e* changes to *i* in all forms of the shoe except *nosotros* and *vosotros*.

preferir *(to prefer)*

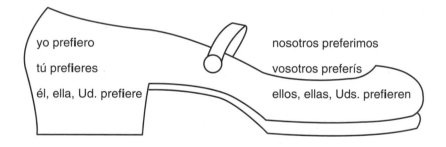

yo prefiero   nosotros preferimos
tú prefieres   vosotros preferís
él, ella, Ud. prefiere   ellos, ellas, Uds. prefieren

Other verbs that can be conjugated just like *preferir* include the following.

Verb	Pronunciation	Meaning
advertir	*ahd-behr-teer*	to notify, to warn
consentir	*kohn-sehn-teer*	to consent
mentir	*mehn-teer*	to lie
referir	*rreh-feh-reer*	to refer
sentir	*sehn-teer*	to feel; to regret

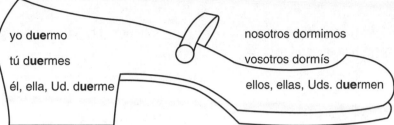

dormir *(to sleep)*

Another verb conjugated like *dormir* is the following.

Verb	Pronunciation	Meaning
morir	*moh-reer*	to die

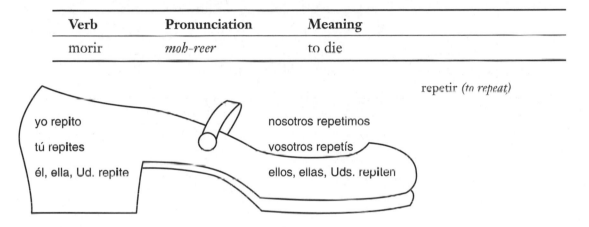

repetir *(to repeat)*

Other verbs that can be conjugated just like *repetir* include the following.

Verb	Pronunciation	Meaning
impedir	*eem-peh-deer*	to prevent
medir	*meh-deer*	to measure
pedir	*peh-deer*	to ask
reír*	*rreh-yeer*	to laugh
servir	*sehr-beer*	to serve

*Reír *keeps the accent over the* i *in all forms of the present tense.*

Verbs Ending in *-uir*

For verbs ending in *-uir* (except those ending in *-guir*; see Chapter 11), insert a *y* after the *u* in all forms except *nosotros* and *vosotros*.

concluir *(to conclude, end)*

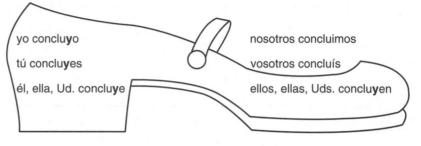

yo conclu**y**o   nosotros concluimos

tú conclu**y**es   vosotros concluís

él, ella, Ud. conclu**y**e   ellos, ellas, Uds. conclu**y**en

Other verbs that can be conjugated just like *concluir* include the following.

Verb	Pronunciation	Meaning
construir	*kohn-stroo-eer*	to build
contribuir	*kohn-tree-boo-eer*	to contribute
destruir	*dehs-troo-eer*	to destroy
incluir	*een-kloo-eer*	to include
sustituir	*soos-tee-too-eer*	to substitute

Verbs Ending in *-iar* and *-uar*

Some verbs ending in *-iar* and *-uar* require an accent in all forms except *nosotros*.

guiar *(to guide)*

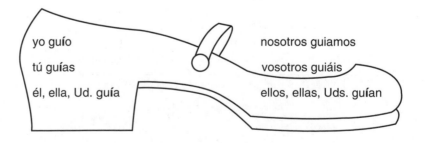

yo guío   nosotros guiamos

tú guías   vosotros guiáis

él, ella, Ud. guía   ellos, ellas, Uds. guían

Other verbs that can be conjugated just like *guiar* include the following.

Verb	Pronunciation	Meaning
confiar (en)	*kohn-fee-yahr (ehn)*	to confide (in), to rely (on)
enviar	*ehn-bee-yahr*	to send
variar	*bah-ree-yahr*	to vary

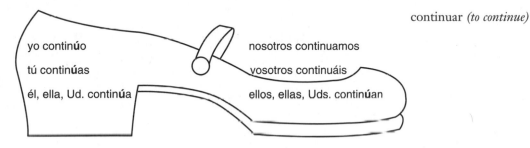

continuar *(to continue)*

yo continúo   nosotros continuamos

tú continúas   vosotros continuáis

él, ella, Ud. continúa   ellos, ellas, Uds. continúan

Another verb that can be conjugated just like *continuar* is *actuar* (*ahk-too-ahr*; to act).

In the vosotros form of *-iar* and *-uar* verbs, be sure to put the accent on the *a:*

Vosotros confiáis en vuestros amigos.   Vosotros continuáis.
You confide in your friends.   You continue.

Some verbs in Spanish have both spelling changes and stem changes. The most common verb of this type is *seguir*. The *e* in the stem of *seguir* changes to *i*, except in the *nosotros* and *vosotros* forms. The *gu* changes to *g* in the *yo* form. Here's what the verb looks like when it's conjugated:

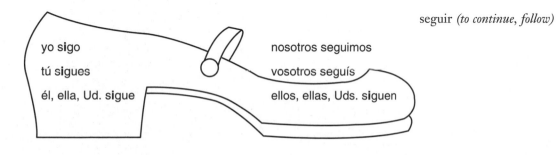

seguir *(to continue, follow)*

yo sigo   nosotros seguimos

tú sigues   vosotros seguís

él, ella, Ud. sigue   ellos, ellas, Uds. siguen

Using "Shoe" Verbs

Review the present tense of "shoe" verbs and then complete the questions you ask your friends:

1. (almorzar) ¿A qué hora _____ Uds?

2. (preferir) ¿Cuándo _____ Uds. salir?

3. (enviar) ¿ _____ Uds. esas cartas?

4. (continuar) ¿ _____ Uds. trabajando?

5. (volver) ¿ _____ Uds. temprano?

6. (dormir) ¿ _____ Uds. en casa?

7. (server) ¿Cuándo _____ Uds. la cena?

8. (contribuir) ¿Qué _____ Uds. al periódico escolar?

Answer Key

Using Ordinal Numbers

1. quinto   3. cuarto   5. primer

2. noveno   4. tercer   6. séptimo

Using "Shoe" Verbs

1. almuerzan   3. envían   5. vuelven   7. sirven

2. prefieren   4. continúan   6. duermen   8. contribuyen

Part 3 Having Fun

No trip is complete without some time for fun, games, amusements, and diversions. Whatever the weather conditions, there's always something to do, no matter where you are. Sightseeing is often at the top of everyone's list. You can also sometimes find exciting activities such as windsurfing, parasailing, scuba diving, and countless other sports. Cultural opportunities abound: museums, concerts, ballets, and operas. For some people, traveling is a shopping experience; for others, it's a gastronomic feast.

The six chapters in Part 3 cover the many ways to get the most out of the countries you visit. You'll learn how to do what you want when you want to do it and how to enjoy yourself to the fullest.

Chapter 13

How's the Weather?

In This Chapter

◆ Weather conditions

◆ Days and months

◆ The four seasons

◆ All about *dar* (to give)

Your hotel room is exactly what you'd hoped for, and you're feeling great. Everything is in working condition, and you even have plenty of towels. Now you're eager to go out and have a wonderful time. When you look outside, however, you see clouds looming overhead. There's no sun in sight. What should you plan for the day?

Your first impulse will probably be to turn on the radio or TV to get the latest weather report. Unfortunately, all the forecasters are babbling away in rapid-fire Spanish, and your knowledge of cognates isn't helping you very much. No problem. This chapter provides you with all the vocabulary you need to understand the forecast and plan your sightseeing.

It's 20 Degrees and They're Wearing String Bikinis!

You've opened your Spanish newspaper to the weather page. The weather forecaster has predicted a temperature of 20 degrees. You open your hotel window, and you're greeted with a balmy sea breeze and a view of a beach studded with bikini-clad bathers. Something must be amiss. Could *el pronóstico* (the forecast) be wrong? It's time to consult with someone in the know at *la recepción*. The following table lists phrases that will enable you to discuss the weather.

Weather Expressions

Expression	Pronunciation	Meaning
¿Qué tiempo hace?	*keh tee-yehm-poh ah-seh*	What's the weather?
Hace buen tiempo.	*ah-seh bwehn tee-yehm-poh*	It's beautiful.
Hace calor.	*ah-seh kah-lohr*	It's hot.
Hace sol.	*ah-seh sohl*	It's sunny.
Hace mal tiempo.	*ah-seh mahl tee-yehm-poh*	It's nasty (bad).
Hace frío.	*ah-seh free-yoh*	It's cold.
Hace fresco.	*ah-seh frehs-koh*	It's cool.
Hace viento.	*ah-seh bee-yehn-toh*	It's windy.
Hay relámpagos.	*ah-yee rreh-lahm-pah-gohs*	It's lightning.
Truena.	*troo-weh-nah*	It's thundering.
Hay niebla (neblina).	*ah-yee nee-yeh-blah (neh-blee-nah)*	It's foggy.
Hay humedad.	*ah-yee oo-meh-dahd*	It's humid.
Hay nubes./ Está nublado.	*ah-yee noo-behs/ ehs-tah noo-blah-doh*	It's cloudy.
Está cubierto.	*ehs-tah koo-bee-yehr-toh*	It's overcast.
Llueve./ Está lloviendo.	*yoo-weh-beh/ ehs-tah yoh-bee-yehn-doh*	It's raining.
Hay lluvias torrenciales.	*ahy yoo-bee-yahs toh-rrehn-see-yahl-ehs*	It's pouring.
Nieva./ Está nevando.	*nee-yeh-bah/ ehs-tah neh-bahn-doh*	It's snowing.
Hay un vendaval.	*ah-yee oon behn-dah-bahl*	There's a windstorm.
Hay granizo.	*ah-yee grah-nee-soh*	There's hail.
Hay lloviznas.	*ah-yee yoh-bees-nahs*	There are showers.

If you want to use the present progressive tense (as discussed in Chapter 8) to stress that a particular weather condition is in existence at the moment, conjugate the verb *estar.* Drop the *-ar, -er,* or *-ir* infinitive ending from the verb and add *-ando* for *-ar* verbs or *-iendo* for *-er* and *-ir* verbs, respectively:

> Está nevando. Está lloviendo.

So why *is* everyone wearing shorts and bikinis when it's 20 degrees out? The answer is really quite simple. Most of the Spanish-speaking world uses Celsius (centigrade) rather than Fahrenheit to tell the temperature (0°C = 32°F). To change Fahrenheit to Centigrade, subtract 32 from the Fahrenheit temperature and multiply the remaining number by ⁵⁄₉. To change Centigrade to Fahrenheit, multiply the Centigrade temperature by ⁹⁄₅ and add 32 to the remaining number.

Baby, It's Cold Outside

Should you bring along a sweater? Will you need a winter coat? How about your new bathing suit? If you want to dress appropriately and be comfortable, you'll want to know what the temperature is. To find out, you would ask the following:

> ¿Cuál es la temperatura?
> *kwahl ehs lah tehm-peh-rah-too-rah*
> What's the temperature?

To answer this question, simply give the number of degrees followed by the word *grados* (*grah-dohs*; degrees). To be more formal, you could say, "Hay una temperatura de *XX* grados" (*ah-yee oo-nah tehm-peh-rah-too-rah deh XX grah-dohs*). If it's below zero, you need to add *menos* (*meh-nohs*; minus) before the number. If the temperature is 1 degree, be sure *grado* is used in the singular, *un grado.* For example:

> Menos cinco grados.
> *meh-nohs seen-koh grah-dohs*
> It's five below.

> Hay una temperatura de cuarenta grados.
> *ah-yee oo-nah tehm-peh-rah-too-rah deh kwah-rehn-tah grah-dohs*
> It's forty degrees.

> **Memory Master**
>
> The verbs *llover* (ue), *tronar* (ue), and *nevar* (ie) are stem changing verbs. Remember to make the necessary changes when conjugating them:
>
> > *Llueve.* It's raining.
> >
> > *Truena.* It's thundering.
> >
> > *Nieva.* It's snowing.

The Forecast Is ...

You're reading the complimentary newspaper available at your hotel in Uruguay. You're curious about the weather and turn to that section. Study the symbols in the following table to help you interpret the symbols on a weather map. Learn what each symbol means. If you ever want to know the weather in the countries you visit (and you will), you're going to love this visual vocabulary.

Symbol	Weather Expression	Pronunciation	Meaning
	cielo despejado	*see-yeh-loh dehs-peh-hah-doh*	clear sky
	algo nublado	*ahl-goh noo-blah-doh*	slightly cloudy
	nublado	*noo-blah-doh*	cloudy
	inestable	*een-ehs-tah-bleh*	changeable
	lluvioso	*yoo-bee-yoh-soh*	rainy
	tormenta eléctrica	*tohr-mehn-tah eh-lehk-tree-kah*	electrical storm
	frente frío	*frehn-teh free-yoh*	cold front
	frente cálido	*frehn-teh kah-lee-doh*	warm front
	frente estacionario	*frehn-teh ehs-tah-see-yoh-nah-ree-yoh*	stationary front
20	temperatura máxima	*tehm-peh-rah-too-rah mahk-see-mah*	maximum temperature

What Day Is It?

In the midst of a glorious vacation, do you ever have to pause for a moment to remember what day it is? It happens to me all the time. For me, the best part of vacation—besides the rest and relaxation—is that time is not of the essence, and I don't have to scurry to get things done. I become totally caught up in having fun, and every day seems like a Saturday.

Occasionally, because I don't want to miss my flight home, I ask "What day is it, anyway?" You might also want to keep track of what day it is so you don't end up at the attraction you're dying to see on a day it's closed. Study the days of the week in the following table to ensure that you get to do everything you want.

Days of the Week

Day	Spanish	Pronunciation
Monday	lunes	*loo-nehs*
Tuesday	martes	*mahr-tehs*
Wednesday	miércoles	*mee-yehr-koh-lehs*
Thursday	jueves	*hweh-behs*
Friday	viernes	*bee-yehr-nehs*
Saturday	sábado	*sah-bah-doh*
Sunday	domingo	*doh-meen-goh*

Note: The days of the week in Spanish (which are all masculine) are not capitalized (unless they are at the beginning of a sentence). Unlike our calendars, Spanish calendars start with Monday. To say that something is happening "on" a certain day, the Spanish use the definite article *el:*

El martes yo voy al centro.
ehl mahr-tehs yoh boy ahl sehn-troh
On Tuesday I go downtown.

The Best Month for a Visit

If your travels or business take you to Latin America, you can see why it's important to know the names of the months. You wouldn't want to sit by a pool in Argentina in July, and you couldn't indulge in winter sports in Chile in December. Be sure you plan your trip wisely. With one slip of the tongue, you could wind up being in the wrong place at the wrong time. The following table will help you identify the months.

Months of the Year

Month	Spanish	Pronunciation
January	enero	*eh-neh-roh*
February	febrero	*feh-breh-roh*
March	marzo	*mahr-soh*
April	abril	*ah-breel*
May	mayo	*mah-yoh*
June	junio	*hoo-nee-yoh*
July	julio	*hoo-lee-yoh*
August	agosto	*ah-gohs-toh*
September	septiembre	*sehp-tee-yehm-breh*
October	octubre	*ohk-too-breh*
November	noviembre	*noh-bee-yehm-breh*
December	diciembre	*dee-see-yehm-breh*

To express "in" a certain month, the Spanish use the preposition *en:*

> Vamos a España en julio.
> *bah-mohs ah ehs-pah-nyah ehn hoo-lee-yoh*
> We are going to Spain in July.

The Four Seasons

Some people like it hot; they go to Spain in the summer or Chile in the winter. Some like it cold; they go to Argentina in the summer and to Costa Rica in the winter.

Whatever you like, be sure you plan your trip when the weather will be perfect. Keep in mind that in countries south of the Equator, the seasons are opposite those in the United Sates. You don't want to worry about hurricanes, storms, or other adverse weather conditions. The following table gives you the names of the seasons.

The Seasons of the Year

Season	Spanish	Pronunciation
winter	el invierno	*ehl een-bee-yehr-noh*
spring	la primavera	*lah pree-mah-beh-rah*
summer	el verano	*ehl beh-rah-noh*
autumn, fall	el otoño	*ehl oh-toh-nyoh*

To express "in" with the seasons, the Spanish use the preposition *en* + the definite article for all the seasons. Here's some wishful thinking to show you how it's done:

Voy a Puerto Rico en el invierno, en la primavera, en
el verano, y en el otoño.
*boy ah pwehr-toh rree-koh ehn ehl een-bee-yehr-noh, ehn lah pree-mah-beh-rah, ehn
ehl beh-rah-noh, ee ehn ehl oh-toh-nyoh*
I go to Puerto Rico in the winter, in the spring, in the summer, and in the fall.

When You Have a Date

When you have a lot on your mind, it's common to lose track of the date. That might be why so many of us have watches equipped with the date to help us remember. If you're traveling for pleasure, one day seems to run into the next, and somewhere along the line the date often gets lost. When you do get around it, dates are expressed as follows:

◆ Day of week + *el* + cardinal number + *de* + month + *de* + year

martes el siete de mayo de dos mil cinco

◆ The first day of each month is called *el primero*. Cardinal numbers are used for all other days.

el primero de enero   el dos de febrero
January 1   February 2

◆ In Spanish, the year is expressed in thousands and hundreds, not just in hundreds as in English. In Spanish, for example, 2006 is expressed as *dos mil seis*.

◆ To express "on" with dates, use the definite article *el*:

Salgo el tres de mayo.
I'm leaving on May 3.

When the Spanish write a date in numbers, the sequence is day + month + year. This is the reverse of the month + day + year sequence we use. Notice how different this looks in the following table.

Spanish	English
el 22 de abril de 1977	April 22, 1977
22.4.77	4/22/77
el cinco de febrero de 1995	February 5, 1995
5.2.95	2/5/95

In a Flash

The new year has just begun, and you're starting to fill out your date book. Of course, some dates are especially important to you. Give the day and dates for these important events of the year: your birthday, a friend's birthday, Thanksgiving, New Year's, Mother's Day, Valentine's Day, Father's Day, and Memorial Day.

To get information about the date, you can ask the following questions:

¿Cuál es la fecha de hoy?
kwahl ehs lah feh-chah deh oy
What is today's date?

¿A cuánto estamos hoy?
ah kwahn-toh ehs-tah-mohs oy
What's today's date?

¿Qué día es hoy?
keh dee-yah ehs oy
What day is today?

The answer to your question would be one of the following:

> Hoy es lunes (el) primero de abril.
> *oy ehs loo-nehs pree-meh-roh deh ah-breel*
> Today is Monday, April 1.

> Estamos a lunes (el) primero de abril.
> *ehs-tah-mohs ah loo-nehs pree-meh-roh deh ah-breel*
> Today is Monday, April 1.

Words and expressions commonly used with days, weeks, and months help you schedule your time. Keep the expressions in the following table in mind when you make your plans.

Time Expressions

Expression	Pronunciation	Meaning
en	*ehn*	in
hace	*ah-seh*	ago
por	*pohr*	per
durante	*doo-rahn-teh*	during
próximo(a)	*prohk-see-moh(mah)*	next
último(a)	*ool-tee-moh(mah)*	last
pasado(a)	*pah-sah-doh(dah)*	last
la víspera	*lah bees-peh-rah*	eve
anteayer	*ahn-teh-ah-yehr*	day before yesterday
ayer	*ah-yehr*	yesterday
hoy	*oy*	today
mañana	*mah-nyah-nah*	tomorrow
pasado mañana	*pah-sah-doh mah-nyah-nah*	day after tomorrow
el día siguiente	*ehl dee-yah see-gee-yehn-teh*	the next day
desde	*dehs-deh*	from
de hoy en una semana	*deh oy ehn oo-nah seh-mah-nah*	a week from today
de mañana en dos semanas	*deh mah-nyah-nah ehn dohs seh-mah-nahs*	two weeks from tomorrow

The adjectives *próximo*, *último*, and *pasado* must agree with their noun in gender:

el próximo (último) día	el mes pasado
the next (last) day	the past month
la próxima (última) noche	la semana pasada
the next (last) night	the past week

What's the Date?

Imagine you're at an important business meeting in which you must use your Spanish to refer to certain past and future dates. If today is *el siete de agosto*, give the date for the following:

1. anteayer
2. de mañana en dos semanas
3. la víspera
4. mañana
5. de mañana en una semana
6. hace siete días

Give Me Good Weather

Don't you always pray for good weather when you travel? One time, when my husband and I had travel plans abroad, we checked the Internet and found that miserable weather was scheduled for our entire stay. Fortunately, we didn't give in to our first inclination to cancel our plans. To our surprise and delight, we got meterogically lucky and the weather was gorgeous the whole week. Sometimes you have to go for it and give it your best shot. Study the following table to learn how to use the verb *dar* (*dahr*), which means "to give" and has an irregular *yo* form only.

The Verb *Dar* (to Give)

Conjugation	Pronunciation	English
yo doy	*yoh doy*	I give
tú das	*too dahs*	you give
él, ella, Ud. da	*ehl, eh-yah, oo-stehd dah*	he, she, you give(s)
nosotros damos	*noh-soh-trohs dah-mohs*	we give
vosotros dáis	*boh-soh-trohs dah-yees*	you give
ellos, ellas, Uds. dan	*eh-yohs, eh-yahs, oo-stehd-ehs dahn*	they, you give

Imagine you're walking along the Paseo del Prado in Madrid. A young man approaches and says, "*Quiero dar un paseo con Ud.*" Is this guy trying to make a pass at you? Before you give him *una bofetada* (oo-nah boh-feh-tah-dah; a slap), familiarize yourself with the following idioms with *dar*.

Idioms with *Dar*

Idiom	Pronunciation	Meaning
dar a	*dahr ah*	to face
dar un abrazo	*dahr oon ah-brah-soh*	to hug
dar con	*dahr kohn*	to run into
dar de beber (comer)	*dahr deh beh-behr (koh-mehr)*	to give a drink (feed)
dar las gracias a	*dahr lahs grah-see-yahs ah*	to thank
dar un paseo	*dahr oon pah-seh-yoh*	to take a walk, to go for a ride
dar recuerdos (a)	*dahr rreh-kwehr-dohs (ah)*	to give regards (to)
dar una vuelta	*dahr oo-nah bwehl-tah*	to take a stroll

Using *Dar*

Use the correct form of the verb *dar* to express what is going on with each of the following subjects:

1. (to take a stroll) Ellos _____.

2. (to give regards) Vosotros _____ a Ana.

3. (to thank) Nosotros _____ al hombre.

4. (to hug) Yo _____ a mi novio.

5. (to run into) Tú _____ con Julio en el parque.

Answer Key

What's the Date?

1. el cinco de agosto
2. el veintidós de agosto
3. el seis de agosto
4. el ocho de agosto
5. el quince de agosto
6. el treinta y uno de julio

Using *Dar*

1. dan un paseo
2. dáis recuerdos
3. damos gracias
4. doy un abrazo
5. das con

Let's See the Sights

In This Chapter

- Sights you can see
- How to make suggestions and plans
- Tips on giving your opinion
- Other countries to visit

You've looked out the window and listened to the weather report for the day. You've consulted your guidebook and decided what activities you'd like to have fun doing. The next step is to take out a map of the city and locate some important tourist attractions. Plan your itinerary so you don't have to run back and forth across town, wasting time instead of having fun.

This chapter presents interesting places to visit and a wide variety of things to do in Spanish-speaking countries. In no time flat, you'll develop the proficiency you need to make suggestions and plans and to give your impressions and opinions. Because there are so many countries you might choose to visit, you'll also learn the Spanish names of the most popular ones.

Super Sights

Do you have a Type A personality? Are you a super-active person who loves to fly from one activity to the next? Or are you the laid-back, mellow Type B, who just feels like relaxing and soaking up the sun? Whatever your preference, Spanish-speaking countries offer a variety of things to do and see. Travel brochures available at hotels and tourist offices propose countless suggestions. When you're ready to make a decision, consult the following table, which lists common activities and sites.

Where to Go and What to Do

El Lugar	The Place	La Actividad	The Activity
el acuario	aquarium	ver los peces	see the fish
la plaza de toros	ring	ver la corrida de toros	see the bullfights
el estadio	stadium	ver un partido de fútbol	see a soccer match
el carnaval	carnival	mirar el desfile, las carrozas	look at the parade, floats
el castillo	castle	ver los cuartos	see the rooms
la catedral	cathedral	ver las vidrieras	see the stained-glass windows
el circo	circus	ver los espectáculos	see the shows
el club	nightclub	ver un espectáculo	see a show
la feria	fair	mirar las exposiciones	look at the exhibits
la fuente	fountain	mirar el chorro de agua	look at the spray of water
la iglesia	church	ver la arquitectura	see the architecture
el museo	museum	ver las pinturas, las esculturas	see the paintings, sculptures
el parque de atracciones	amusement park	montar en los tiovivos	go on the rides

What Shall We See?

Are you off to the Prado to see the famous artwork? Or are you really curious about bullfighting? Perhaps you want to admire the stained-glass windows of a famous church or the statues in a public square. To express what you would like to see, use the irregular verb *ver* (to see) presented in the following table. *Ver* is an easy verb to learn because it's only irregular in the *yo* form (an extra *e* is added). All other forms follow the rules for regular *-er* verbs.

The Verb *Ver* (to See)

Conjugated Form	Pronunciation	Meaning
yo veo	*yoh beh-yoh*	I see
tú ves	*too behs*	you see
él, ella, Ud. ve	*ehl, eh-yah, oo-stehd beh*	he, she, you see(s)
nosotros vemos	*nohs-oh-trohs beh-mohs*	we see
vosotros véis	*bohs-oh-trohs beh-yees*	you see
ellos, ellas, Uds. ven	*eh-yohs, eh-yahs, oo-stehd-ehs behn*	they, you see

Suggest Away!

Have you always had your heart set on a romantic second honeymoon in Cancún? The seductive brochures, the enticing ads, and your friends' pictures have convinced you that this is a vacation spot you'd really enjoy. How will your spouse feel about this? Will your enthusiasm be shared? Here's how to find out.

One way to make a suggestion in Spanish is to ask this simple question:

> *¿Por qué no?* + a verb in the nosotros form

For example:

> ¿Por qué no vamos a Cancún?
> *pohr keh noh bah-mohs ah kahn-koon*
> Why don't we go to Cancún?

You can also tell someone what you'd like to do and then ask how he or she feels about the idea. Of course, they might think you're a little pushy. But what the heck. Go for it!

Quiero ir a Cancún.	¿Qué piensa(s)[cree(s)]?
kee-yeh-roh eer ah kahn-koon	*keh pee-yehn-sah(s)*
I want to go to Cancún.	What do you think?

To express the English "Let's," use the *nosotros* form of the irregular verb *ir* + *a* + the infinitive of the activity you're suggesting:

Vamos a viajar a Cancún.
bah-mohs ah bee-yah-hahr ah kahn-koon
Let's travel to Cancún.

Vamos a partir mañana.
bah-mohs ah pahr-teer mah-nyah-nah
Let's leave tomorrow.

The other way to make a polite suggestion is to use the *nosotros* form of the present subjunctive tense. (Remember to check irregular verb forms, which must be memorized.) Although this sounds complicated, it really is quite simple. Just insert the letter that is the opposite of the infinitive ending, like you did with commands using *Ud.* For regular *-ar* verbs, change the *-a* ending to *-e*. For regular *-er* and *-ir* verbs, change the *-e* or *-i* ending to *-a*:

> **Memory Master**
>
> When using the command form that expresses "Let's," the subject pronoun *nosotros* never is used.

Viajemos a Cancún.
bee-yah-heh-mohs ah kahn-koon
Let's travel to Cancun.

Partamos mañana.
pahr-tah-mohs mah-nyah-nah
Let's leave tomorrow.

Veamos esa película.
Beh-yah-mohs eh-sah peh-lee-koo-lah
Let's see that film.

Making Suggestions

The weather is simply beautiful, and you're itching to go out and have a great time. Suggest five things you and I can do together.

> *Example:* ¿Por qué no vamos al parque?
> Quiero nadar en el mar.
> ¿Qué piensas?

Other Useful Phrases

I bet you're thinking that asking for what you want is pretty easy. Now that you're feeling good about your progress, let's try a more colloquial approach. You can use a number of phrases, as shown in the following table. To complete your thought, just tack on the infinitive of the verb and maybe an object for the verb.

The familiar forms are in parentheses. Note the use of the polite pronoun *le* (to you) and the familiar pronoun *te* (to you) in some of the following expressions. These pronouns are used to ask about "you" and are placed before the verb. (A more detailed explanation of these pronouns appears in Chapter 15.)

In a Flash _____

Look at today's weather. Make as many suggestions as you can in Spanish for appropriate activities for the day.

Phrase	Pronunciation	Meaning
¿Le (te) gustaría …?	*leh (teh) goos-tah-ree-yah*	Would you like …?
¿Tiene(s) ganas de …?	*tee-yeh-neh(s) gah-nahs deh*	Do you feel like …?
¿Quiere(s) …?	*kee-yeh-reh(s)*	Do you want …?

For example:

> ¿Tiene(s) ganas de ver una corrida de toros?
> Do you feel like going to a bullfight?

> ¿Le (te) gustaría ir al cine?
> Would you like to go to the movies?

> ¿Quiere(s) ver las exposiciones?
> Do you want to see the exhibits?

The phrases in the preceding list can be made negative by using *no*:

> ¿No tiene(s) ganas de ver una corrida de toros?
> Don't you feel like seeing a bullfight?

> ¿No le (te) gustaría ir al cine?
> Wouldn't you like to go to the movies?

> ¿No quiere(s) ver las exposiciones?
> Don't you want to see the exhibits?

Are you acquainted with any grouchy-from-lack-of-sleep teenagers who give abrupt "yes" or "no" answers to questions? The rest of us are usually more polite and say "Yes, but …" or "No, because …."

In Spanish, if you'd like to elaborate on your answer, here's what you have to do: if you see the pronoun *le* or *te* (to you) in the question, simply use *me* (to me) before the verb in your answer to express how *you* feel:

> Sí, me gustaría ir al cine.
> Yes, I'd like to go to the movies.

> No, no me gustaría ir al cine.
> No, I wouldn't like to go to the movies.

For the other sentences, you can give the *yo* form of the verb in the present:

> Sí, tengo ganas de ver una corrida de toros.
> Yes, I feel like seeing a bullfight.

> No, no tengo ganas de ver una corrida de toros.
> No, I don't feel like seeing a bullfight.

> Sí, quiero mirar las exposiciones.
> Yes, I'd like to see the exhibits.

> No, no quiero mirar las exposiciones.
> No, I wouldn't like to see the exhibits.

What Do You Think?

Someone suggested an activity to you. How do you feel about it? Are you interested in pursuing it further? Does it have appeal? If the answer is yes, you might say:

Me gusta (encanta) la música clásica.
meh goos-tah (ehn-kahn-tah) lah moo-see-kah klah-see-kah
I like (adore) classical music.

Soy aficionado(a) al arte.
soy ah-fee-see-yoh-nah-doh(ah) ahl ahr-the
I'm an art fan.

To express what you like or dislike, use *(no) me gusta (me encanta)* + the singular noun or infinitive:

Me gusta (encanta) el español.	Me gusta (encanta) hablar español.
I like (adore) Spanish.	I like to speak (adore speaking) Spanish.

> ### Memory Master
>
> Use *me gusta* and *me encanta* when referring to one thing you like or adore. If there's more than one, use *me gustan* and *me encantan:*
>
> Me gusta la música.
> I like music.
>
> Me encantan las óperas.
> I adore operas.

You also can use *(no) me gustan (me encantan)* + the plural noun. Use *(no) me gusta (me encanta)* with infinitives.

No me gustan (encantan) los libros.   No me gusta (encanta) bailar y cantar.
I don't like (adore) the books.   I don't like (adore) dancing and singing.

Suppose you've tried something totally out of character. Chances are, you'll want to express what you think of the activity. Was it fun? Did you really enjoy it? You can give a positive opinion by using *es (ehs)* followed by an adjective, such as *Es excelente*, or "It's excellent." The following table provides a list of adjectives to help you describe the fun you can have in Spanish-speaking countries.

Phrase	Pronunciation	Meaning
estupendo	*ehs-too-pehn-doh*	stupendous
fenomenal	*feh-noh-meh-nahl*	phenomenal
excelente	*ehk-seh-lehn-teh*	excellent
magnífico	*mag-nee-fee-koh*	magnificent
fantástico	*fahn-tahs-tee-koh*	fantastic
sensacional	*sehn-sah-see-yoh-nahl*	sensational
maravilloso	*mah-rah-bee-yoh-soh*	marvelous
divertido	*dee-behr-tee-doh*	fun
regio	*rreh-hee-yoh*	great
fabuloso	*fah-boo-loh-soh*	fabulous
de película	*deh peh-lee-koo-lah*	out of this world
bárbaro	*bahr-bah-roh*	awesome
extraordinario	*ehks-trah-ohr-dee-nah-ree-yoh*	extraordinary

Maybe the activity is totally unappealing to you. Perhaps you find it boring. Use the following phrases to express your dislikes.

Phrase	Pronunciation	Meaning
No me gusta …	*noh meh goos-tah*	I don't like …
Odio …, Detesto …	*oh-dee-yoh, deh-tehs-toh*	I hate …
No soy aficionado(a) a …	*noh soy ah-fee-see-yoh-nah-doh(ah) ah*	I'm not a fan of …

The following example sentences describe a few activities some people might not enjoy:

No me gusta la música clásica.

Odio (Detesto) la ópera.

No soy aficionado(a) al arte.

Are you the type of person who will try anything once? Maybe something you tried just wasn't your cup of tea. If you want to give a negative opinion about an activity, you might say "*Es aburrido*," or "It's boring." Here is a list of adjectives you could use to describe something you don't like.

Adjective	Pronunciation	Meaning
aburrido	*ah-boo-rree-doh*	boring
asqueroso	*ahs-keh-roh-soh*	loathsome; disgusting
feo	*feh-yoh*	ugly
un horror	*oon oh-rrohr*	a horror
un desastre	*oon dehs-ahs-treh*	a disaster
desagradable	*dehs-ah-grah-dah-bleh*	disagreeable, unpleasant
terrible	*teh-rree-bleh*	terrible
tonto	*tohn-toh*	silly
horrible	*oh-rree-bleh*	horrible
ridículo	*rree-dee-koo-loh*	ridiculous

The World Beyond

You might be having a wonderful time in Spain and then, all of a sudden, decide you'd like to see other parts of the world. You'll need to know the names of the countries you want to visit to make your travel plans. If you can't distinguish *Suiza* (Switzerland) from *Suecia* (Sweden), you could wind up eating smorgasbord in Stockholm rather than chocolate fondue in the Alps. The Spanish names of various countries and continents are listed in the following tables.

Countries

Country	Spanish	Pronunciation
Austria	Austria	*ow-stree-yah*
Belgium	Bélgica	*behl-hee-kah*
Belize	Belice	*beh-lee-seh*
Canada	Canadá	*kah-nah-dah*
China	China	*chee-nah*
Dominican Republic	La República Dominicana	*lah rreh-poo-blee-kah doh-mee-nee-kah-nah*
England	Inglaterra	*een-glah-teh-rrah*
France	Francia	*frahn-see-yah*
Germany	Alemania	*ah-leh-mah-nee-yah*
Greece	Grecia	*greh-see-yah*
Italy	Italia	*ee-tahl-ee-yah*
Japan	Japón	*hah-pohn*
Mexico	México	*meh-hee-koh*
Netherlands	Los Países Bajos	*lohs pah-yee-sehs bah-hohs*
Panama	Panamá	*pah-nah-mah*
Peru	Perú	*peh-roo*
Russia	Rusia	*rroo-see-yah*
Spain	España	*ehs-pah-nyah*
Sweden	Suecia	*soo-weh-see-yah*
Switzerland	Suiza	*soo-wee-sah*
United States	Estados Unidos	*ehs-tah-dohs oo-nee-dohs*

In Spanish, names of countries are not preceded by the definite article (*el*, *la*, *los*, or *las*). The exceptions are *El Salvador* and *La République Dominicana* because *El* and *La* are part of the countries' names. Do not make a contraction of *a* + *el* when speaking about El Salvador:

Voy a Argentina.   Voy a El Salvador.

The Continents

Continent	Spanish	Pronunciation
Africa	África	*ah-free-kah*
Antarctica	Antártica	*ahn-tahr-tee-kah*
Asia	Asia	*ah-see-yah*
Australia	Australia	*ow-strah-lee-yah*
Europe	Europa	*eh-yoo-roh-pah*
North America	Norte América,	*nohr-teh ah-meh-ree-kah*
	América del Norte	*ah-meh-ree-kah dehl nohr-teh*
South America	Sud América,	*sood ah-meh-ree-kah,*
	América del Sur	*ah-meh-ree-kah dehl soor*

Going Places

Do you plan to go to Puerto Rico for your next vacation? Will you be staying with relatives who have a beach house in the Condado area? To say that you are going "to" another country or city, use the preposition *a:*

¡Atención!

Use the definite article with geographical names that are modified:

Vivo en la América del Norte.

But:

Vivo en Norte América.

Voy a Puerto Rico.
boy ah pwehr-toh rree-koh
I am going to Puerto Rico.

For staying in a country (or a city or a house or a room, and so on), use the preposition *en:*

Estaré en Puerto Rico.
ehs-tah-reh ehn pwehr-toh rree-koh
I'll be in Puerto Rico.

Where Are You From?

Can you tell whether an American comes from the Northeast or the South? Of course you can. The different regional accents are a dead giveaway. Sometimes, people who speak the same language have difficulty understanding each other. One time, I asked someone to translate what a fellow traveler was saying, only to find out he was speaking to me in English, my native tongue! Always play it safe and avoid embarrassing moments by asking from where a person hails. Use the preposition *de* to express "from."

Soy de Nueva York.
soy deh noo-weh-bah yohrk
I'm from New York.

Where Are You Going?

Tell what country you are going to if you plan to see the following. Start your sentences with *Voy* (I'm going).

1. a bullfight
2. Mexican jumping beans
3. the leaning Tower of Pisa
4. Big Ben
5. the Eiffel Tower
6. home

Answer Key

Making Suggestions

Sample responses:

Quiero ir a la corrida de toros. ¿Qué piensas?

Vamos a ir al carnaval.

Partamos para el castillo.

¿Por qué no vamos al circo?

Where Are You Going?

1. Voy a España.
2. Voy a México.
3. Voy a Italia.
4. Voy a Inglaterra.
5. Voy a Francia.
6. Voy a Estados Unidos.

Chapter 15

A Shopping Spree

In This Chapter

- ◆ Stores and their wares
- ◆ Clothing, colors, sizes, and materials
- ◆ All about *gustar* (to like)
- ◆ Direct and indirect objects
- ◆ *This*, *that*, *these*, and *those* (a.k.a. demonstrative adjectives)

You've finally placed a checkmark next to every tourist attraction on your "Don't Miss" list. It's time for a change. Why not concentrate on picking up some souvenirs for friends back home?

When I visit a foreign country, I try to bring back crafts that will remind me of my vacation for years to come. T-shirts, scarves, ashtrays, and wallets hold no appeal to me. Instead, give me a wide-brimmed Mexican sombrero and a multicolored serape, a set of ornate Spanish maracas, a painted mask from Puerto Rico, a carved stone statue from the Dominican Republic, or a simple doll made from hemp. No matter what your preference, this chapter can help you purchase items that will make you and your loved ones happy.

Stores Galore

It's been decided. Today you're going shopping. Will you join the crowds in the open markets, browse the small shops of local artisans, rub shoulders with the rich and famous in boutiques, or search out a large mall (*un centro comercial; oon sehn-troh koh-mehr-see-yahl*) where you can purchase anything and everything? The following table will help you find your way.

Stores (*Las Tiendas, lahs tee-yehn-dahs*)

La Tienda	The Store	*Las Mercancías*	The Merchandise
la juguetería	toy store	los juguetes	toys
la librería	bookstore	los libros	books
la florería	florist	las flores	flowers
la tienda de ropa	clothing store	la ropa	clothing
el almacén	department store	todo	everything
la tabaquería	tobacco store	el tabaco	tobacco
		los cigarrillos	cigarettes
		los cigarros	cigars
		las pipas	pipes
		los fósforos	matches
		los encendedores	lighters
el quiosco de periódicos	newsstand	los periódicos	newspapers
		las revistas	magazines
la tienda de discos	record store	los discos	records
		los casetes	cassette tapes
		los CD	compact discs
la joyería	jewelry store	las joyas	jewels
		los relojes	watches
		los collares	necklaces
		el anillo, la sortija	ring
		la pulsera	bracelet
		los aretes	earrings
la marroquinería	leather goods store	las carteras	wallets
		las bolsas	pocketbooks
		las maletas	suitcases
		las carteras	briefcases

La Tienda	**The Store**	*Las Mercancías*	**The Merchandise**
la tienda de recuerdos	souvenir shop	las camisetas	T-shirts
		los carteles	posters
		los monumentos en miniatura	miniature monuments
		las máscaras	masks
		las pinturas	paintings

Gems and Jewels

You can get a good bargain on jewelry in some foreign countries because you can avoid local taxes and import duties. On our last trip to Puerto Rico, my husband purchased a beautiful gold necklace for me for my birthday. Before making our purchase, we went to several different stores to price gold by the ounce. When we found the best deal, we bargained with the sales clerk. It was, overall, a very friendly and amusing experience. Imagine how lucky I felt when I got home and saw a comparable piece in a discount store for almost twice the price. If you know your prices and are a good shopper, use the following table to get exactly what you want.

Jewels (*Las Joyas, lahs hoh-yahs*)

Jewel	Spanish	Pronunciation
amethyst	la amatista	*lah ah-mah-tees-tah*
aquamarine	el aguamarina	*ehl ah-gwah-mah-ree-nah*
diamond	el diamante	*ehl dee-yah-mahn-teh*
emerald	la esmeralda	*lah ehs-meh-rahl-dah*
ivory	el marfil	*ehl mahr-feel*
jade	el jade	*ehl hah-deh*
onyx	el ónix	*ehl oh-neeks*
pearls	las perlas	*lahs pehr-lahs*
ruby	el rubí	*ehl rroo-bee*
sapphire	el zafiro	*ehl sah-fee-roh*
topaz	el topacio	*ehl toh-pah-see-yoh*
turquoise	la turquesa	*lah toor-keh-sah*

If you're buying jewelry, you might want to ask the following questions:

¿Es oro macizo? ¿Es plata?
ehs oh-roh mah-see-soh *ehs plah-tah*
Is it solid gold? Is it silver?

Clothing

Maybe you're curious about Spanish fashions and have decided to try your luck at buying a typical item of clothing. Perhaps you'll choose a T-shirt, or maybe you've always craved a big sombrero to protect you from the sun. Whatever you decide to buy, the following table will help you in your quest for something *a la última moda* (*ah lah ool-tee-mah moh-dah;* in the latest style) or *tradicional* (*trah-dee-see-yoh-nahl;* traditional).

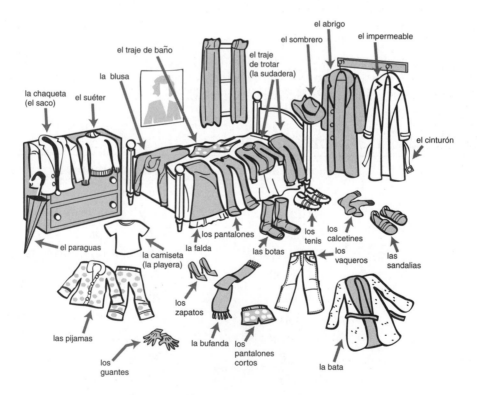

Clothing (*La Ropa, lah roh-pah*)

Article	Spanish	Pronunciation
bathing suit	el traje de baño	*ehl trah-heh deh bah-nyoh*
belt	el cinturón	*ehl seen-too-rohn*
boots	las botas	*lahs boh-tahs*
gloves	los guantes	*lohs gwahn-tehs*
hat	el sombrero	*ehl sohm-breh-roh*
jacket	la chaqueta, el saco	*lah chah-keh-tah, ehl sah-koh*
jeans	los jeans, los vaqueros	*lohs geens, lohs bah-keh-rohs*
jogging suit	el traje de trotar, la sudadera	*ehl trah-heh deh troh-tahr, lah soo-dah-deh-rah*
overcoat	el abrigo	*ehl ah-bree-goh*
pajamas	las pijamas	*lahs pee-hah-mahs*
pants	los pantalones	*lohs pahn-tah-loh-nehs*
raincoat	el impermeable	*ehl eem-pehr-meh-yah-bleh*
robe	la bata	*lah bah-tah*
sandals	las sandalias	*lahs sahn-dah-lee-yahs*
scarf	la bufanda	*lah boo-fahn-dah*
shoes	los zapatos	*lohs sah-pah-tohs*
shorts	los pantalones cortos	*lohs pahn-tah-loh-nehs kohr-tohs*
sneakers	los tenis	*lohs teh-nees*
socks	los calcetines	*lohs kahl-seh-tee-nehs*
sweater	el suéter	*ehl sweh-tehr*
T-shirt	la camiseta, la playera	*lah kah-mee-seh-tah, lah plah-yeh-rah*
umbrella	el paraguas	*ehl pah-rah-gwahs*

Because most countries use the metric system, their sizes are different from ours. Look at the following conversion chart to determine the sizes you would wear.

CONVERSION TABLES FOR CLOTHING SIZES

WOMEN												
SHOES												
American	4	$4\frac{1}{2}$	5	$5\frac{1}{2}$	6	$6\frac{1}{2}$	7	$7\frac{1}{2}$	8	$8\frac{1}{2}$	9	$9\frac{1}{2}$	10
Continental	35	35	36	36	37	37	38	38	39	39	40	40	41

DRESSES, SUITS						
American	8	10	12	14	16	18
Continental	36	38	40	42	44	46

BLOUSES, SWEATERS						
American	32	34	36	38	40	42
Continental	40	42	44	46	48	50

MEN									
SHOES									
American	7	$7\frac{1}{2}$	8	$8\frac{1}{2}$	9	$9\frac{1}{2}$	10	$10\frac{1}{2}$	11	$11\frac{1}{2}$
Continental	39	40	41	42	43	43	44	44	45	45

SUITS, COATS								
American	34	36	38	40	42	44	46	48
Continental	44	46	48	50	52	54	56	58

SHIRTS								
American	14	$14\frac{1}{2}$	15	$15\frac{1}{2}$	16	$16\frac{1}{2}$	17	$17\frac{1}{2}$
Continental	36	37	38	39	40	41	42	43

If you're shopping and want to be sure you get the right size shoes or clothing, use one of the following phrases:

Llevo el tamaño …
yeh-boh ehl tah-mah-nyoh
I wear …

Mi talla es …
mee tah-yah ehs
My size is …

pequeño
peh-keh-nyoh
small

pequeña
peh-keh-nyah
small

mediano
meh-dee-yah-noh
medium

mediana
meh-dee-yah-nah
medium

grande
grahn-deh
large

grande
grahn-deh
large

When you make purchases in a foreign country, remember to save your receipts. Some countries refund sales tax, or value-added tax (VAT), to foreign visitors. Look for rebate information in stores or at the airport before you leave the country.

Colors

When I look at the world, I usually describe things as red, yellow, green, blue, and so on. My sister Susan, on the other hand, *una artista*, talks about tangerine, burnt sienna, aubergine, and turquoise. I rarely understand the shade she means. Let's keep things simple. The following table will help you with the basic colors you'll need in everyday situations.

Colors (*Los Colores, los koh-lohr-ehs*)

Color	Spanish	Pronunciation
beige	beige	*beh-heh*
black	negro	*neh-groh*
blue	azul	*ah-sool*
brown	marrón, pardo	*mah-rrohn, pahr-doh*
gray	gris	*grees*
green	verde	*behr-deh*
orange	anaranjado	*ah-nah-rahn-hah-doh*
pink	rosado	*rroh-sah-doh*
purple	púrpura, morado	*poor-poo-rah, moh-rah-doh*
red	rojo	*rroh-hoh*
white	blanco	*blahn-koh*
yellow	amarillo	*ah-mah-ree-yoh*

To describe a color as light, add the word *claro* (*klah-roh*) after the color. To describe a color as dark, add the word *oscuro* (*oh-skoo-roh*).

verde claro	verde oscuro
light green	dark green

Colors are adjectives and must agree with the noun they are describing:

Quiero comprar esa camisa blanca.
I want to buy that white shirt.

Materials

Do you bring along a travel iron, or do you hang your travel-wrinkled clothes in a steamy bathroom and hope for the best? Do you insist on permanent press, or do you prefer more exotic materials? If you plan to make a clothing purchase while on vacation, the following table will help you pick the right fabric.

Materials (*Las Telas, lahs teh-lahs*)

Material	Spanish	Pronunciation
cashmere	casimir	*kah-see-meer*
corduroy	pana	*pah-nah*
cotton	algodón	*ahl-goh-dohn*
denim	tela tejana	*teh-lah teh-hah-nah*
flannel	franela	*frah-neh-lah*
knit	tejido de punto	*teh-hee-doh deh poon-toh*
lace	encaje	*ehn-kah-heh*
leather	cuero	*kweh-roh*
linen	lino	*lee-noh*
satin	raso	*rrah-soh*
silk	seda	*seh-dah*
suede	gamuza	*gah-moo-sah*
velvet	terciopelo	*tehr-see-yoh-peh-loh*
wool	lana	*lah-nah*

The Object of My Affection

I have an absolutely fabulous black dress. Imagine I am telling you about it: "I wear my black dress often. I put on my black dress to go to parties. I love my black dress."

In a Flash

Make a list of all the new clothes you need. Be sure to include the color and material you prefer.

How tedious! It would be much easier to say: "I wear my black dress often. I put it on to go to parties. I love it."

What did I do to improve my conversation? I stopped repeating "my black dress" (a direct object noun) and replaced it with "it" (a direct object pronoun). What exactly are direct objects? Let's take a closer look.

Direct objects (which can be nouns or pronouns) answer whom or what the subject of the sentence is acting upon. They can refer to people, places, things, or ideas:

I see the boy.	I like the dress.	He pays Jane, Mike, and me.
I see him.	I like it.	He pays us.

¡Atención!

Be careful! Some verbs such as *escuchar* (to listen to), *buscar* (to look for), *pagar* (to pay for), and *mirar* (to look at) take direct objects in Spanish because the English prepositions are built directly into the meaning of the Spanish verbs.

Direct object nouns can be replaced by the direct object pronouns shown in the following table.

Direct Object Pronoun	Meaning
me (meh)	me
te (teh)	you (familiar)
le (leh)	you, him (used primarily in Spain)
lo (loh)	you, him (used primarily in Spanish America), it
la (lah)	you, her, it
nos (nohs)	us
os (ohs)	you (familiar)
los (lohs)	them, you
las (lahs)	them, you (feminine)

Indirect objects can be replaced by indirect object pronouns. Take the story of my friend Marta, who is crazy about her new boyfriend, Paco. This is what she told me: "I write to Paco. Then I read my love letters to Paco. I buy presents for Paco. I bake cookies for Paco. I cook dinners for Paco." To get to the point more efficiently, all she had to say was: "I write

Memory Master

In Spanish America, *lo* generally is used instead of *le* as the direct object to express "him" and "you":

Lo veo.
I see him (it).

to Paco and then I read him (to him) my love letters. I buy him (for him) presents. I bake him (for him) cookies, and I cook him (for him) dinners."

How do indirect objects differ from direct objects? Take a closer look. Indirect objects answer the question: "To whom is the subject doing something?" or "For whom is the subject acting?"

I speak to the boys.	I buy a gift for Mary.
I speak to them.	I buy a gift for her.
I buy her a gift.	He gives (to) me a tie every Christmas.

Indirect objects only refer to people and animals. Indirect object nouns can be replaced by indirect object pronouns. The Spanish preposition *a* (and the forms *al*, *a la*, *a los*, *a las*), meaning "to" or "for," indicates that an indirect object is needed.

Indirect Object Pronoun	Meaning
me (meh)	(to) me
te (teh)	(to) you (familiar)
le (leh)	(to) him, her, you, it
nos (nohs)	(to) us
os (ohs)	(to) you
les (lehs)	(to) them

The Personal A

The clue to the correct usage of an indirect object is the Spanish preposition *a* (and the forms *al*, *a la*, *a los*, *a las*) followed by the name of or reference to a person. The verb *telefonear* is always followed by *a* + indirect object. It, therefore, always takes an indirect object pronoun:

¿Le telefonea a Paco?	¿Le telefonea?
Are you calling Paco?	Are you calling him?

This rule can be somewhat tricky because of the personal *a*. What is the personal *a?* It's the preposition *a* used before the direct object of the verb, if the direct object is a person, a pet, or a pronoun referring to a person. The personal *a* has no meaning and merely indicates a reference to a person.

> Visito a mi amigo.

> Lo visito.
> I visit him.

> **¡Atención!**
>
> Never use the personal *a* with *ser* (to be) or *tener* (to have).
>
> Ella es mi amiga.
> She is my friend.
> Tengo dos hijos.
> I have two sons.

Choose Your Words

To correctly choose between a direct or indirect pronoun, remember to see whether adding the word *to* or *for* makes sense in your sentence. If it does, choose an indirect object pronoun. If not, you must use the direct object pronoun. Look at the following English sentences:

> I write (to) him love letters.

> I buy (for) him presents.

Notice that the "to" or "for" often is understood but not used in English. Be careful in Spanish when choosing a direct or indirect object pronoun. If the words *to* or *for* make sense in the sentence even though they don't actually appear, use an indirect object pronoun.

You should have little problem using the direct or indirect object pronouns for *me/to me* (me), *you/to you* (te, nos), or *us/to us* (nos) because these pronouns are exactly the same. You must be careful, however, when differentiating between *him* (her, it, you, them) and *to (for) him* (her, it, you, them) because there are now two sets of pronouns:

him (it, you)	lo, le (in Spain)	to him (it, you)	le
her (it, you)	la	to her (it, you)	le
them	los, las	to them	les

Sometimes this gets a bit tricky. Remember to choose the pronoun that reflects the number and gender of the noun to which you are referring:

Ella lleva el vestido rojo. Él le habla a Ana.
Ella lo lleva. Él le habla.

Él lleva la camisa blanca. Él le habla a Pablo.
Él la lleva. Él le habla.

Llevo mis zapatos negros. Él les habla a Ana y Pablo.
Los llevo. Él les habla.

Ellas llevan sandalias amarillas.
Las llevan.

The Position of Object Pronouns

Although we can automatically put object pronouns in their proper place in English, correct placement in Spanish does not follow English rules and requires some practice. Let's take a closer look:

- ◆ Object pronouns are normally placed before the verb:

  Yo lo llevo. Yo le hablo.
  Yo no lo llevo. Yo no le hablo.
  ¡No lo lleve! ¡No le hable!

- ◆ When direct and indirect object pronouns are used with an infinitive or a gerund (*estar* + *-ando*, *-iendo* endings) (preceded by a conjugated verb form), they can be placed before the conjugated verb or after the infinitive or gerund and attached to it:

  Quiero llevarla.
  La quiero llevar.

- ◆ When the gerund is followed by the object pronoun, count back three vowels and add an accent to obtain the proper stress:

  Estoy llevándola.
  La estoy llevando.

- ◆ In an affirmative command, the object pronoun follows the verb form and is attached to it. Again, count back three vowels (if there are only two vowels:

Dilo. [Say it.] Then no accent is needed.) and add an accent for proper stress. Note in the preceding example that, in a negative command, the object pronoun precedes the verb, as follows:

¡No lo (la) lleve!
¡Llévela!

I Like It Like That

When you go on vacation, I hope you will enjoy everything, from the food you eat to your accommodations to the places you visit. To express that something is pleasing to you, use the verb *gustar*.

Translated literally, *gustar* means "to be pleasing to." You can't simply say "I like …" in Spanish. You must say "_____ is pleasing to me." The word *to* is very important. It instructs you to use an indirect object pronoun to get your point across. The verb *gustar* must agree with the noun because that word is the subject of the sentence. In general, the verb will be in either the third-person singular (*él, ella, Ud.*) or plural (*ellos, ellas, Uds.*) form:

> Les gusta el sombrero.
> The hat is pleasing to them.
> They like the hat.

Memory Master
If you want to specify who likes what, use the preposition *a* + the person's name before the *gustar* construction.
A Marta le gustan los casetes. Marta likes the cassettes.
A Roberto y a Juan no les gusta la música. Roberto and Juan don't like the music.

In this example, *gusta* agrees with *sombrero*, which is the subject of the sentence:

> Le gustan las camisas.
> The shirts are pleasing to him.
> He likes the shirts.

Gustan agrees with *camisas*, which is the subject of the sentence.

Let's say you've gone shopping and have picked out some shirts you really love. The following sentences show how to express your likes:

Me gusta la camisa.
I like the shirt.
The shirt is pleasing to me.

Me gustan las camisas.
I like the shirts.
The shirts are pleasing to me.

Don't let the reverse word order trick you. Pick the indirect object that expresses the person to whom the noun is pleasing. If you remember that the subject follows the verb *gustar*, you'll have little trouble. Let's take a look at a few more sentences to see how *gustar* works:

¿Te gusta el sombrero?
Do you like the hat?

Nos gusta la falda.
We like the skirt.

Le gustan los zapatos.
He (She, You) likes (like) the shoes.

No os gusta el traje.
You don't like the suit.

Les gusta la blusa.
They like the blouse.

Two other verbs that work exactly like *gustar* are *encantar* (*ehn-kahn-tahr*; to like very much) and *faltar* (*fahl-tahr*; to lack, to need):

Les encanta el abrigo.
They love the coat.

Me falta un vestido.
I need a dress.

Using Object Pronouns

Speak about what happens in a store by substituting a direct or indirect object for the noun object:

1. Ud. habla a la empleada.
2. Compro un pantalón azul.
3. Un muchacho admira los tennis.
4. Pagamos la factura.
5. Tú pones el sombrero negro.
6. El empleado les contesta a sus clientes.

You Want It? Ask for It!

Do you get annoyed when a sales clerk hovers over your shoulder as you examine the merchandise? Or do you crave the assistance of someone in the know? Here are some phrases to help you deal with common shopping situations. Upon entering a store, an employee might ask you the following:

¿En qué puedo servirle?
ehn keh pweh-doh sehr-beer-leh
How may I help you?

¿Qué desea?
keh deh-seh-yah
What would you like?

¿Los están atendiendo?
lohs ehs-tahn ah-tehn-dee-yehn-doh
Is someone helping you?

If you are just browsing, you would answer:

No, gracias. Simplemente estoy buscando.
noh grah-see-yahs. seem-pleh-mehn-teh ehs-toy boos-kahn-doh
No, thank you. I am (just) looking.

If you want to see or buy something, you would answer:

Sí, estoy buscando un (una) _____, por favor.
see ehs-toy boos-kahn-doh oon (oo-nah) _____ pohr fah-bohr
Yes, I'm looking for a _____, please.

Of course, if you're a shopper like me, you'd want to know:

¿Hay ventas (gangas)?
ah-yee behn-tahs (gahn-gahs)
Are there any sales?

¿Hay rebajas (descuentos)?
ah-yee rreh-bah-hahs (dehs-kwehn-tohs)
Are there any discounts?

To ask which item a person prefers, use *¿qué?* before the noun:

¿Qué camiseta prefiere(s)?

To ask which of many someone prefers, use *¿cuál?*

¿Cuál de los dos (pantalones) prefiere(s)?
¿Cuál quiere(s)?
¿Cuáles te gustan?

You can answer using the appropriate definite article and an adjective:

El azul.
The blue one.

Las pequeñas.
The small ones.

Expressing Opinions

That shirt is you. You just love those pants. What a perfect jacket! If you are happy with an item, you can express your pleasure using one of the phrases in the following table.

Phrase	Pronunciation	Meaning
Me gusta (mucho).	*meh goos-tah(n) (moo-choh)*	I like it (a lot).
Me queda muy bien.	*meh keh-dah mwee bee-yehn*	It suits (fits) me very well.
Me queda perfecta-mente.	*meh keh-dah pehr-fehk-tah-mehn-teh*	It suits (fits) me perfectly.
Está bien.	*ehs-tah(n) bee-yehn*	It's nice.
Es elegante.	*ehs eh-leh-gahn-teh*	It's elegant.
Es práctico(a).	*ehs prahk-tee-koh(kah)*	It's practical.
Siempre es bonito(a).	*see-yehm-preh ehs boh-nee-toh(tah)*	It's always attractive.

Face it! The cookies you ate all winter are showing on your hips. This is, of course, the fault of your clothing. If you are disappointed with the way you look, you might use one of the comments in the following table.

Phrase	Pronunciation	Meaning
No me gusta.	*noh meh goos-tah(n)*	I don't like it.
No me queda bien.	*noh meh keh-dah bee-yehn*	It doesn't suit (fit) me.
Es horrible.	*ehs oh-rree-bleh*	It's horrible.
Es pequeño(a).	*ehs peh-keh-nyoh(nyah)*	It's small.
Es apretado(a).	*ehs ah-preh-tah-doh(dah)*	It's tight.
Es corto(a).	*ehs kohr-toh(tah)*	It's short.
Es largo(a).	*ehs lahr-goh(gah)*	It's long.
Es chillón(ona)	*ehs chee-yohn(yoh-nah)*	It's loud.
Es estrecho(a).	*ehs ehs-treh-choh(chah)*	It's narrow.

If you're not satisfied and you want something else, use the following:

> Estoy buscando algo más (menos) + *adjective*
> *ehs-toy boos-kahn-doh ahl-goh mahs (meh-nohs)*
> I'm looking for something more (less) …

If something is "too" long or short, simply add the adverb *demasiado* (*deh-mah-see-yah-doh*) before the adjective:

> Es demasiado corto.
> *Ehs deh-mah-see-yah-doh kohr-toh*
> It's too small.

Remember to change verbs and adjectives to accommodate plural subjects. Adverbs do not need to agree in Spanish; therefore, the adverb *demasiado* (too) does not change:

> Los pantalones son demasiado cortos.
> La blusa es demasiado apretada.

I'll Take This, That, and Some of Those

When I go shopping, I want a consultant. I either bring along a friend, or I rely on the opinion of a well-put-together salesperson. It's common practice to ask how this shirt, that blouse, these pants, or those skirts look on the person buying them. A demonstrative adjective points out someone or something being referred to and allows you to be specific by expressing this, that, these, and those, as shown in the following table.

Demonstrative Adjectives

Demonstrative Adjective	Masculine	Feminine
this (near speaker)	este	esta
these (near speaker)	estos	estas
that (near listener)	ese	esa
those (near listener)	esos	esas
that (away from both)	aquel	aquella
those (away from both)	aquellos	aquellas

Notice that the demonstrative adjective you choose depends on how close the noun is to the subject.

◆ *Este* (*esta* and so on) refers to someone or something near or directly concerning the speaker:

Este vestido es bonito.　　　　　Estos relojes son caros.
This dress is pretty.　　　　　　These watches are expensive.

◆ *Ese* (*esa*, and so on) refers to someone or something nearer the person being addressed than the speaker:

Ese hombre es guapo.　　　　　Esas bufandas son baratas.
That man is handsome.　　　　　Those scarves are inexpensive.

◆ *Aquel* (*aquella*, and so on) refers to someone or something quite remote from both the speaker and the person being addressed and that concerns neither of them directly:

Aquel país es grande.　　　　　Aquella ciudad es bella.
That country is big.　　　　　　That city is beautiful.

Memory Master

The tags *aquí* (here), *ahí* or *allí* (there), and *allá* (over there) are used respectively with *este*, *ese*, and *aquel*.

Me gusta esta falda aquí.　　　　　Nos falta aquel libro allá.
I like this skirt here.　　　　　　We need that book (over) there.

No le encantan esos zapatos allí.
He doesn't love those shoes there.

What Do You Think?

Look at the gifts your friends bought. Using the demonstrative adjectives you've just learned, express how you feel about them. Give as much detail as possible.

Answer Key

Using Object Pronouns

1. Ud. le habla.
2. Lo compro.
3. Un muchacho los admira.
4. La pagamos.
5. Lo pones.
6. El empleado les contesta.

What Do You Think?

Sample responses:

Esta corbata larga es horrible.

Esta camisa es demasiado chillona.

Estos pantalones cortos son prácticos.+

Esta pequeña camiseta es elegante.

Chapter 16

A Home-Cooked Meal

In This Chapter

- ◆ Specialty food stores
- ◆ Ways to express quantity
- ◆ Tips on using demonstrative pronouns

You've been shopping all day, and you've picked up some great souvenirs. Armed with your metric conversion charts, you even were able to select some fabulous native fashions in the correct sizes. Shopping 'til you drop really works up a voracious appetite, though. Dinner's not until after 7 P.M., and it's only 4.30 P.M. now. How should you proceed to ease that rumbling in your stomach?

One great idea is to drop into a local grocery store or specialty food store and grab something yummy to tide you over until your next meal. Why not try *un taco* filled with meat, *una tortilla* topped with *salsa verde*, or a pastry? Many different food choices are presented in this chapter. You'll also learn how to get the quantity you desire. This is important because the Spanish system of weights differs from ours. Let's get eating!

Shopping Around

When I travel, the height of luxury for me is having a refrigerator in my room stocked with drinks and snacks. No matter where I'm traveling, after I reach my destination and unpack, the first thing I do is scout out the nearest food supply and stock up. If you get the midnight munchies, come to my room. I'm always well supplied with native drinks and delicacies. If there's a stove in my room, however, I usually ignore it. I don't cook on vacation, but perhaps this is something you enjoy doing. Purchase your favorite culinary delights from the shops listed in the following table.

Depending on the country you're in, the word for "grocery store" can vary. You might see *una tienda de comestibles, una tienda de abarrotes, una aborrotería, una pulpería, una tienda de ultramarinos,* or *una bodega.* In Spain, a *bodega* is a store that sells only wine from barrels, so you won't be able to purchase any food there. When in doubt, go to the local *supermercado!*

Food Shops

The Store	*La Tienda*	Pronunciation
bakery	la panadería	*lah pah-nah-deh-ree-yah*
butcher shop	la carnicería	*lah kahr-nee-seh-ree-yah*
candy store	la confitería	*lah kohn-fee-teh-ree-yah*
dairy store	la lechería	*lah leh-cheh-ree-yah*
delicatessen	la salchichonería	*lah sahl-chee-choh-neh-ree-yah*
fish store	la pescadería	*lah pehs-kah-deh-ree-yah*
fruit store	la frutería	*lah froo-teh-ree-yah*
grocery store	la abacería	*lah ah-bah-seh-ree-yah*
liquor store	la tienda de licores	*lah tee-yehn-dah deh lee-koh-rehs*
pastry shop	la pastelería	*lah pahs-teh-leh-ree-yah*
supermarket	el supermercado	*ehl soo-pehr-mehr-kah-doh*

Are you ready to try something new? It's always interesting to taste a specialty that's new to your palate. If you wanted to savor a typical food, would you try a fruit? a vegetable? a dessert? Do you prefer meat? fish? poultry? game? What foods (*alimentos*) tempt you? The following tables can help you select something you'll enjoy.

At the Grocery Store

Vegetables	*Las Legumbres*	Pronunciation
asparagus	los espárragos	*lohs ehs-pah-rrah-gohs*
broccoli	el brécol	*ehl breh-kohl*
carrot	la zanahoria	*lah sah-nah-oh-ree-yah*
corn	el maíz	*ehl mah-yees*
eggplant	la berenjena	*lah beh-rehn-heh-nah*
lettuce	la lechuga	*lah leh-choo-gah*
mushroom	el champiñón	*ehl chahm-pee-nyohn*
onion	la cebolla	*lah seh-boh-yah*
pepper	la pimienta	*lah pee-mee-yehn-tah*
potato	la papa, la patata	*lah pah-pah, lah pah-tah-tah*
rice	el arroz	*ehl ah-rrohs*
spinach	la cspinaca	*lah ehs-pee-nah-kah*
sweet potato	la batata	*lah bah-tah-tah*
tomato	el tomate	*ehl toh-mah-teh*

At the Fruit Store

Fruits	*Las Frutas*	Pronunciation
apple	la manzana	*lah mahn-sah-nah*
apricot	el albaricoque	*ehl ahl-bah-ree-koh-keh*
banana	la banana, el plátano	*lah bah-nah-nah, el pleh-tah-noh*
cherry	la cereza	*lah seh-reh-sah*
grape	la uva	*lah oo-bah*
grapefruit	la toronja	*lah toh-rohn-hah*
guava	la guayaba	*lah gwah-yah-bah*
lemon	el limón	*ehl lee-mohn*
melon	el melón	*ehl meh-lohn*
orange	la naranja	*lah nah-rahn-hah*
peach	el melocotón	*ehl meh-loh-koh-tohn*

continues

At the Fruit Store   (continued)

Fruits	*Las Frutas*	Pronunciation
pear	la pera	*lah peh-rah*
pineapple	la piña	*lah pee-nyah*
raisin	la pasa	*lah pah-sah*
raspberry	la frambuesa	*lah frahm-bweh-sah*
strawberry	la fresa	*lah freh-sah*

Nuts	*Las Nueces*	Pronunciation
almond	la almendra	*lah ahl-mehn-drah*
chestnut	la castaña	*lah kahs-tah-nyah*
hazelnut	la avellana	*lah ah-beh-yah-nah*
walnut	la nuez	*lah nwehs*

At the Butcher or Delicatessen

Meats	*Las Carnes*	Pronunciation
bacon	el tocino	*ehl toh-see-noh*
beef	la carne de vaca (res)	*lah kahr-neh deh bah-kah (rrehs)*
ham	el jamón	*ehl hah-mohn*
lamb	la carne de cordero	*lah kahr-neh deh kohr-deh-roh*
liver	el hígado	*ehl ee-gah-doh*
pork	la carne de cerdo	*lah kahr-neh deh sehr-doh*
roast beef	el rosbif	*ehl rrohs-beef*
sausage	las salchichas	*lahs sahl-chee-chahs*
veal	la carne de ternera	*lah kahr-neh deh tehr-neh-rah*

Fowl and Game	*La Carne de Ave y de Caza*	Pronunciation
chicken	el pollo	*ehl poh-yoh*
duck	el pato	*ehl pah-toh*
goose	el ganso	*ehl gahn-soh*
turkey	el pavo	*ehl pah-boh*

At the Fish Store

Fish and Seafood	*El Pescado y los Mariscos*	Pronunciation
clam	la almeja	*lah ahl-meh-hah*
crab	el cangrejo	*ehl kahn-greh-hoh*
flounder	el lenguado	*ehl lehn-gwah-doh*
lobster	la langosta	*lah lahn-gohs-tah*
mussel	el mejillón	*lah meh-hee-yohn*
oyster	la ostra	*lah ohs-trah*
red snapper	el pargo colorado	*ehl pahr-goh koh-loh-rah-doh*
salmon	el salmón	*ehl sahl-mohn*
scallops	las conchas de peregrino	*lahs kohn-chahs deh peh-reh-gree-noh*
shrimp	los camarones, las gambas	*lohs kah mah roh nehs, lahs gahm-bahs*
sole	el lenguado	*ehl lehn-gwah-doh*
squid	el calamar	*ehl kah-lah-mahr*
swordfish	el pez espada	*ehl pehs ehs-pah-dah*
trout	la trucha	*lah troo-chah*
tuna	el atún	*ehl ah-toon*

At the Dairy

Dairy Products	*Productos Lácteos*	Pronunciation
butter	la mantequilla	*lah mahn-teh-kee-yah*
cheese	el queso	*ehl keh-soh*
cream	la crema	*lah kreh-mah*
eggs	los huevos	*lohs hweh-bohs*
yogurt	el yogur	*ehl yoh-goor*

At the Bakery and Pastry Shop

Breads and Desserts	*Pan y Postres*	Pronunciation
biscuit	el bizcocho	*ehl bees-koh-choh*
bread	el pan	*ehl pahn*
cake	el pastel, la torta	*ehl pahs-tehl, lah tohr-tah*
cookie	la galleta	*lah gah-yeh-tah*
custard (caramel)	la crema catalana (el flan)	*lah kreh-mah kah-tah-lah-nah (ehl flahn)*
marzipan	el mazapán	*ehl mah-sah-pahn*
meringue	el merengue	*ehl meh-rehn-geh*
pie	el pastel	*ehl pahs-tehl*
pudding (cream)	la natilla	*lah nah-tee-yah*
rice pudding	el arroz con leche	*ehl ah-rrohs kohn leh-cheh*
rolls (sweet)	los panecillos (dulces)	*lohs pah-neh-see-yohs (dool-sehs)*
tart	la tarta	*lah tahr-tah*

At the Candy Store

Sweets	*Los Dulces*	Pronunciation
candy	los dulces	*lohs dool-sehs*
chocolate	el chocolate	*ehl choh-koh-lah-teh*
gum	el chicle	*ehl chee-kleh*

Serious Shopping

Tell where you would go to purchase the following items.

1. _____   2. _____   3. _____   4. _____   5. _____

At the Supermarket

Drinks	*Las Bebidas*	Pronunciation
cider	la sidra	*lah see-drah*
coffee (iced)	el café (helado)	*ehl kah-feh (eh-lah-doh)*
juice	el jugo, el zumo	*ehl hoo-goh, ehl soo-moh*
milk	la leche	*lah leh-cheh*
soda	la gaseosa	*lah gah-seh-yoh-sah*
tea (iced)	el té (helado)	*ehl teh (eh-lah-doh)*
water	el agua	*ehl ah-gwah*
mineral	mineral	*mee-neh-rahl*
carbonated	con gas	*kohn gahs*
noncarbonated	sin gas	*seen gahs*
wine	el vino	*ehl bee-noh*

If you want to be specific about a type of juice, use *jugo de* + the name of the fruit:

    jugo de naranja   jugo de manzana
    orange juice   apple juice

In a Flash

Label the foods in your refrigerator. Keep the labels on until you learn the names of your favorite foods. Then, remove the labels and practice naming what's on hand.

Quantity Counts

Because most of us are used to dealing with ounces, pounds, pints, quarts, and gallons, I've included a conversion chart to help you out until the metric system becomes second nature.

Measuring Quantities of Food*

Solid Measures		Liquid Measures	
U.S. Customary	Metric Customary	U.S. System Equivalent	Metric System Equivalent
1 ounce	28 grams	1 ounce	30 milliliters
¼ pound	125 grams	16 ounces (1 pint)	475 milliliters
½ pound	250 grams (1 quart)	32 ounces (approximately 1 liter)	950 milliliters

continues

Measuring Quantities of Food* (continued)

Solid Measures		Liquid Measures	
U.S. Customary	Metric Customary	U.S. System Equivalent	Metric System Equivalent
¼ pound	375 grams	1 gallon	3.75 liters
1.1 pound	500 grams		
2.2 pound	1,000 grams (1 kilogram)		

All weight and measurement comparisons are approximate.

When I was a kid, no one ever told us about the metric system. If you're a bit confused as to how it works, trust me, I understand perfectly. You can make measurements easier by simply asking for a box, a bag, or a can or by memorizing the amounts you think you'll need: a pound, a quart, or whatever. Consult the following table to help you get the right amount.

Getting the Amount You Want

Amount	Spanish	Pronunciation
a bag of	un saco de	*oon sah-koh deh*
a bar of	una barra de	*oo-nah bah-rrah deh*
a bottle of	una botella de	*oo-nah boh-teh-yah deh*
a box of	una caja de	*oo-nah kah-hah deh*
a bunch of	un atado de	*oon ah-tah-doh deh*
a can of	una lata de	*oo-nah lah-tah deh*
a dozen	una docena de	*oo-nah doh-seh-nah deh*
a half-pound of	una media libra de	*oo-nah meh-dee-yah lee-brah deh*
a jar of	un pomo de	*oon poh-moh deh*
a package of	un paquete de	*oon pah-keh-teh deh*
a piece of	un pedazo de	*oon peh-dah-soh deh*
a pound of	una libra de	*oo-nah lee-brah deh*
a quart of	un litro de	*oon lee-troh deh*
a slice of	un trozo de	*oon troh-soh deh*

If you want to get a true feel for Hispanic cultures, you have to go off your diet every now and then. You know you want to taste the *dulce de zapote* (*dool-seh deh sah-poh-teh*) that your Mexican friend has prepared for you. Never mind the caloric content of the zapote pulp, orange juice, and sugar. Taste it, and savor its creamy texture and tangy flavor. Your friend offers you more. Don't allow yourself to completely blow your diet. Use the following expressions to limit the quantity you receive.

Quantity	Spanish	Pronunciation
a little	un poco de	*oon poh-koh deh*
a lot	mucho(a)	*moo-choh(ah)*
enough	bastante, suficiente	*bahs-tahn-teh, soo-fee-see-yehn-teh*
too much	demasiado	*deh-mah-see-yah-doh*

What Would You Like?

When you go into a store, do you sometimes drive the clerk crazy by pointing to this item and then that one? Do you make demands because you must have that brand and not this one? When you finally think you've made the best choice, do you notice that one over there and then spend several minutes debating your choice? If this is the case, you'll certainly need demonstrative pronouns.

These nifty little words are extremely useful and easy to learn. In fact, except for an accent mark, they are exactly the same as the demonstrative adjectives studied in Chapter 15. The following table will help you make your selections.

Demonstrative Pronouns

Demonstrative Pronoun	Masculine	Feminine
this one	éste	ésta
these	éstos	éstas
that one (near speaker)	ése	ésa
those (near speaker)	ésos	ésas
that one (away from speaker, over there)	aquél	aquélla
those (away from speaker, over there)	aquéllos	aquéllas

- Demonstrative pronouns indicate a person, place, or thing when the noun itself is not mentioned:

  Prefiero ésta.
  I prefer this one.

- Demonstrative pronouns agree in number and gender with the nouns they replace:

  esta botella y aquélla
  this bottle and that (one)

  Este vino es rojo, ése blanco, y aquél rosado.
  This wine is red, that one white, and that one (over there) rosé.

Getting What You Want

In a small, neighborhood store, someone always is eager to help you. Be prepared for the questions you might be asked and have the proper answer ready so you get what you want:

¿Qué desea?	¿En qué puedo servirle?
keh deh-seh-yah	*ehn keh pweh-doh sehr-beer-leh*
What would you like?	How may I help you?

Your answer might begin one of these ways:

Deseo …?	¿Podría darme …?	Por favor.
deh-seh-yoh	*poh-dree-yah dahr-meh*	*pohr fah-bohr*
I would like …	Could you give me …?	Please.

You might then be asked one of the following:

¿Y con eso?	¿Es todo?
ee kohn eh-soh	*ehs toh-doh*
And with that?	Is that all?

The appropriate response is either to name additional items you want or to answer as follows:

Sí, es todo, gracias.
see ehs toh-doh grah-see-yahs
Yes, that's all, thank you.

I Would Like …

Okay, you're on your own. Tell a shopkeeper you would like the following items:

1. A pound of ham
2. A liter of soda
3. A chocolate bar
4. A box of cookies
5. A bag of candy
6. A half-pound of turkey

Answer Key

Serious Shopping

1. A la lechería
2. A la carnicería
3. A la panadería
4. A la frutería
5. A la pescadería

I Would Like …

1. Deseo una libra de jamón.
2. ¿Podría darme un litro de gaseosa?
3. Una barra de chocolate, por favor.
4. Deseo una caja de galletas.
5. Un saco de dulces, por favor.
6. ¿Podría darme una media libra de pavo?

17

Dining Out

In This Chapter

◆ Tips on ordering in a restaurant

◆ What to say to get the dish you want

◆ Info for those of you on special diets

◆ Exclamations!

Let's say you're in Cancún. You shopped all morning and then stopped at a local store to pick up some snacks. You used what you learned about the metric system in Chapter 16 to purchase appropriate quantities of all your favorite goodies. Before you took your *siesta*, you lounged around your room munching on *tacos* and *tortillas* and sipping *piña coladas*.

Now you've awakened and your stomach is growling again. It's time to venture out and find an enjoyable eating spot. Perhaps you'll stop at a *tapas* bar for some appetizers and a drink before your main meal, or maybe it's late and you're ready for dinner. This chapter teaches you how to order food from a Spanish menu, even if your diet is limited and requires certain restrictions. If you're not perfectly satisfied with every aspect of your meal, you'll be able to send back the food and get exactly what you want.

Pick a Place You Like

Whether you're just a little hungry and crave a small bite or you're ravenous and in search of a quality meal, a variety of establishments will cater to your needs and your pocketbook. If you want an informal setting, try one of the options in the following list. If you prefer a more formal meal, head for the nearest *restaurante (rehs-tow-rahn-teh)*.

◆ *Un café (oon kah-feh).* A small neighborhood restaurant where residents socialize.

◆ *Una cafetería (oo-nah kah-feh-teh-ree-yah).* Not at all the self-service type of establishment you would expect. A small, informal café serving snacks and drinks.

◆ *Un bar, una tasca, una taberna (oon bahr, oo-nah tahs-kah, oo-nah tah-behr-nah).* Pubs or bars in which drinks and small snacks known as *tapas (tah-pahs)* or *pinchos (peen-chohs)* are served.

◆ *Una fonda, una hostería, una venta, una posada (oo-nah fohn-dah, oo-nah ohs-teh-ree-yah, oo-nah behn-tah, oo-nah poh-sah-dah).* Inns specializing in regional dishes.

◆ *Un merendero, un chiringuito (oon meh-rehn-deh-roh, oon chee-reen-gee-toh).* Outdoor stands, usually at the beach, that sell seafood, drinks, and ice cream.

◆ *Una cervecería (oo-nah sehr-beh-seh-ree-yah).* A pub that specializes in German beer in the barrel as well as wine.

◆ *Una hacienda (oo-nah ah-see-yehn-dah).* A ranch-style restaurant found in Spanish America.

◆ *Una cantina (oo-nah kahn-tee-nah).* A men's bar found in Spanish America. (Sorry, ladies. There's nothing illicit going on, though; the men simply want their privacy.)

Making a Reservation

Should you decide to eat in a popular restaurant, you might find it necessary to reserve a table. When you call, you will be asked for a lot of information. Be sure you know what to say:

Quisiera hacer una reservación.　　　　　　　　para esta noche
kee-see-yeh-rah ah-sehr oo-nah rreh-sehr-bah-see-yohn　　*pah-rah ehs-tah noh-cheh*
I would like to reserve a table.　　　　　　　for this evening

para mañana (el sábado)
por la noche
pah-rah mah-nyah-nah (ehl sah-bah-doh)
pohr lah noh-cheh
for tomorrow (Saturday) evening

para dos personas
pah-rah dohs pehr-soh-nahs
for two people

cerca de la ventana
sehr-kah deh lah behn-tah-nah
near the window

para las ocho y media
pah-rah lahs oh-choh ee meh-dee-yah
for 8:30 P.M.

en la terraza (el rincón), por favor
ehn lah teh-rrah-sah (ehl rreen-kohn) pohr fah-bohr
on the terrace (in the corner), please

At the Restaurant

Let's say you didn't reserve a table and you show up at a restaurant unannounced. *El jefe del comedor (ehl heh-feh dehl koh-meh-dohr;* the headwaiter) will most certainly ask the following:

¿Una mesa para cuántas personas?
oo-nah meh-sah pah-rah kwahn-tahs pehr-soh-nahs
A table for how many?

You respond:

Una mesa para tres, por favor.
oo-nah meh-sah pah-rah trehs pohr fah-bohr
A table for three, please.

Setting a Place

It's just been one of those days. You dropped your fork, and as you bent down to retrieve it, you spilled water on your suit and had to mop it up with your napkin. Your elbow hit your empty plate, which is now on the floor. After all this, you need a new place setting. The following table gives you the vocabulary you need to ask the waiter for cutlery or other items.

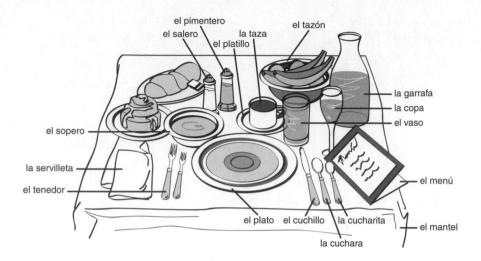

A Table Setting

Tableware	Spanish	Pronunciation
bowl	el tazón	*ehl tah-sohn*
carafe	la garrafa	*lah gah-rrah-fah*
cup	la taza	*lah tah-sah*
dinner plate	el plato	*ehl plah-toh*
fork	el tenedor	*ehl teh-neh-dohr*
glass	el vaso	*ehl bah-soh*
knife	el cuchillo	*ehl koo-chee-yoh*
menu	el menú	*ehl meh-noo*
napkin	la servilleta	*lah sehr-bee-yeh-tah*
pepper shaker	el pimentero	*ehl pee-mehn-teh-roh*
place setting	el cubierto	*ehl koo-bee-yehr-toh*
salt shaker	el salero	*ehl sah-leh-roh*
saucer	el platillo	*ehl plah-tee-yoh*
soup dish	el sopero	*ehl soh-peh-roh*
soup spoon	la cuchara	*lah koo-chah-rah*
tablecloth	el mantel	*ehl mahn-tehl*
teaspoon	la cucharita	*lah koo-chah-ree-tah*
wine glass	la copa	*lah koh-pah*

"How May I Help You?"

Is something missing from your table? Do you want to make a request of the head waiter, waiter, or wine steward? If you do, the following information and phrases will help you get what you want:

◆ Use an indirect object pronoun. Remember that the verb *faltar* must agree with the number of items lacking. If it's just one, use *falta*. For more than one, use *faltan*.

Showing Need	Pronunciation	Spanish
Me falta(n) …	*meh fahl-tah(n)*	I need …
Te falta(n) …	*teh fahl-tah(n)*	You need …
Le falta(n) …	*leh fahl-tah(n)*	He, she, you need(s) …
Nos falta(n) …	*nohs fahl-tah(n)*	We need …
Os falta(n) …	*ohs fahl-tah(n)*	You need …
Les falta(n) …	*lehs fahl-tah(n)*	They, you need …

◆ You also can use the verb *necesitar* (to need).

Showing Need	Pronunciation	Spanish
Necesito …	*neh-seh-see-toh*	I need …
Necesitas …	*neh-seh-see-tahs*	You need …
Él necesita …	*ehl neh-seh-see-tah*	He needs …
Ella necesita …	*eh-yah neh-seh-see-tah*	She needs …
Ud. necesita …	*oo-stehd neh-seh-see-tah*	You need …
Necesitamos …	*neh-seh-see-tah-mohs*	We need …
Necesitáis …	*neh-seh-see-tah-yees*	You need …
Ellos necesitan …	*eh-yohs neh-seh-see-tahn*	They need …
Ellas necesitan …	*eh-yahs neh-seh-see-tahn*	They need …
Uds. necesitan …	*oo-steh-dehs neh-seh-see-tahn*	You need …

"Oh, Waiter!"

Use what you've learned to tell your server you need the following items:

1. salt shaker
2. napkin
3. fork
4. knife
5. plate
6. teaspoon

"*Camarero* [Waiter], What Do You Recommend?"

Let's assume you've had a drink at a pub or bar before arriving at the restaurant. You'll probably want to order right away. The following phrases will help you ask the waiter for the specials of the day or for his own personal recommendations:

¿Cuál es el plato del día?
kwahl ehs ehl plah-toh dehl dee-yah
What is today's specialty?

¿Cuál es la especialidad de la casa?
kwahl ehs lah ehs-peh-see-yah-lee-dahd deh lah kah-sah
What is the house specialty?

¿Qué recomienda Ud.?
keh rreh-koh-mee-yehn-dah oo-stehd
What do you recommend?

This Mexican Menu Is Greek to Me

A menu could prove a bit difficult to understand unless you're acquainted with certain culinary terms. If you're traveling in Mexico and your waiter is too busy or speaks too fast, you might wind up with something you didn't really want or don't particularly like. The following table gives you the terms you need to interpret what's being offered.

What's on the Menu?

Salsas (Sauces)	Pronunciation	Description
ají de queso	*ah-hee deh keh-soh*	cheese sauce
adobo	*ah-doh-boh*	chili sauce made with sesame seeds, nuts, and spices
mole	*moh-leh*	chili sauce made with sesame seeds, cocoa, and spices
pipián	*pee-pee-yahn*	chili and pumpkin seed sauce spiced with coriander and served with breadcrumbs
salsa cruda	*sahl-sah kroo-dah*	an uncooked tomato sauce dip
salsa de perejil	*sahl-sah deh peh-reh-heel*	parsley sauce

Salsas (Sauces)	Pronunciation	Description
salsa de tomatillo verde	*sahl-sah deh toh-mah tee-yoh behr-deh*	Mexican green tomato sauce

Chiles (Chilies)	Pronunciation	Description
ancho	*ahn-choh*	medium hot
chipotle	*chee-poht-leh*	hot, smokey-flavored
jalapeño	*hah-lah-peh-nyoh*	hot, meaty-flavored
pasilla	*pah-see-yah*	hot, rich, sweet-flavored
pequín	*peh-keen*	hot
pimiento	*pee-mee-yehn-toh*	peppery
poblano	*poh-blah-noh*	medium hot, rich-flavored
serrano	*seh-rrah-noh*	hot

Tortillas (Tortillas)	Pronunciation	Description
burrito	*boo-rree-toh*	flour tortilla with a cheese and meat filling served with salsa
chalupas	*chah-loo-pahs*	cheese or ground pork filling served with a green chili sauce
chilaquiles	*chee-lah-kee-lehs*	baked layers of tortillas filled alternately with beans, meat, chicken, and cheese
enchiladas	*ehn-chee-lah-dahs*	soft corn tortillas filled with meat, rice, and cheese and topped with spicy sauce
flautas	*flow-tahs*	rolled, flute-shaped, deep-fried tortilla sandwich
quesadillas	*keh-sah-dee-yahs*	deep-fried tortillas covered with cheese, tomato, and pepper
tacos	*tah-kohs*	crisp toasted tortillas filled with meat, poultry, or beans and topped with shredded lettuce, cheese, and sauce
tamal	*tah-mahl*	cooked corn husks stuffed with meat, chicken, and chile peppers (known as *tamales* in English)
tostada	*tohs-tah-dah*	tortilla chip with different pepper and cheese toppings

Let's Eat!

You might choose to sample an appetizer from the restaurant before beginning your meal. Then it's on to the soup and the main course. The following tables list the interesting prospects awaiting you.

Appetizers (Los Aperitivos, lohs ah-peh-ree-tee-bohs)

Los Aperitivos	Pronunciation	Spanish
alcachofas	*ahl-kah-choh-fahs*	artichokes
almejas	*ahl-meh-hahs*	clams
anguilas ahumadas	*ahn-gee-lahs ah-oo-mah-dahs*	smoked eels
calamares	*kah-lah-mah-rehs*	squid
camarones	*kah-mah-roh-nehs*	shrimp
caracoles	*kah-rah-koh-lehs*	snails
champiñones	*chahm-pee-nyoh-nehs*	mushrooms
chorizo	*choh-ree-soh*	spicy sausage
cigales	*see-gah-lehs*	crayfish
guacamole	*gwah-kah-moh-leh*	avocado spread
huevos	*weh-bohs*	eggs
melón	*meh-lohn*	melon
moluscos	*moh-loos-kohs*	mussels
ostras	*ohs-trahs*	oysters
sardinas	*sahr-dee-nahs*	sardines
tostadas	*tohs-tah-dahs*	tortilla chips

Soups (Las Sopas, lahs soh-pahs)

Las Sopas	Pronunciation	Spanish
gazpacho	*gahs-pah-choh*	puréed, uncooked tomatoes, served cold
potaje madrileño	*poh-tah-heh mah-dree-leh-nyoh*	thick, puréed cod, spinach, and chickpeas

Las Carnes	Pronunciation	Spanish
sopa de ajo	*soh-pah deh ah-hoh*	garlic soup
sopa de albóndigas	*soh-pah deh ahl-bohn-dee-gahs*	meatball soup
sopa de cebolla	*soh-pah deh seh-boh-yah*	onion soup
sopa de fideos	*soh-pah deh fee-deh-yohs*	noodle soup
sopa de gambas	*soh-pah deh gahm-bahs*	shrimp soup
sopa de mariscos	*soh-pah deh mah-rees-kohs*	seafood soup
sopa de pescado	*soh-pah deh pehs-kah-doh*	fish soup
sopa de verduras	*soh-pah deh behr-doo-rahs*	soup made from puréed green vegetables

Meats (Las Carnes, lahs kahr-nehs)

Las Carnes	Pronunciation	Spanish
el asado	*ehl ah-sah-doh*	roast
el bistec	*ehl bees-tehk*	steak
el cabrito	*ehl kah-bree-toh*	goat
la carne de vaca	*lah kahr-neh deh bah-kah*	beef
el cerdo	*ehl sehr-doh*	pork
la chuleta	*lah choo-leh-tah*	chop, cutlet
el churrasco	*ehl chuh-rrahs-koh*	steak, charcoal-grilled
el cordero	*ehl kohr-deh-roh*	lamb
el estofado, el guisado	*ehl ehs-toh-fah-doh, ehl gee-sah-doh*	stew
la hamburguesa	*lah ahm-boor-geh-sah*	hamburger
el jamón	*ehl hah-mohn*	ham
el solomillo	*ehl soh-loh-mee-yoh*	sirloin
el lomo fino	*ehl loh-moh fee-noh*	filet mignon
la morcilla	*lah mohr-see-yah*	blood pudding
el rosbif	*ehl rrohs-beef*	roast beef
la salchicha	*lah sahl-chee-chah*	sausage
el tocino	*ehl toh-see-noh*	bacon
la ternera	*lah tehr-neh-rah*	veal

That's the Way I Like It

Even if you know how to order your hamburger or veal chops, you want to be certain your entrée is cooked to your specifications. The waiter might ask the following question:

> ¿Comó lo (la, los, las) quiere?
> *koh-moh loh (lah, lohs, lahs) kee-yeh-reh*
> How do you want it (them)?

Do you prefer your fish baked or broiled? Do you want your meat medium-rare or well-done? If you want to be sure your food is prepared to your liking, use the following table to express your wants and needs.

Proper Preparation

Meats and Vegetables	Spanish	Pronunciation
baked	asado	*ah-sah-doh*
boiled	cocido	*koh-see-doh*
breaded	empanado	*ehm-pah-nah-doh*
broiled	a la parrilla	*ah lah pah-rree-yah*
fried	frito	*free-toh*
grilled	asado a la parrilla	*ah-sah-doh ah lah pah-rree-yah*
marinated	escabechado	*ehs-kah-beh-chah-doh*
medium	término medio	*tehr-mee-noh meh-dee-yoh*
medium-rare	un poco rojo pero no crudo	*oon poh-koh rroh-hoh peh-roh noh kroo-doh*
poached	escalfado	*ehs-kahl-fah-doh*
rare	poco asado	*poh-koh ah-sah-doh*
roasted	asado	*ah-sah-doh*
steamed	al vapor	*ahl bah-pohr*
very rare	casi crudo	*kah-see kroo-doh*
well-done	bien asado (hecho, cocido)	*bee-yehn ah-sah-doh (eh-choh, koh-see-doh)*

Eggs	Spanish	Pronunciation
fried	fritos	*free-tohs*
hard-boiled	duros	*doo-rohs*
poached	escalfados	*ehs-kahl-fah-dohs*
scrambled	revueltos	*rreh-bwehl-tohs*
soft-boiled	pasados por agua	*pah-sah-dohs pohr ah-gwah*
omelette	una tortilla	*oo-nah tohr-tee-yah*
plain omelette	una tortilla a la francesa	*oo-nah tohr-tee-yah ah lah frahn-seh-sah*
herb omelette	una tortilla con hierbas	*oo-nah tohr-tee-yah kohn yehr-bahs*

Hot and Spicy

You should expect a variety of spices to be used in Spain and in the Spanish American countries. Menu descriptions or your waiter can usually help you determine if a dish will be to your liking—whether you prefer bland or spicy. The following table will help you become acquainted with many of the spices you might encounter.

Herbs, Spices, and Condiments

Spice	Spanish	Pronunciation
basil	la albahaca	*lah ahl-bah-ah-kah*
bay leaf	la hoja de laurel	*lah oh-hah deh low-rehl*
butter	la mantequilla	*lah mahn-teh-kee-yah*
caper	el alcaparrón	*ehl ahl-kah-pah-rrohn*
chives	el cebollino	*ehl seh-boh-yee-noh*
dill	el eneldo	*ehl eh-nehl-doh*
garlic	el ajo	*ehl ah-hoh*
ginger	el jengibre	*ehl hehn-hee-breh*
honey	la miel	*lah mee-yehl*
ketchup	la salsa de tomate	*lah sahl-sah deh toh-mah-teh*
mustard	la mostaza	*lah mohs-tah-sah*

continues

Herbs, Spices, and Condiments (continued)

Spice	Spanish	Pronunciation
oil	el aceite	*ehl ah-seh-yee-teh*
paprika	el pimentón dulce	*ehl pee-mehn-tohn dool-seh*
parsley	el perejil	*ehl peh-reh-heel*
pepper	la pimienta	*lah pee-mee-yehn-tah*
rosemary	el romero	*ehl rroh-meh-roh*
saffron	el azafrán	*ehl ah-sah-frahn*
salt	la sal	*lah sahl*
sesame	el ajonjolí	*ehl ah-hohn-hoh-lee*
sugar	el azúcar	*ehl ah-soo-kahr*

Diet Do's and Don'ts

Does your diet require certain restrictions? Are you a person with specific likes and dislikes of which your server should be aware? If so, you'll want to remember the phrases in the following table.

Dietary Restrictions

Phrase	Spanish	Pronunciation
I am on a diet.	Estoy a régimen.	*ehs-toy ah rreh-hee-mehn*
I'm a vegetarian.	Soy vegetariano(a).	*soy beh-heh-tah-ree-yah-noh(ah)*
Do you serve kosher food?	¿Sirven Uds. comida permitida por la religión judia?	*seer-behn oo-steh-dehs koh-mee-dah pehr-mee-tee-dah pohr lah rreh-lee-hee-yohn hoo-dee-yah*
I can't eat anything made with …	No puedo comer nada con …	*noh pweh-doh koh-mehr nah-dah kohn*

I can't have any …
  dairy products
  alcohol
  saturated fats
  shellfish
	No puedo tomar …
	  productos lácteos
	  alcohol
	  grasas saturadas
	  mariscos
		noh pweh-doh toh-mahr
		  proh-dook-tohs lahk-teh-yohs
		  ahl-koh-ohl
		  grah-sahs sah-too-rah-dahs
		  mah-rees-kohs

I'm looking for a dish …	Estoy buscando un plato …	*ehs-toy boos-kahn-doh oon plah-toh*

Phrase	Spanish	Pronunciation
high in fiber	con mucha fibra	*kohn moo-chah fee-brah*
low in cholesterol	con poco colesterol	*kohn poh-koh koh-lehs-teh-rohl*
low in fat	con poca grasa	*kohn poh-kah grah-sah*
low in sodium	con poca sal	*kohn poh-kah sahl*
nondairy	no lácteo	*noh lahk-teh-yoh*
salt-free	sin sal	*seen sahl*
sugar-free	sin azúcar	*seen ah-soo-kahr*
without artificial coloring	sin colorantes artificiales	*seen koh-loh-rahn-tehs ahr-tee-fee-see-yah-lehs*
without preservatives	sin preservativos	*seen preh-sehr-bah-tee-bohs*

I'm Sending It Back

The dish you ordered just doesn't seem right. Perhaps something is missing. Maybe you ordered it rare, but it looks and tastes like shoe leather. The waiter said it wouldn't be too hot, but you can't seem to get enough water to cool your palate. If there's a problem, you'll want to be able to communicate exactly what it is. The following table will help you send back that disappointing dish and get something more to your liking.

Possible Problems with Your Food

Problem	Spanish	Pronunciation
… is cold	está frío	*ehs-tah free-yoh*
… is too rare	está demasiado crudo	*ehs-tah deh-mah-see-yah-doh kroo-doh*
… is overcooked	está sobrecocido	*ehs-tah soh-breh-koh-see-doh*
… is tough	está duro	*ehs-tah doo-roh*
… is burned	está quemado	*ehs-tah keh-mah-doh*
… is too salty	está muy salado	*ehs-tah mwee sah-lah-doh*
… is too sweet	está muy dulce	*ehs-tah mwee dool-seh*
… is too spicy	está demasiado picante	*ehs-tah deh-mah-see-yah-doh pee-kahn-teh*
… is spoiled	está pasado	*ehs-tah pah-sah-doh*
… is bitter (sour)	está agrio (cortado)	*ehs-tah ah-gree-yoh (kohr-tah-doh)*
… is dirty	está sucio	*ehs-tah soo-see-yoh*

Fancy Finales

Finally, it's time for dessert! You'll surely have some interesting specialties from which to choose. The following table will help you make your decision.

Divine Desserts

Dessert	Spanish	Pronunciation
caramel custard	el flan	*ehl flahn*
cookies	las galletas	*lahs gah-yeh-tahs*
gelatin	la gelatina	*lah heh-lah-tee-nah*
ice cream	el helado	*ehl eh-lah-doh*
pie	el pastel	*ehl pahs-tehl*
rice pudding	el arroz con leche	*ehl ah-rrohs kohn leh-cheh*
sponge cake	el bizcocho	*ehl bees-koh-choh*
tart	la tarta	*lah tahr-tah*
yogurt	el yogur	*ehl yoh-goor*

Here's an important distinction to make: if you're eating *ensalada* (salad), be sure to order *galletas saladas* (crackers). For dessert, order *galletas* (cookies); they are sweet.

If you'd rather have ice cream, the following terms will help you get the serving and *el sabor* (*ehl sah-bohr*; flavor) you prefer.

Ice Cream	Spanish	Pronunciation
cone	un barquillo	*oon bahr-kee-yoh*
cup	una taza	*oo-nah tah-sah*
chocolate	de chocolate	*deh choh-koh-lah-teh*
vanilla	de vainilla	*deh bah-yee-nee-yah*
strawberry	de fresa	*deh freh-sah*

Drink to Me Only

Spaniards usually drink wine with dinner. The wines you might order include those in the following table.

Beverage	Spanish	Pronunciation
red wine	el vino tinto	*ehl bee-noh teen-toh*
rosé wine	el vino rosado	*ehl bee-noh rroh-sah-doh*
white wine	el vino blanco	*ehl bee-noh blahn-koh*
dry wine	el vino seco	*ehl bee-noh seh-koh*
sweet wine	el vino dulce	*ehl bee-noh dool-seh*
sparkling wine	el vino espumoso	*ehl bee-noh ehs-poo-moh-soh*
champagne	el champán	*ehl chahm-pahn*

If you don't choose to have wine with your meal, you will, of course, want to order something else. You might even want to order different drinks with different courses. The following table lists other beverages you might enjoy with or after dinner.

Beverages

Beverage	Spanish	Pronunciation
coffee	un café	*oon kah-feh*
with milk	con leche	*kohn leh-cheh*
espresso	exprés	*ehks-prehs*
with cream	con crema	*kohn kreh-mah*
black	solo	*soh-loh*
iced	helado	*eh-lah-doh*
decaffeinated	descafeinado	*dehs-kah-feh-yee-nah-doh*
tea	un te	*oon teh*
with lemon	con limón	*kohn lee-mohn*
with sugar	con azúcar	*kohn ah-soo-kahr*
herbal	herbario	*ehr-bah-ree-yoh*
soda	una soda, una gaseosa	*oo-nah soh-dah, oo-nah gah-seh-yoh-sah*
mineral water	un agua mineral	*oon ah-gwah mee-neh-rahl*
carbonated	con gas	*kohn gahs*
noncarbonated	sin gas	*seen gahs*
juice	un jugo	*oon hoo-goh*
milk	una leche	*oo-nah leh-cheh*
skim milk	desnatada	*dehs-nah-tah-dah*

You Can't Have It All

De is used after nouns of quantity, as follows:

un vaso de leche   una botella de agua
a glass of milk   a bottle of water

There is no Spanish equivalent for "some" when the noun can't be counted. To express what you want, simply use the word *quisiera* (*kee-see-yeh-rah*), which means "I would like," and a noun. In general, "some" is understood when a noun is used:

Quisiera carne, por favor.
I'd like some meat, please.

When the noun can be counted, use *unos* or *unas* before the noun:

Quisiera unos huevos, por favor.
I'd like some eggs, please.

¡Delicioso!

How was your meal? Would you tell your friends about it and recommend it highly? Or would you rate it as just so-so? If you're really happy with your meal and the food was exceptional, you might want to express your pleasure using the word *¡Qué …!* to say "What a …!"

¡Qué comida!   ¡Qué servicio!
What a meal!   What service!

To make the exclamation more intense, add an adjective that agrees with the noun and place the word *tan* (*tahn*) or *más* (*mahs*) before the adjective. (Both words mean "so" in this context, although we do not use "so" in our English equivalent of the phrase.)

¡Qué comida tan rica!   ¡Qué platos tan sabrosos!
What a rich meal!   What tasty dishes!

¡Qué servicio tan excelente!
What excellent service!

Muchas Gracias

The meal was great. Tell the person who recommended the restaurant how much you enjoyed it. Use *que* + noun + *tan* (*más*) + adjective to express how you felt about what you ate and drank:

1. soup
2. steak
3. wine
4. salad
5. dessert

Don't forget to ask for the check at the end of your meal:

La cuenta, por favor.
lah kwehn-tah pohr fah-bohr
The check, please.

On many occasions, the tip is included in the bill. Look for the words *servicio incluído*.

Answer Key

"Oh, Waiter!"

1. Necesito un salero.
2. Me falta una servilleta.
3. Necesito un tenedor.
4. Me falta un cuchillo.
5. Necesito un plato.
6. Me falta una cucharita.

Muchas Gracias

Sample responses:

1. ¡Qué sopa tan excelente!
2. ¡Qué bistec tan delicioso!
3. ¡Qué vino más sabroso!
4. ¡Qué ensalada tan magnífica!
5. ¡Qué postre tan rico!

Play Time!

In This Chapter

- ◆ Things to do to have fun
- ◆ Invitations: extending, accepting, and refusing
- ◆ Ways to use adverbs to describe abilities

You've visited countless tourist attractions, collected souvenirs, and purchased gifts for people you love. The meals you've eaten have been superb, and your appetite is truly sated. Now you want to have some fun, engage in your favorite sport, or simply lie back and relax.

You can go off to the sea to swim, snorkel, parasail, or windsurf. Or would you prefer to ski or hike on snow-covered mountains? Are you drawn to the links for a round of golf or to the courts for a friendly tennis match? Are you a film *aficionado* or a theater buff? An opera lover or a fan of the ballet? Would you like to gamble and spend some time in a Dominican casino? After studying this chapter, you'll be able to discuss any of these activities, invite someone to join you, and even brag about your skills and talents.

Sports Are My Life

I love a challenging tennis match, and my racquet has seen nearly as many countries as I have. My husband prefers the pool and likes nothing better than trying to surpass his daily record of laps. Whether you're into sports or you'd rather spend some relaxing time at the pool or the beach, you'll need certain words and expressions to discuss your preferences.

Outdoor activities and sports are listed in the following table. The verbs *hacer* and *jugar* + *a* + definite article are commonly used to describe participation in a sport. Words with one star (*) use *hacer*; those with two (**) use *jugar*. The verbs in parentheses are used in place of *jugar* or *hacer*.

Ella hace el ciclismo.   Juego al tenis.
She goes cycling.   I play tennis.

Vamos de pesca.
We go fishing.

If you want to say you like or dislike a sport, use the phrase *(no) me gusta* + definite article (*el, la, los, las*) + sport.

When using the verb *jugar* + *a* + definite article, remember that *a* contracts with *el* to form *al:*

Juego al tenis.
I play tennis.

Sports

Sport	Spanish	Pronunciation
aerobics	los aeróbicos*	*lohs ah-yee-roh-bee-kohs*
baseball	el béisbol**	*ehl beh-yees-bohl*
basketball	el baloncesto,** el básquetbol**	*ehl bah-lohn-sehs-toh, ehl bahs-keht-bohl*
bicycling	el ciclismo* (montar en bicicleta)	*ehl see-klees-moh (mohn-tahr ehn bee-see-kleh-tah)*
boating	(dar) un paseo en barco	*(dahr) oon pah-seh-yoh ehn bahr-koh*
bodybuilding	el fisiculturismo*	*ehl fee-see-kool-too-rees-moh*

Sport	Spanish	Pronunciation
canoeing	el piragüismo*	*ehl pee-rah-gwees-moh*
diving	el clavado	*ehl klah-bah-doh*
fishing	la pesca (ir de pesca)	*lah pehs-kah (eer deh pehs-kah)*
football	el fútbol americano**	*ehl foot-bohl ah-meh-ree-kah-noh*
golf	el golf**	*ehl gohlf*
horseback riding	la equitación*	*lah eh-kee-tah-see-yohn*
ice-skating	el patinaje sobre hielo* (patinar)	*ehl pah-tee-nah-heh soh-breh yeh-loh (pah-tee-nahr)*
jogging	el footing* (trotar)	*ehl foo-teeng (troh-tahr)*
mountain climbing	el alpinismo*	*ehl ahl-pee-nees-moh*
sailing	la navegación* (navegar)	*lah nah-beh-gah-see-yohn (nah-beh-gahr)*
scuba (skin) diving	el buceo	*ehl boo-seh-yoh*
skating	el patinaje*	*ehl pah-tee-nah-heh*
skiing	el esquí* (esquiar)	*ehl ehs-kee (ehs-kee-yahr)*
soccer	el fútbol**	*ehl foot-bohl*
surfing	el surf* (surfear)	*ehl soorf (soor-feh-yahr)*
swimming	la natación* (nadar)	*lah nah-tah-see-yohn (nah-dahr)*
tennis	el tenis**	*ehl teh-nees*
volleyball	el voleibol**	*ehl boh-lee-bohl*
waterskiing	el esquí acuático*	*ehl ehs-kee ah-kwah-tee-koh*

Please Join Us

If you prefer to play with a partner, you might find it necessary to extend an invitation to someone you don't know very well. To ask someone to join you, you can use the stem-changing verbs *querer* (ie), "to want," or *poder* (ue), "to be able to," plus the infinitive of the verb *jugar* (ue), "to play." Remember that these verbs change in the shape of the shoe—within the stem of the verb, *e* changes to *ie* and *o* changes to *ue* in all present tense forms except *nosotros* and *vosotros*. Here's a quick memory refresher from Chapter 12:

querer (to want, to wish)

poder (to be able)

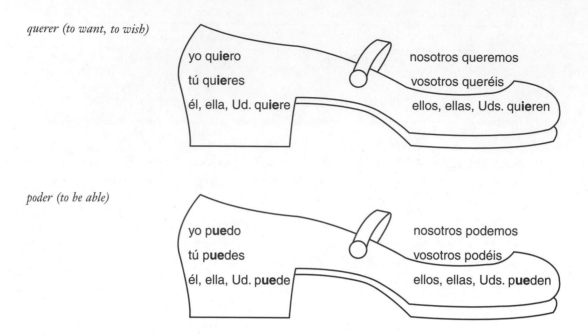

Now you're ready to ask someone to join you. First you have to find out whether he or she plays or enjoys the same activity as you. If the answer is yes, go ahead and extend an invitation using the following structure:

¿Le (Te) gusta + jugar + a + definite article + sport?

The following are some examples:

¿Le (Te) gusta jugar al tenis?   ¿Le (Te) gusta el alpinismo?
Do you like to play tennis?   Do you like to go mountain climbing?

You also could ask something like:

¿Quiere (Quieres) acompañarme (acompañarnos)?
Do you want to join me (us)?

¿Puede (Puedes) acompañarme (acompañarnos)?
Can you accompany me (us)?

Let's Play

If you're going to play a sport in which there is a match, you would say the following:

> Voy a jugar un partido de....
> *boy ah hoo-gahr oon pahr-tee-doh deh*
> I'm going to play a game of....

If you want to say you're going to engage in an activity, refer to the earlier "Sports" table and use *ir + a +* the infinitive of the verb in parentheses. You also could use *ir + a + hacer +* a sport. Here are some examples:

Voy a nadar.	Voy a hacer equitación.
boy ah nah-dahr	*boy ah ah-sehr eh-kee-tah-see-yohn*
I'm going to go swimming.	I'm going to go horseback riding.

Note the following irregularities:

Voy de pesca.	Voy a jugar al ping-pong.
boy deh pehs-kah	*boy ah hoo-gahr ahl peeng-pohng*
I'm going fishing.	I'm going to play Ping-Pong.

It's time to get some exercise. Remember that each sport is played in a particular environment: a court, a field, a course, a rink, and so on. The following table will help you choose the proper venue for the sport that interests you.

Where to Go

Sports Venue	Spanish	Pronunciation
beach	la playa	*lah plah-yah*
course (golf)	el campo	*ehl kahm-poh*
court	la cancha	*lah kahn-chah*
court (jai alai)	el frontón	*ehl frohn-tohn*
field	el campo	*ehl kahm-poh*
gymnasium	el gimnasio	*ehl heem-nah-see-yoh*
mountain	la montaña	*lah mohn-tah-nyah*
ocean	el océano	*ehl oh-seh-yah-noh*
park	el parque	*ehl pahr-keh*
path	el camino	*ehl kah-mee-noh*

continues

Where to Go (continued)

Sports Venue	Spanish	Pronunciation
pool	la piscina	*lah pee-see-nah*
rink	la pista	*lah pees-tah*
sea	el mar	*ehl mahr*
slope	la pista	*lah pees-tah*
stadium	el estadio	*ehl ehs-tah-dee-yoh*
track	la pista	*lah pees-tah*

Play by the Rules

When a sentence contains one subject noun or pronoun, be sure to conjugate the verb that immediately follows it. Any verb or verbs after that should remain in the infinitive. Express "in" and "to the" by using *a* + definite article (*al, a la*):

Yo quiero jugar al golf.
yoh kee-yeh-roh hoo-gahr ahl gohlf
I want to play golf.

¿Quiere (Quieres) ir al parque a jugar un partido de fútbol?
kee-yeh-reh (kee-yeh-rehs) eer ahl pahr-keh ah hoo-gahr oon pahr-tee-doh deh foot-bohl
Do you want to go to the park to play soccer?

¿Puede (Puedes) acompañarme a la playa?
pweh-deh (pweh-dehs) ah-kohm-pah-nyahr-meh ah lah plah-yah
Can you go with me to the beach?

If the sentence contains two subject nouns or pronouns, a verb must be conjugated after each:

Susana va a la playa, pero ella no quiere nadar.
soo-sah-nah bah ah lah plah-yah peh-roh eh-yah noh kee-yeh-reh nah-dar
Susana is going to the beach, but she doesn't want to swim.

Invite Your Friends Along

Today is a beautiful day, and you're in the mood to get some exercise. Phone a friend and invite her to go with you to the best place for the following activities.

Example: ¿Quieres ir al parque a jugar al tenis?
Would you like to go to the park to play tennis?

1. hiking
2. skiing
3. swimming
4. skating
5. mountain climbing
6. golfing

Accepting the Invitation

It's always a friendly gesture to graciously accept an invitation offered to you. Perhaps you've been asked to play doubles tennis, to accompany someone on a sightseeing trip, or to eat dinner at someone's house. Whatever the situation, the following phrases will help you in your social encounters:

Phrase	Pronunciation	Meaning
Con mucho gusto.	*kohn moo-choh goos-toh*	With pleasure.
Por supuesto.	*pohr soo-pwehs-toh*	Of course.
Claro.	*klah-roh*	Of course.
Es una buena idea.	*ehs oo-nah bweh-nah ee-deh-yah*	That's a good idea.
¡Magnífico!	*mahg-nee-fee-koh*	Great!
De acuerdo.	*deh ah-kwehr-doh*	Okay. (I agree.)
Sin duda.	*seen doo-dah*	There's no doubt about it.
¿Por qué no?	*pohr keh noh*	Why not?
Si tú quieres (Ud. quiere).	*see too kee-yeh-rehs (oo-stehd kee-yeh-reh)*	If you want to.
Con placer.	*kohn plah-sehr*	Gladly.

A Polite Refusal

There are times when you would like to accept an invitation but truly cannot. Maybe you have a previous appointment. Perhaps you're tired and would like to be alone for a while. Of course, you wouldn't want to offend anyone, so you need to turn down the invitation politely. The following table shows you how to do just that.

Phrase	Pronunciation	Meaning
Es imposible.	*ehs eem-poh-see-bleh*	It's impossible.
No tengo ganas.	*noh tehn-goh gah-nahs*	I don't feel like it.
No puedo.	*noh pweh-doh*	I can't.
No estoy libre.	*noh ehs-toy lee-breh*	I'm not free.
No quiero.	*noh kee-yeh-roh*	I don't want to.
Lo siento.	*loh see-yehn-toh*	I'm sorry.
Estoy cansado(a).	*ehs-toy kahn-sah-doh(dah)*	I'm tired.
Estoy ocupado(a).	*ehs-toy oh-koo-pah-doh(dah)*	I'm busy.

I Don't Care

We've all received invitations we can't decide whether to accept. If you can't make up your mind or are feeling indifferent toward an idea, use one of the phrases in the following table.

Phrase	Pronunciation	Meaning
Depende.	*deh-pehn-deh*	It depends.
No me importa.	*noh meh eem-pohr-tah*	I don't care.
Me da lo mismo.	*meh dah loh mees-moh*	It's all the same to me.
Lo que Ud. prefiera (tú prefieras).	*loh keh oo-stehd preh-fee-yeh-rah (too preh-fee-yeh-rahs)*	Whatever you want.
Lo que Ud. quiera (tú quieras).	*loh keh oo-stehd kee-yeh-rah (too kee-yeh-rahs)*	Whatever you want.
No tengo preferencia.	*noh tehn-goh preh-feh-rehn-see-yah*	I don't have any preference.
Yo no sé.	*yoh noh seh*	I don't know.
Tal vez.	*tahl behs*	Perhaps. (Maybe.)

Other Diversions

You like sports, and you're a cultured, refined person. Now it's time for a change of pace. Why not try some of the activities listed in the following table? If you choose to see an opera, a ballet, or a concert, don't forget to bring along *los gemelos* (binoculars).

Places to Go and Things to Do

El Lugar	Place	La Actividad	Activity
ir a la opera	go to the opera	escuchar a los cantantes	listen to the singers
ir a la playa	go to the beach	nadar, tomar sol	swim, sunbathe
ir a una discoteca	go to the disco	bailar	dance
ir a un ballet	go to the ballet	ver a los bailadores	see the dancers
ir a un casino	go to the casino	jugar	play, gamble
ir al centro comercial	go to the mall	mirar los escaparates	window-shop
ir al cine	go to the movies	ver una película	see a film
ir a un concierto	go to a concert	escuchar la orquesta	listen to the orchestra
ir al teatro	go to the theater	ver un drama	see a play
ir de excursión	go on an excursion	ver los puntos de interés	see the sights
quedarse en su habitación (casa)	stay in one's room (home)	jugar a los naipes	play cards
		jugar a las damas	play checkers
		jugar al ajedrez	play chess
		leer una novela	read a novel

At the Shore

Have you ever been so excited to finally see the sea that you jumped into the ocean without a second thought? When you finally came out, you might have realized you forgot to get a towel, and now you're standing there dripping wet. If you want to have a pleasant day at the beach or the pool, remember to take along the items in the following table.

Spanish	Pronunciation	Beach Items
una pelota de playa	*oo-nah peh-loh-tah deh plah-yah*	beach ball
un sillón de playa	*oon see-yohn deh plah-yah*	beach chair
una toalla de playa	*oo-nah toh-wah-yah deh plah-yah*	beach towel
una sombrilla	*oo-nah sohn-bree-yah*	beach umbrella
una nevera portátil	*oo-nah neh-beh-rah pohr-tah-teel*	cooler
una radio	*oo-nah rrah-dee-yoh*	radio
las gafas de sol	*lahs gah-fahs deh sohl*	sunglasses
la loción bronceadora	*lah loh-see-yohn brohn-seh-yah-doh-rah*	suntan lotion

Film at Eleven

You're all played out, you're all walked out, and your belly is full. If you're a film buff, you might want to catch the latest film or even your favorite show on TV. If you want some quiet entertainment, ask these questions and then consult the following table:

¿Qué tipo de película están pasando?
keh tee-poh deh peh-lee-koo-lah ehs-tahn pah-sahn-doh
What kind of film are they showing?

¿Qué hay en la televisión?
keh ah-yee ehn lah teh-leh-bee-see-yohn
What's on TV?

Movies and Television Programs

Type of Program	Spanish	Pronunciation
adventure film	una película de aventura	*oo-nah peh-lee-koo-lah deh ah-behn-too-rah*
cartoon	los dibujos animados	*lohs dee-boo-hohs ah-nee-mah-dohs*
comedy	una comedia	*oo-nah koh-meh-dee-yah*
documentary	un documental	*oon doh-koo-mehn-tahl*
drama	un drama	*oon drah-mah*
game show	un juego	*oon hweh-goh*
horror movie	una película de horror	*oo-nah peh-lee-koo-lah deh oh-rrohr*
love story	una película de amor	*oo-nah peh-lee-koo-lah deh ah-mohr*
mystery	un misterio	*oon mees-teh-ree-yoh*
news	las noticias	*lahs noh-tee-see-yahs*
police story	una película policíaca	*oo-nah peh-lee-koo-lah poh-lee-see-yah-kah*
reality show	una demonstración de la realidad	*oo-nah deh-mohn-strah-see-yohn deh lah rreh-yah-lee-dad*
science fiction film	una película de ciencia ficción	*oo-nah peh-lee-koo-lah deh see-yehn-see-yah feek-see-yohn*
soap opera	una telenovela	*oo-nah teh-leh-noh-beh-lah*
spy movie	una película de espionaje	*oo-nah peh-lee-koo-lah deh ehs-pee-yoh-nah-heh*
talk show	un programa de entrevistas	*oon proh-grah-mah deh ehn-treh-bees-tahs*
weather	el parte meteorológico, el pronóstico	*ehl pahr-teh meh-teh-yoh-roh-loh-hee-koh, ehl proh-nohs-tee-koh*
western	una película del oeste, un western	*oo-nah peh-lee-koo-lah dehl oh-wehs-teh, oon wehs-tehrn*

How Did You Like It?

Use the phrases in the following table to express your enjoyment of a film or program.

Positive Review	Spanish	Pronunciation
I love it!	¡Me encanta!	*meh ehn-kahn-tah*
It's a good movie.	¡Es una buena película!	*ehs oo-nah bweh-nah peh-lee-koo-lah*
It's amusing!	¡Es divertida!	*ehs dee-behr-tee-dah*
It's great!	¡Es fantástica!	*ehs fahn-tahs-tee-kah*
It's moving!	¡Me conmueve!	*meh kohn-mweh-beh*
It's original!	¡Es original!	*ehs oh-ree-hee-nahl*

If you're less than thrilled with the show, try the phrases in the following table.

Negative Review	Spanish	Pronunciation
It's a bad movie!	¡Es una película mala!	*ehs oo-nah peh-lee-koo-lah mah-lah*
It's a loser!	¡Es un desastre!	*ehs oon deh-sahs-treh*
It's garbage!	¡Es una porquería!	*ehs oo-nah pohr-keh-ree-yah*
It's the same old thing!	¡Es lo mismo de siempre!	*ehs loh mees-moh deh see-yehm-preh*
It's too violent!	¡Es demasiado violenta!	*ehs deh-mah-see-yah-doh bee-yoh-lehn-tah*

At a Concert

On a trip to Spain, you discover your favorite rock group will be performing there during your visit. Or maybe you're more into classical guitar or chamber music. One young student of mine received an all-expenses-paid trip to Europe to sing opera with a choir. Whatever your taste in music, the following table will help you with the names of the musical instruments you will hear.

Musical Instruments

Instrument	Spanish	Pronunciation
accordion	el acordeón	*ehl ah-kohr-deh-yohn*
cello	el violoncelo	*ehl bee-yoh-lohn-seh-loh*
clarinet	el clarinete	*ehl klah-ree-neh-teh*
drum	el tambor	*ehl tahm-bohr*
drum set	la batería	*lah bah-teh-ree-yah*
flute	la flauta	*lah flah-oo-tah*
guitar	la guitarra	*lah gee-tah-rrah*
harp	el arpa	*ehl ahr-pah*
horn	el cuerno	*ehl kwehr-noh*
oboe	el oboe	*ehl oh-boh-weh*
piano	el piano	*ehl pee-yah-noh*
piccolo	el flautín	*ehl flah-oo-teen*
saxophone	el saxofón	*ehl sahk-soh-fohn*
trombone	el trombón	*ehl trohm-bohn*
trumpet	la trompeta	*lah trohm-peh-tah*
violin	el violín	*ehl bee-yoh-leen*

Jugar vs. *Tocar*

In English, whether we're talking about engaging in a sport or playing an instrument, we use the verb "to play." In Spanish, however, a distinction is made. The verb *jugar* + *a* + definite article (*al, a la, a los, a las*) is used before the name of a sport or game. *Jugar* is a stem-changing shoe verb that changes *u* to *ue* in all forms except *nosotros* and *vosotros*. Here's a quick refresher course (or refer to Chapter 12):

jugar *(to play)*

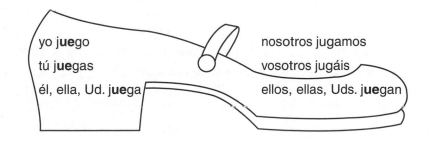

yo **jue**go   nosotros jugamos
tú **jue**gas   vosotros jugáis
él, ella, Ud. **jue**ga   ellos, ellas, Uds. **jue**gan

<table>
<tr><td>Jugamos a los naipes.</td><td>Juego al tenis.</td></tr>
<tr><td>*hoo-gah-mohs ah lohs nah-yee-pehs*</td><td>*hweh-goh ahl teh-nees*</td></tr>
<tr><td>We play cards.</td><td>I play tennis.</td></tr>
</table>

Use the verb *tocar* when you're talking about playing a musical instrument:

Me gusta tocar el piano.
meh goos-tah toh-kahr ehl pee-yah-noh
I like to play the piano.

How Good Are You?

Adverbs are often used to describe how someone does something, as in "He plays the classical guitar beautifully." (In English, most adverbs end in *-ly*.) In Spanish, adverbs are used for the same purpose, and they generally end in *-mente*.

To form most adverbs in Spanish, add *-mente* to the feminine singular form of the adjective. This works well as long as you look for the proper letter at the end of the adjective and know the feminine forms. (See Chapter 9 if you need a refresher.) The following table shows you how easy this is.

Adverbs Formed from Feminine Adjectives

Feminine Adjective	Adverb	Meaning
atenta	atentamente	attentively
cariñosa	cariñosamente	affectionately
completa	completamente	completely
especial	especialmente	especially
fácil	fácilmente	easily
final	finalmente	finally
frecuente	frecuentemente	frequently
inteligente	inteligentemente	intelligently
lenta	lentamente	slowly
rápida	rápidamente	quickly
triste	tristemente	sadly

When you need to describe an action with two or more adverbs, add *-mente* only to the last one. The other adverbs should be in the feminine singular adjective form, to which it is assumed that *-mente* would be added had they stood alone. Here's an example:

> Enrique habla clara, lenta, fácil, y elocuentemente.
> Henry speaks clearly, slowly, easily, and eloquently.

If you can't think of the adverb or if one does not exist, use the preposition *con* + the noun.

Con + Noun	Adverb	Meaning
con alegría	alegremente	happily
con cortesía	cortésmente	courteously
con cuidado	cuidadosamente	carefully
con habilidad	hábilmente	skillfully
con paciencia	pacientemente	patiently

Is your Spanish good? Do you speak the language well? How about your accent, is it good or bad? (Of course it's good—you're using the pronunciation guide and listening to the CD!) Be careful with the adverbs *well* and *badly*. They have distinctively different forms from the adjectives *good* and *bad*.

Adjective	Meaning	Adverb	Meaning
bueno	good	bien	well
malo	bad	mal	badly

> Ella es buena, y habla bien el español.
> *eh-yah ehs bweh-nah ee ah-blah bee-yehn ehl ehs-pah-nyohl*
> She is good, and she speaks Spanish well.

> Son malos músicos, y tocan mal la guitarra.
> *sohn mah-lohs moo-see-kohs ee toh-kahn mahl lah gee-tah-rrah*
> They are bad musicians, and they play the guitar poorly.

Some adverbs and adverbial expressions are not formed from adjectives at all; therefore, they do not end in *-mente*. The following table provides some of the most common adverbs that follow this rule.

Adverbs and Adverbial Expressions Not Formed from Adjectives

Adverb/Adverbial Expression	Pronunciation	Meaning
ahora	*ah-oh-rah*	now
allá	*ah-yah*	there
aquí	*ah-kee*	here
peor	*peh-yohr*	worse
mejor	*meh-hohr*	better
más	*mahs*	more
menos	*meh-nohs*	less
a menudo	*ah meh-noo-doh*	often
muy	*mwee*	very
siempre	*see-yehm-preh*	always
también	*tahm-bee-yehn*	also, too
tan	*tahn*	as, so
tarde	*tahr-deh*	late
temprano	*tehm-prah-noh*	soon, early
todavía	*toh-dah-bee-yah*	still, yet
ya	*yah*	already

Adverbs are generally placed after the verb they modify. Sometimes, however, the position of the adverb is variable, and it is placed where we would logically put an English adverb. Notice the position of the adverbs in the following examples:

> Juega bien al fútbol.
> *hweh-gah bee-yehn ahl foot-bohl*
> He plays soccer well.

> Juega muy bien al fútbol.
> *hweh-gah mwee bee-yehn ahl foot-bohl*
> He plays soccer very well.

Generalmente juega bien.
geh-neh-rahl-mehn-teh hweh-gah bee-yehn
Usually he plays well.

Do You Do It Well?

How's your flamenco dancing? Do you make a perfect flan? Can you sing like a nightingale? Or do you wail like a sick cat? Naturally, everyone's abilities differ. We're all good at some things and awful at others. How do you think you measure up? Use adverbs to express how you feel you perform the following activities:

Example: hablar español
Hablo español lentamente.

1. hablar español (speak Spanish)
2. cocinar (cook)
3. pensar (think)
4. trabajar (work)
5. bailar (dance)
6. nadar (swim)

Answer Key

Invite Your Friends Along

1. ¿Quieres ir al parque?

2. ¿Puedes acompañarme a la pista?

3. ¿No quieres acompañarme a la piscina? a la playa?

4. ¿No puedes ir a la pista?

5. ¿Quieres ir a la montaña?

6. ¿Puedes acompañarme al campo?

Do You Do It Well?

Sample responses:

1. Hablo español rápidamente.
2. Cocino bien.
3. Pienso inteligentemente.
4. Trabajo cuidadosamente.
5. Bailo lentamente.
6. Nado bastante mal.

Part 4 Problem-Solving

Traveling is perfect when everything goes the way it should. Unfortunately, sometimes problems arise through no fault of your own. In Part 4, you learn how to deal with annoying inconveniences that can interfere with your daily routines. You certainly wouldn't want them to ruin your good time.

Some situations are relatively minor, such as forgetting your toothpaste, staining your clothing, running out of film, breaking the heel on your shoe, or making a phone call or sending a letter or package. Other situations are more serious and require immediate attention: an injury, a lost contact lens, broken glasses, or a forgotten prescription.

Part 4 covers a wide range of problems that might arise when you least expect them. The good news is that you'll be able to deal with any or all of them quite expeditiously.

Chapter **19**

Getting Great Service

In This Chapter

- ◆ Personal services
- ◆ Problems and solutions
- ◆ Tips on using pronouns after prepositions
- ◆ Ways to make comparisons

You're having the time of your life traveling throughout the Spanish-speaking world. You've been gone so long, however, that little by little, problems are starting to surface. First, have you looked at yourself in the mirror lately? It's time for a change. Your new tweed jacket has a hole in it, and you just dropped your glasses and broke the frames. And if that isn't enough, your shoes need resoling, and the flash in your camera no longer works. Don't fret! Ask around or consult *las páginas amarillas* (*lahs pah-hee-nahs ah-mah-ree-yahs;* the Yellow Pages). Just explain your problems, and expert technicians will see to all of them. This chapter will help you get the job done.

Dealing with a Bad Hair Day

Imagine you've spent the day relaxing in the sun. Now it's time to prepare for an important conference, meeting, or date you have planned for this evening. Upon returning to your room, you cast a quick glance at yourself in the mirror. Good grief! You have terminal hat head, and your beautiful curls are as flat as a board. For a quick fix-me-up, run to the nearest *peinador* (*peh-yee-nah-dohr*; hairstylist).

Gone are the days when men were treated solely *en la barbería* (*ehn lah bahr-beh-ree-yah*; at the barbershop) while women went *al salón de belleza* (*ahl sah-lohn deh beh-yeh-sah*; to the beauty parlor). Thanks to the modern unisex trend, many establishments today cater to the needs of everyone because both men and women frequently demand the same services. Use the following sentences when your hair needs help:

¿Puede darme   Quisiera …
pweh-deh dahr-meh   *kee-see-yeh-rah*
Can you give me …   I would like …

Do you want a quick fix-up or a whole new look? Check out the services listed in the following table.

Hair Care

Type of Service	Spanish	Pronunciation
a blunt cut	un corte en cuadrado	*oon kohr-teh ehn kwah-drah-doh*
a coloring (vegetable)	un tinte (vegetal)	*oon teen-teh (beh-heh-tahl)*
a facial	un masaje facial	*oon mah-sah-heh fah-see-yahl*
a haircut	un corte de pelo	*oon kohr-teh deh peh-loh*
a manicure	una manicura	*oo-nah mah-nee-koo-rah*
a pedicure	una pedicura	*oo-nah peh-dee-koo-rah*
a permanent	una permanente	*oo-nah pehr-mah-nehn-teh*
a set	un marcado	*oon mahr-kah-doh*
a shampoo	un champú	*oon chahm-poo*
a trim	un recorte	*oon rreh-kohr-teh*
a waxing	una depilación	*oo-nah deh-pee-lah-see-yohn*
highlights	reflejos	*rreh-fleh-hohs*
layers	un corte en degradación	*oon kohr-teh ehn deh-grah-dah-see-yohn*

Do you need other services? The following table provides the phrases you need to explain exactly what you want. Here's how to preface your request:

Podría _____, por favor.
poh-dree-yah _____, pohr fah-bohr
Could you _____, please.

Other Services

Type of Service	Spanish	Pronunciation
blow-dry my hair	secarme el pelo	*seh-kahr-meh ehl peh-loh*
curl my hair	rizarme el pelo	*rree-sahr-meh ehl peh-loh*
shave	afeitarme	*ah-feh-yee-tahr-meh*
my beard	la barba	*lah bahr-bah*
my mustache	el bigote	*ehl bee-goh-teh*
my head	la cabeza	*lah kah-beh-sah*
straighten my hair	estirarme el pelo	*ehs-tee-rahr-meh ehl peh-loh*
trim my bangs	recortarme el flequillo	*rreh-kohr-tahr-meh ehl fleh-kee-yoh*
trim	recortarme	*rreh-kohr-tahr-meh*
my beard	la barba	*lah bahr-bah*
my mustache	el bigote	*ehl bee-goh-teh*
my sideburns	las patillas	*lahs pah-tee-yahs*

Just a Trim?

We all know what it's like to go to a hair salon and explain in very clear English exactly what we want. A half-hour later when the hair stylist is done, however, we end up shrieking at the mirror. That was *not* what we asked for. Imagine the same situation with a language barrier. The following tables can help.

Quisiera un peinado _____.   Prefiero mi pelo _____.
kee-see-yeh-rah oon peh-yee-nah-doh   *preh-fee-yeh-roh mee peh-loh*
I'd like a _____ style.   I prefer my hair _____.

Hairstyles

Hairstyle	Spanish	Pronunciation
long	largo	*lahr-goh*
medium	mediano	*meh-dee-yah-noh*
short	corto	*kohr-toh*
wavy	ondulado	*ohn-doo-lah-doh*
curly	rizado	*rree-sah-doh*
straight	lacio (liso)	*lah-see-yoh (lee-soh)*

Asking for the Perfect Hair Color

Hair Color	Spanish	Pronunciation
auburn	rojizo	*rroh-hee-soh*
black	negro	*neh-groh*
blond	rubio	*rroo-bee-yoh*
brunette	castaño	*kahs-tah-nyoh*
chestnut brown	pardo	*pahr-doh*
red	pelirrojo	*peh-lee-rroh-hoh*
a darker color	un color más oscuro	*oon koh-lohr mahs oh-skoo-roh*
a lighter color	un color más claro	*oon koh-lohr mahs klah-roh*
the same color	el mismo color	*ehl mees-moh koh-lohr*

Memory Master

You may use both a direct and an indirect object in the same sentence. The indirect object (a person) precedes the direct object (usually a thing):

¿Puede Ud. arreglármelo?
Can you fix it for me?

The indirect object pronouns *le* and *les* become *se* before the direct objects *lo, la, los,* and *las:*

¿Puede Ud. arreglárselo?
Can you fix it for him/her/them?

Problems and More Problems

When you need to have certain services performed or when something you own needs repair, you should have some key phrases on hand. Make use of the following sentences when you go to the dry cleaner, the shoemaker, the optometrist, the jeweler, or the camera store:

¿A qué hora abre (cierra) Ud.?
ah keh oh-rah ah-breh (see-yeh-rah) oo-stehd
At what time do you open? (close?)

¿Qué días abre (cierra) Ud.?
keh dee-yahs ah-breh (see-yeh-rrah) oo-stehd
What days are you open? (closed?)

¿Puede arreglarme _____.
pweh-deh ah-rreh-glahr-meh _____.
Can you fix _____ for me?

¿Puede arreglármelo (la, los, las) hoy (temporalmente, mientras espero)?
pweh-deh ah-rreh-glahr-meh-loh (lah, lohs, lahs) oy (tehm-poh-rahl-mehn-the, mee-yehn-trahs yoh ehs-peh-roh)
Can you fix it (them) today (temporarily, while I wait)?

¿Me puede dar un recibo?
meh pweh-deh dahr oon rreh-see-boh
May I have a receipt?

At the Dry Cleaner's *(En la Tintorería)*

My friends think I'm crazy, but I like to travel with a compact travel iron. I can't stand that rumpled look. My husband believes that hanging anything in a damp bathroom will do the trick just fine. When you unpack, do you hate the way your clothes come out? Did you spill sangria on your favorite shirt? No problem. Every country has dry-cleaning and laundry establishments that can deal with all your spots, stains, wrinkles, and tears. Here's how to explain your problem:

Tengo un problema.	¿Cuál es el problema?
tehn-goh oon proh-bleh-mah	*kwahl ehs ehl proh-bleh-mah*
I have a problem.	What's the problem?

Hay …
ah-yee
There is (are) …

Problem	Spanish	Pronunciation
a hole	un roto	*oon rroh-toh*
a missing button	(le falta) un botón	*(leh fahl-tah) oon boh-tohn*
a spot, stain	una mancha	*oo-nah mahn-chah*
a tear	un desgarrón	*oon dehs-gah-rrohn*

Memory Master

If you'd like a service performed for someone else, use the appropriate indirect object pronoun: *te* (for you), *le* (for him, her, you), *nos* (for us), *os* (for you), *les* (for them):

¿Puede tejerle este abrigo?
Can you please weave this coat for him?

Congratulations! You've successfully explained your problem. Now you're ready to state what you'd like done about it.

¿Puede _____ este (esta, estos, estas)?
pweh-deh _____ ehs-teh (ehs-tah, ehs-tohs, ehs-tahs)
Can you _____ this (these) for me?

lavarme en seco	remendarme
lah-bahr-meh ehn seh-koh	*rreh-mehn-dahr-meh*
dry clean	mend
plancharme	almidonarme
plahn-chahr-meh	*ahl-mee-doh-nahr-meh*
press	starch
tejerme	
teh-hahr-meh	
weave	

At the Laundry (*En la Lavandería*)

Whether you're on the road or enjoying a leisurely vacation in a hotel, your laundry will pile up. If it can't wait until you get home, the following phrases will help you get started:

Quiero lavarme la ropa.
kee-yeh-roh lah-bahr-meh lah rroh-pah
I'd like to wash my clothes.

Quisiera que me laven la ropa.
kee-see-yeh-rah keh meh lah-behn lah rroh-pah
I'd like to have my clothes washed.

You don't want anyone to see that ring around your collar, or perhaps you're embarrassed by that tomato-sauce stain on your white shirt. Maybe you think no one does a better job washing clothes than you, or you're afraid that your new wool sweater will shrink. If you're intent on doing the job yourself, here are some phrases that might prove useful:

¿Hay una lavadora (secadora) desocupada?
ah-yee oo-nah lah-bah-doh-rah (seh-kah-doh-rah) deh-soh-koo-pah-dah
Is there a free washing machine (dryer)?

¿Dónde puedo comprar jabón en polvo?
dohn-deh pweh-doh kohm-prahr hah-bohn ehn pohl-boh
Where can I can buy soap powder?

At the Shoemaker's (*En la Zapatería*)

Have you walked so much that your shoes need new soles? Perhaps you're going out on the town and it's time for a shine. If you're a jeans-and-sneakers type of person, maybe it's time for some new laces. Use the following phrases to help you:

¿Puede remendarme …?
pweh-deh rreh-mehn-dahr-meh
Can you repair _____ for me?

estos zapatos
ehs-tohs sah-pah-tohs
these shoes

este tacón
ehs-teh tah-kohn
this heel

estas botas
ehs-tahs boh-tahs
these boots

esta suela
ehs-tah sweh-lah
this sole

¿Vende cordones de zapatos?
behn-deh kohr-doh-nehs deh sah-pah-tohs
Do you sell shoelaces?

Quisiera que me lustre los zapatos.
kee-see-yeh-rah keh meh loos-treh lohs sah-pah-tohs
I'd like a shoe shine.

At the Optician's (*En la Óptica*)

People who wear contact lenses know that they tend to disappear or rip at the most inopportune moments. For people who rely on glasses, a broken lens or frame while on vacation could be a real disaster. Familiarize yourself with the following useful phrases:

¿Puede arreglarme estos lentes (estas gafas)?
pweh-deh ah-rreh-glahr-meh ehs-tohs lehn-tehs (ehs-tahs gah-fahs)
Can you repair these glasses for me?

¿Puede darme otra lentilla (otro lente) de contacto?
pweh-deh dahr-meh oh-trah lehn-tee-yah (oh-troh lehn-teh) deh kohn-tahk-toh
Can you replace this contact lens?

¿Tiene lentes progresivos?
tee-yeh-neh lehn-tehs proh-greh-see-bohs
Do you have progressive lenses?

¿Vende lentes (gafas) de sol?
behn-deh lehn-tehs (gah-fahs) deh sohl
Do you sell sunglasses?

At the Jeweler's (*En la Joyería*)

What bad luck! Your watch battery just went dead right in the middle of your trip. You'll have to stop in a jewelry store or a *la relojería* (*la rreh-loh-heh-ree-yah;* watchmaker's) for a quick repair.

¿Puede arreglarme este reloj?
pweh-deh ah-rreh-glahr-meh ehs-teh rreh-loh
Can you repair this watch?

Mi reloj no funciona.
mee rreh-loh noh foon-see-yoh-nah
My watch doesn't work.

Mi reloj está parado.
mee rreh-loh ehs-tah pah-rah-doh
My watch has stopped.

¿Vende pulsos (baterías)?
behn-deh pool-sohs (bah-teh-ree-yahs)
Do you sell bands (batteries)?

At the Camera Shop (*En la Tienda de Fotografía*)

If you're like me, you take your camera and a huge supply of film on every trip. You wouldn't want to miss any precious moments. Besides, when you get back, you like to look at the shots you snapped. In a way, this enables you to relive the vacation many times. If you need more supplies, a repair, or simply want to develop your film, the words in the following table will help you.

Photo Supply	Spanish	Pronunciation
a camera	una cámara	*oo-nah kah-mah-rah*
film	una película	*oo-nah peh-lee-koo-lah*
slides	las diapositivas	*lahs dee-yah-poh-see-tee-bahs*
a video camera	una videocámara	*oo-nah bee-deh-yoh-kah-mah-rah*

If you have special needs, you might ask the following.

¿Vende películas a color (en blanco y negro)
de 20 (36) exposiciones?
behn-deh peh-lee-koo-lahs ah koh-lohr (ehn blahn-koh ee neh-groh)
deh behn-teh (treh-een-tah ee seh-yees) ehks-poh-see-see-yoh-nehs
Do you sell rolls of 20 (36) exposure film in color (black and white)?

Quisiera que me revele este carrete (rollo).
kee-see-yeh-rah keh meh rreh-beh-leh ehs-teh kah-rreh-teh (rroh-yoh)
I would like to have this film developed.

Finding Help

In addition to needing repairs, you might find that you need other services. Should you lose important papers or documents or need special assistance, you might find yourself in need of the police or the American embassy. Don't be afraid to ask for a translator, if necessary. Although you've become quite good at this, if you're nervous or upset, you might not be able to get your thoughts across in any language. The following phrases should help you get started:

¿Dónde está …?
dohn-deh ehs-tah
Where is …

la comisaría de policía
lah koh-mee-sah-ree-yah deh poh-lee-see-yah
the police station?

el consulado americano
ehl kohn-soo-lah-doh ah-meh-ree-kah-noh
the American consulate?

la embajada americana
lah ehm-bah-hah-dah ah-meh-ree-kah-nah
the American embassy?

Yo perdí … mi pasaporte	mi cartera
yoh pehr-dee mee pah-sah-pohr-teh	*mee kahr-teh-rah*
I lost … my passport	my wallet

Ayúdeme, por favor.
ah-yoo-deh-meh pohr fah-bohr
Help me, please.

Necesito un intérprete.
neh-seh-see-toh oon een-tehr-preh-teh
I need an interpreter.

¿Hay alguien aquí que hable inglés?
ah-yee ahl-gee-yehn ah-kee keh ah-bleh een-glehs
Does anyone here speak English?

Prepositional Pronouns

To get the services you need, you'll have to use prepositions. Prepositions are words used to show the relationship of a noun to another word in the sentence.

A prepositional pronoun replaces a noun as the object of a preposition. This pronoun always follows the preposition. The following table shows subject pronouns with their corresponding prepositional pronouns.

Prepositional Pronouns

Subject	Prepositional Pronoun	Meaning
yo	mí	me
tú	ti	you (familiar)
él	él	him, it
ella	ella	her, it
Ud.	Ud.	you (formal)
nosotros (as)	nosotros (as)	us
vosotros (as)	vosotros (as)	you (familiar)
ellos	ellos	them
ellas	ellas	them
Uds.	Uds.	you (formal)

Be sure to use the correct pronoun in a prepositional phrase. The only prepositional pronouns that differ from subject pronouns are *mí* and *ti*, so this is fairly simple.

> Este regalo no es para ti, es para mí.
> *ehs-teh rreh-gah-loh noh ehs pah-rah tee ehs pah-rah mee*
> This present isn't for you, it's for me.

> No podemos partir sin ellos.
> *noh poh-deh-mohs pahr-teer seen eh-yohs*
> We can't leave without them.

Because indirect object pronouns often need clarification in Spanish, it's common to add the preposition *a* + a prepositional pronoun to avoid confusion:

> Le doy a él (ella, Ud.) la respuesta.
> I give him (her, you) the answer.

Memory Master

Mí and *ti* combine with the preposition *con* (kohn), which means "with," as follows:

Él va al centro conmigo.
He's going downtown with me.

No puedo ir contigo.
I can't go with you.

To stress to whom an action has importance, add *a* + a prepositional pronoun:

A mí me gusta el chocolate.
I like chocolate.

A él no le encantan los deportes.
He doesn't adore sports.

Using These Pronouns

You're talking about some of the activities you and your friends do together. Use prepositions to complete the following sentences:

1. (you/fam.) Yo voy al cine con _____.

2. (you/pl.) Nosotros estudiamos sin _____.

3. (me) Tú vives cerca de _____.

4. (them/m.) Ella trabaja lejos de _____.

5. (us) Ellos siempre llegan después de _____.

6. (him) Este regalo es para _____.

Memory Master

Prepositional pronouns replace a noun that's the object of a preposition:

Este regalo no es para ti, es para mí.
This present isn't for you, it's for me.

Refer to the preceding "Prepositional Pronouns" table for a quick review. Remember, the only prepositional pronouns that differ from subject pronouns are *mí* and *ti*.

Making Comparisons

Which airline company has the best airfare to a Spanish-speaking country? Which hotel has the best facilities? Which car rental gives you the best deal? Who is the most reliable tour guide in the city? Every day, we make comparisons. Sometimes we're looking for the most; sometimes the least. Use the following table to help you with comparisons.

Comparison of Adjectives: Inequality

	Adjective	Pronunciation	Meaning
Positive	triste	*trees-teh*	sad
Comparative	más triste	*mahs trees-teh*	sadder
	menos triste	*meh-nohs trees-teh*	less sad
Superlative	el (la, los, las) _____ más triste(s)	*ehl (lah, lohs, lahs) _____ mahs trees-teh(s)*	the saddest _____
	el (la, los, las) _____ menos triste(s)	*ehl (lah, lohs, lahs) _____ meh-nohs trees-teh(s)*	the least sad _____

The word *que* may or may not be used after the comparative. When used, *que* expresses "than":

> ¿Quién es más sincero?
> Who is more sincere?

> Roberto es más sincero (que Rafael).
> Roberto is more sincere (than Rafael).

> Amalia es menos sincera (que Ana).
> Amalia is less sincere (than Ana).

The comparative and superlative forms of adjectives must agree in gender and number with the nouns they describe:

> Julio es menos fuerte que su amigo.
> Juanita es más linda que su hermana.

> Estas camisetas son las menos caras.
> Esos coches son los más deportivos.

The preposition *de* + a definite article (*del, de la, de los, de las*) can be used to express *in (of) the:*

> Este hombre es simpático.
> This man is nice.

> Este hombre es más simpático que él.
> This man is nicer than he.

Este hombre es el más simpático del pueblo.
This man is the nicest in the city.

Esas mujeres son ricas.
Those women are rich.

Esas mujeres son las más ricas.
Those women are the richest.

Aquellas mujeres son las menos ricas de la ciudad.
Those women are the least rich in the city.

That's Highly Irregular

Beware of irregular comparisons. Never use *más* or *menos* with the adjectives *bueno* and *malo*. Special comparative forms are used to express *better* and *best*.

Spanish	Positive English	Comparative Spanish	Superlative English	Spanish	English
bueno (-a, -os, -as)	good	mejor (-es)	better	el (la) mejor, los (las) mejores	best
malo (-a, -os, -as)	bad	peor (-es)	worse	el (la) peor, los (las) peores	worst

When *grande* and *pequeño* refer to age (older or younger), do not use *más* or *menos*. Instead, use the comparative forms shown in the following table.

Spanish	Positive English	Comparative Spanish	Superlative English	Spanish	English
grande	big	mayor (-es)	older	el (la) mayor, los (las) mayores	oldest
pequeño	small	menor (-es)	younger	el (la) menor, los (las) menores	youngest

Su hermano mayor es pequeño.
His older brother is small.

Comparisons of Inequality

Each person in my family has different levels of artistic talent. When my husband picks up a pencil and a piece of paper, his drawings are quite good. My son, Michael, has the second-best genes and seems rather talented. I have the worst ability, which I passed on to my other son, Eric. He also draws horribly. No one can ever tell exactly what it is I've put on the paper. At least I make everyone laugh. Not only can people be compared, but the ways in which they do things can also be compared. The following table shows how to make comparisons using adverbs (to describe actions).

Comparison of Adverbs: Inequality

	Adverb	Pronunciation	Meaning
Positive	rápidamente	*rrah-pee-dah-mehn-teh*	rapidly
Comparative	más rápidamente	*mahs rrah-pee-dah-mehn-teh*	more rapidly
	menos rápidamente	*meh-nohs rrah-pee-dah-mehn-teh*	less rapidly
Superlative	más rápidamente	*mahs rrah-pee-dah-mehn-teh*	more rapidly
	menos rápidamente	*meh-nohs rrah-pee-dah-mehn-teh*	less rapidly

No distinction is made between the comparative and superlative forms of adverbs. For the comparative and superlative, use *que* to express "than":

Yo camino rápidamente.
I walk fast.

Carlos camina más rápidamente (the fastest).
Carlos walks faster.

Carlos camina más rápidamente que yo.
Carlos walks faster than I.

Comparisons of Equality

You've done a lot of sightseeing on your trip. Did you find the modern museums as entertaining as museums that hold the treasures of antiquity? Did you spend as much time visiting the Picasso exhibits as you did those of Velázquez? If all things are equal, it becomes necessary to form a comparison of equality using either adjectives or adverbs. To do this, use the following formula:

tan + adjective or adverb + *como* ("as … as")

Él es tan elegante como su amigo.
He is as elegant as his friend.

Ella trabaja tan diligentemente como él.
She works as hard as he does.

Absolutely Superlative

When no comparison is involved and you want to express that something is absolutely superlative, you can attach *-ísimo*, *-ísima*, *-ísimos*, or *-ísimas* to the adjective (according to the number and gender of the noun being described). If the adjective ends in a vowel, drop the vowel before adding the superlative ending. The *-ísimo* ending means the same as using *muy* + adjective. In the following sentence pairs, both sentences have the same meaning:

El hotel es muy grande.   Esta película es muy popular.
Es un hotel grandísimo.   Es una película popularísima.

Adjectives with certain endings make the following changes: *c* changes to *qu*, *g* changes to *gu*, and *z* becomes *c* before adding *-ísimo*. Notice these changes in the following, equivalent sentences:

Es un postre muy rico.   Es una avenida muy larga.
Es un postre riquísimo.   Es una avenida larguísima.

El tigre es muy feroz.
El tigre es ferocísimo.

Adverbs also can be made absolutely superlative, but you probably won't be hearing or saying this often because the words seem to be tongue twisters. If you'd like to give it a shot, add *-mente* to the feminine form of the adjective to which you are adding *-ísima*:

Él trabaja lentísimamente.
He works very slowly.

How Do You Measure Up?

How do you compare to people you know? Are you shorter? Thinner? More charming? Do you dance better? Work more seriously? Listen more patiently? Use what you've learned to compare yourself to friends or family members.

Answer Key

Using These Pronouns

1. contigo
2. Uds.
3. mí
4. ellos
5. nosotros
6. él

How Do You Measure Up?

Sample responses:

Soy menos grande que mi hermano.

Soy más gorda que mi madre.

Soy tan encantadora como mi hermana.

Bailo mejor que mi esposo.

Trabajo tan diligentemente como mi amiga.

Escucho más pacientemente que mi hijo.

Chapter 20

"Is There a Doctor in the House?"

In This Chapter

- ◆ Your body
- ◆ Symptoms, complaints, and illnesses
- ◆ Ways to express "how long"
- ◆ All about *decir* (to say, to tell)
- ◆ Tips on using reflexive verbs

In Chapter 19, you learned to cope with minor, everyday hassles. You should now feel assured that you can make yourself look presentable and obtain necessary repairs with a fair amount of expediency. In this chapter, you'll learn the words and expressions to help you deal with a more serious problem—an illness.

Of course, we often think "it can't happen to me." People travel far and wide all the time without ever having to visit a doctor. But let's face it: at the most inopportune moments, people can get sick or have freak accidents. My best friend passed a kidney stone in France, my son shattered a tooth in the Dominican Republic, my mother fell and fractured her wrist in Puerto Rico, and I got violently seasick on a two-day cruise to nowhere.

Life's medical annoyances really can bring us down when all we want to do is relax and have a good time. The situation can become even more frustrating if we can't communicate what's wrong. In this chapter, you will learn to describe what ails you and how long you've had your symptoms.

Love Your Body!

My Aunt Harriet drools over the sexy ads for Cancún, and she covets a genuine turquoise jewelry collection. Why hasn't she flown the coop and jumped on an Aeronaves de México flight during the winter snows? The answer is simple—Montezuma's Revenge (severe diarrhea). She's convinced that if she just looks at a glass of water, she'll wind up in *un consultorio* (*oon kohn-sool-toh-ree-yoh;* a doctor's office), or worse yet, she'll spend the entire week in *el baño* (*ehl bah-nyoh;* the bathroom).

Logically, she knows she can travel with a bottle of Lomotil and always keep mineral water on hand. But she's heard too many horror stories from friends who ate salad (washed in tap water) or had drinks on the rocks (with ice cubes made from local water). Everyone says that, with today's modern technology and advanced hygienic conditions, the curse of Montezuma is a thing of the past. Perhaps one day you'll see my aunt on that flight. If you go, however, you'll want to learn the words in the following table so you can tell somebody you're sick and where it hurts—just in case.

Body Part	Spanish	Pronunciation
ankle	el tobillo	*ehl toh-bee-yoh*
arm	el brazo	*ehl brah-soh*
back	la espalda	*lah ehs-pahl-dah*
body	el cuerpo	*ehl kwehr-poh*
brain	el cerebro	*ehl seh-reh-broh*
chest	el pecho	*ehl peh-choh*
chin	la barbilla	*lah bahr-bee-yah*
ear	la oreja	*lah oh-reh-hah*
eye	el ojo	*ehl oh-hoh*
face	la cara	*lah kah-rah*
finger	el dedo	*ehl deh-doh*
foot	el pie	*ehl pee-yeh*
hand	la mano	*lah mah-noh*

Body Part	Spanish	Pronunciation
head	la cabeza	*lah kah-beh-sah*
heart	el corazón	*ehl koh-rah-sohn*
knee	la rodilla	*lah rroh-dee-yah*
leg	la pierna	*lah pee-yehr-nah*
mouth	la boca	*lah boh-kah*
nail	la uña	*lah oo-nyah*
neck	el cuello	*ehl kweh-yoh*
nose	la nariz	*lah nah-rees*
skin	la piel	*lah pee-yehl*
shoulder	el hombro	*ehl ohm-broh*
spine	la espina dorsal	*lah ehs-pee-nah dohr-sahl*
stomach	el estómago	*ehl ehs-toh-mah-goh*
throat	la garganta	*lah gahr-gahn-tah*
toe	el dedo del pie	*ehl deh-doh dehl pee-yeh*
tongue	la lengua	*lah lehn-gwah*
tooth	el diente	*ehl dee-yehn-teh*
wrist	la muñeca	*lah moo-nyeh-kah*

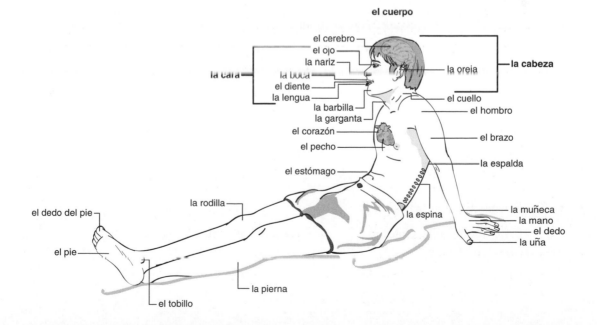

el cuerpo

el cerebro
el ojo
la nariz
la oreja
la cabeza
la cara
la boca
el diente
la lengua
el cuello
la barbilla
el hombro
la garganta
el corazón
el brazo
el pecho
la espalda
el estómago
la rodilla
la muñeca
el dedo del pie
la espina
la mano
el dedo
el pie
la uña
la pierna
el tobillo

"I Have a Headache"

Jet lag is no joke. In the 1970s, when it was popular to backpack around Europe on $5 a day, my husband and I decided to do just that before we started our family. We arrived in England during an extremely hot spell, and we spent our first 3 nights in an unbearably hot trailer—that's what happens when you go without reservations. We hardly slept a wink. When the sun came up, we were exhausted, but we'd still go out sightseeing.

Our next stop was Paris. We had another hot room without a bath in the red-light district. Sleep still wouldn't come. At the end of a week and a half of traveling, when we were delirious from lack of sleep, we finally went to the doctor. The kind man prescribed a sleep aid. Finally, we were able to resume a normal life.

If you run into a problem and have to seek medical help, the obvious first question will be "What's the matter with you?" "*¿Qué le pasa?*" (*keh leh pah-sah*). To say what hurts or bothers you, use the expression *tener dolor de (en)* + the part that hurts.

Tengo dolor de cabeza.	Tiene dolor en el brazo.
tehn-goh doh-lohr deh kah-beh-sah	*tee-yeh-neh doh-lohr ehn ehl brah-soh*
I have a headache.	He has pain in his arm.

It Hurts

You can also choose to talk about your symptoms using the shoe verb *doler* (*doh-lehr*; to hurt). *Doler* is a stem-changing verb and is used in the same way as the verb *gustar*. This means you'll only have to use two verb forms: *duele* (*dweh-leh*) and *duelen* (*dweh-lehn*). Why is that? *Doler* means something is hurting (to) you; therefore, an indirect object pronoun is used to refer to the person in pain.

The indirect object pronouns include *me* (to me), *te* (to you), *le* (to him, her, or you), *nos* (to us), *os* (to you), and *les* (to them or you). The subject of the sentence is the body part causing the pain:

Me duele el pie.	Me duelen los pies.
My foot hurts.	My feet hurt.

To be specific, you may say:

Le duele a ella el pie.	Les duelen a ellos los pies.
Her foot hurts.	Their feet hurt.

Let's take a closer look at how this works. Let's say you've been playing volleyball for the first time in a long while. At the end of the day, your whole body aches. You might say the following to a friend:

Me duele la cabeza.

My head hurts.

(My head is hurting to me.)

Me duelen los dedos.

My fingers hurt.

(My fingers are hurting to me.)

What about the other members of your volleyball team? Don't let the reverse word order fool you. Remember to choose an indirect object pronoun that refers to the person in pain. The subject will follow the verb *doler* and must, therefore, agree with it. Let's see how this works:

¿Te duele el brazo?

teh dweh-leh ehl brah-soh

Does your arm hurt?

¿Le duele el estómago?

leh dweh-leh ehl ehs-toh-mah-goh

Does his (her, your) stomach hurt?

Nos duelen las piernas.

nohs dweh-lehn lahs pee-yehr-nahs

Our legs hurt.

¿Os duelen los dedos?

ohs dweh-lehn lohs deh-dohs

Do your fingers hurt?

No les duelen las manos.

noh lehs dweh-lehn lahs mah-nohs

Their (Your) hands don't hurt.

If you want to emphasize who is in pain, you can add the preposition *a* + a name or prepositional pronoun:

A Julio le duelen las espaldas.

Julio's shoulders hurt.

A ellos les duele la garganta.

Their throats hurt.

Notice that it is unnecessary to use a possessive adjective before the name of the body part because the indirect object pronoun states to whom the pain is occurring.

What's the Matter?

Perhaps your symptoms are indicative of something a bit more complicated than aches or pains. Maybe there's a problem that requires further medical attention. The following table lists some possible symptoms and conditions. These words will come in handy when you need to provide a more detailed description of your aches and pains. Use the word *tengo* (*tehn-goh*; I have) to preface your complaint.

Symptoms and Conditions	Spanish	Pronunciation
broken bone	un hueso roto	*oon weh-soh rroh-toh*
bruise	una contusión	*oo-nah kohn-too-see-yohn*
bump	una hinchazón	*oo-nah een-chah-sohn*
burn	una quemadura	*oo-nah keh-mah-doo-rah*
chills	un escalofrío	*oon ehs-kah-loh-free-yoh*
cough	una tos	*oo-nah tohs*
cramps	un calambre	*oon kah-lahm-breh*
diarrhea	una diarrea	*oo-nah dee-yah-rreh-yah*
fever	una fiebre	*oo-nah fee-yeh-breh*
indigestion	una indigestión	*oo-nah een-dee-hehs-tee-yohn*
lump	un bulto	*oon bool-toh*
migraine	una jaqueca	*oo-nah hah-keh-kah*
pain	un dolor	*oon doh-lohr*
rash	una erupción	*oo-nah eh-roop-see-yohn*
sprain	una torcedura	*oo-nah tohr-seh-doo-rah*
swelling	una inflamación	*oo-nah een-flah-mah-see-yohn*

The following might be useful to help describe your illness as well:

Yo toso.
yoh toh-soh
I'm coughing.

Yo estoy agotado(a).
yoh ehs-toy ah-goh-tah-doh(dah)
I'm exhausted.

Yo no puedo dormir.
yoh noh pweh-doh dohr-meer
I can't sleep.

Yo tengo náuseas.
yoh tehn-goh now-seh-yahs
I'm nauseous.

Yo estornudo.
yoh ehs-tohr-noo-doh
I'm sneezing.

Yo estoy sangrando.
yoh ehs-toy sahn-grahn-doh
I'm bleeding.

Me duele todo
el cuerpo.
meh dweh-leh toh-doh
ehl kwehr-poh
I hurt everywhere.

Me siento mal.
meh see-yehn-toh mahl
I feel bad.

It Hurts Right Here

Now use all you've learned so far to describe your symptoms and complaints to a doctor. Pretend you have the following health problems:

1. flulike symptoms
2. an allergy
3. a sprained ankle
4. a migraine

This Is What's Wrong

Obviously, you won't be the only one doing the talking when you visit the doctor. You will be asked to fill out forms, list any medications you're taking, and answer other questions about your symptoms and general health. The doctor or nurse might ask whether you have some of the symptoms or illnesses listed in the following table.

Symptom/Illness	Spanish	Pronunciation
allergic reaction	una reacción alérgica	*oo-nah rreh-ahk-see-yohn ah-lehr-hee-kah*
appendicitis	la apendicitis	*lah ah-pehn-dee-see-tees*
asthma	el asma	*ehl ahs-mah*
bronchitis	la bronquitis	*lah brohn-kee-tees*
cancer	el cáncer	*ehl kahn-sehr*
cold	un resfriado, un catarro	*oon rrehs-free-yah-doh, oon kah-tah-rroh*
diabetes	la diabetes	*lah dee-yah-beh-tehs*
dizziness	el vértigo	*ehl behr-tee-goh*
flu	la gripe	*lah gree-peh*
German measles	la rubeola	*lah rroo-beh-yoh-lah*
heart attack	un ataque al corazón	*oon ah-tah-keh ahl koh-rah-sohn*
hepatitis	la hepatitis	*lah eh-pah-tee-tees*
measles	el sarampión	*ehl sah-rahm-pee-yohn*
mumps	las paperas	*lahs pah-peh-rahs*
pneumonia	la pulmonía	*lah pool-moh-nee-yah*
stroke	un ataque de apoplejía	*oon ah-tah-keh deh ah-poh-pleh-hee-yah*

How Long Have You Felt This Way?

One of the most frequent questions a doctor asks is, "How long have you been feeling this way?" This question can be asked in one of two ways, and you can also give an appropriate answer in one of two ways. The first question and answer pair is the most common and probably is the easiest to use:

¿Cuánto tiempo hace que + present tense verb?
kwahn-toh tee-yehm-poh ah-seh keh
(For) how long (has) have + present tense verb?

You would answer this question with the following:

Hace + time + *que* + present tense verb

You could also answer the question of how long you've been sick in this way:

¿Desde cuándo + present tense?
dehs-deh kwahn-doh
(For) How long has (have) + present tense?

You would answer this question with the following:

present tense of verb + *desde hace* + time

Here are some examples of what you might be asked and how you might respond to the questions:

¿Cuánto tiempo hace que sufre?
kwahn-toh tee-yehm-poh ah-seh keh soo-freh
(For) How long have you been suffering?

¿Desde cuándo sufre?
dehs-deh kwahn-doh soo-freh
(For) How long have you been suffering?

Hace dos días (que sufro).
ah-seh dohs dee-yahs (keh soo-froh)
(I've been suffering) For two days.

(Sufro) desde ayer.
soo-froh dehs-deh ah-seh ah-yehr
(I've been suffering) Since yesterday.

What Do You Tell the Doctor?

When something's really bothering you and you're somewhat frightened, what do you tell the doctor? Do you tell him what's truly bothering you? Or are you afraid to enumerate all your symptoms? To discuss what you say or tell someone, use the irregular verb *decir* (to tell, to say). Notice that *decir* is a go-go shoe verb. The *yo* form ends in *-go*, and the *e* from the stem changes to *i* in all forms except *nosotros* and *vosotros*.

decir *(to tell, to say)*

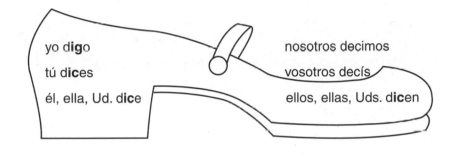

yo di**g**o	nosotros decimos
tú di**c**es	vosotros decís
él, ella, Ud. di**c**e	ellos, ellas, Uds. di**c**en

Me, Myself, and I

Use the irregular, stem-changing shoe verb *sentirse* (*sehn-teer-seh*) to express how you feel. Do you notice something strange about this verb, something that just doesn't look right? Besides the *ie* stem change, this verb does not end like most others: *-se* is attached to the infinitive ending. This actually is a special pronoun, called a reflexive pronoun, which can serve as either a direct or indirect object pronoun.

> **Memory Master**
>
> To say "that" after the verb *decir* use *que*:
>
> He says that I'm not very sick. Él dice que no estoy muy enfermo(a).

Quite simply, a reflexive pronoun shows that the subject is performing an action upon itself. The subject and the reflexive pronoun refer to the same person(s) or thing(s). (She washes herself. They enjoy themselves.) Don't panic about these verbs. They are quite easy to use and will be explained more fully in the next section. For the time being, here's how to conjugate a reflexive verb using the correct reflexive pronouns.

sentirse *(to feel)*

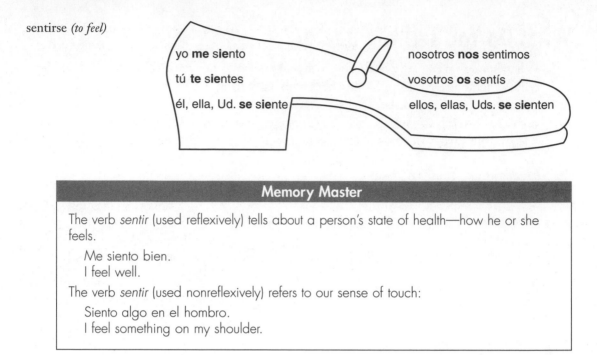

yo **me** siento	nosotros **nos** sentimos
tú **te** sientes	vosotros **os** sentís
él, ella, Ud. **se** siente	ellos, ellas, Uds. **se** sienten

---

Memory Master

The verb *sentir* (used reflexively) tells about a person's state of health—how he or she feels.

Me siento bien.
I feel well.

The verb *sentir* (used nonreflexively) refers to our sense of touch:

Siento algo en el hombro.
I feel something on my shoulder.

Here's how to express how you feel:

Me siento bien (mal, mejor, peor).
meh see-yehn-toh bee-yehn (mahl, meh-hohr, peh-yohr)
I feel well (bad, better, worse).

You've seen the doctor and have gotten *una receta (oo-nah rreh-seh-tah;* a prescription). You're now ready to leave the doctor's office. Wait! Not so fast! Don't forget this very important question that might save you some money:

¿Puede darme un recibo para mi seguro médico?
pweh-deh dahr-meh oon rreh-see-boh pah-rah mee seh-goo-roh meh-dee-koh
May I please have a receipt for my medical insurance?

Is It Reflexive?

Are you the type of person who is always doing favors for someone else and generally tends to put yourself last? Or do you think of yourself first because, after all, who else will if you don't? Are you *generoso* or *egoísta* when it comes to yourself and others? In

Spanish, when you perform an action upon or for yourself, that action (verb) is reflexive and requires a reflexive pronoun. In many instances, you can use the same verb without the reflexive pronoun when performing the action upon or for someone else. In these cases, an object pronoun—direct or indirect—is used:

Me lavo.	Lavo a mi niño.	Lo lavo.
meh lah-boh	*lah-boh ah mee nee-nyoh*	*loh lah-boh*
I wash myself.	I wash my son.	I wash him.

In the right example, the direct object pronoun *lo* expresses "him."

Me compro un libro.	Le compro un libro.	Le compro un libro a Ana.
I buy myself a book.	I buy her a book.	I buy Ann a book.

In the preceding example, the indirect object pronoun *le* expresses "for her."

Some verbs are always or almost always used reflexively. The following table provides a list of the most common reflexive verbs. The verbs followed by an asterisk (*) are shoe verbs.

Common Reflexive Verbs

Reflexive Verb	Pronunciation	Meaning
acordarse (ue)*[de]	*ah-kohr-dahr-seh [deh]*	to remember
acostarse (ue)*	*ah-kohs-tahr-seh*	to go to bed
afeitarse	*ah-feh-yee-tahr-seh*	to shave
alegrarse	*ah-leh-grahr-seh*	to be glad
apresurarse	*ah-preh-soo-rahr-seh*	to hurry
apurarse	*ah-poo-rahr-seh*	to worry, get upset, hurry
bañarse	*bah-nyahr-seh*	to bathe oneself
callarse	*kah-yahr-seh*	to be silent
cepillarse	*seh-pee-yahr-seh*	to brush (hair, teeth)
despertarse (ie)*	*dehs-pehr-tahr-seh*	to wake up
desvestirse (i)*	*dehs-behs-teer-seh*	to undress
divertirse (ie)*	*dee-behr-teer-seh*	to have fun
ducharse	*doo-chahr-seh*	to take a shower

continues

Common Reflexive Verbs (continued)

Reflexive Verb	Pronunciation	Meaning
engañarse	*ehn-gah-nyahr-seh*	to be mistaken
enojarse	*eh-noh-hahr-seh*	to become angry
equivocarse	*eh-kee-boh-kahr-seh*	to be mistaken
fiarse [de]	*fee-yahr-seh [deh]*	to trust
fijarse	*fee-hahr-seh [ehn]*	to notice
irse	*eer-seh*	to go away
lavarse	*lah-bahr-seh*	to wash oneself
levantarse	*leh-bahn-tahr-seh*	to get up
llamarse	*yah-mahr-seh*	to be called, to be named
maquillarse	*mah-kee-yahr-seh*	to put on makeup
olvidarse [de]	*ohl-bee-dahr-seh [deh]*	to forget
pararse	*pah-rah-seh*	to stop oneself
peinarse	*peh-yee-nahr-seh*	to comb one's hair
ponerse	*poh-nehr-seh*	to put on, to become
quedarse	*keh-dahr-seh*	to remain
quejarse	*keh-hahr-seh*	to complain
quitarse	*kee-tahr-seh*	to remove (take off)
reírse [de]	*rreh-yeer-seh [deh]*	to laugh [at]
sentarse (ie)*	*sehn-tahr-seh*	to sit down
sentirse (ie)*	*sehn-teer-seh*	to feel
vestirse (i)*	*behs-teer-seh*	to get dressed

Remember that shoe verbs require appropriate spelling changes. (Refer to Chapter 12 to refresh your memory.) Here are some examples of conjugated shoe verbs in sample sentences:

Yo me acuesto.   Yo me divierto.   Yo me visto.
I go to bed.   I have fun.   I get dressed.

Verbs followed by *a*, *de*, or *en* require those prepositions to make their intentions understood:

Yo me apresuro a partir.
I hurry to leave.

Yo no me olvido de nada.
I don't forget anything.

Who's Doing What to Whom?

My husband is a very fortunate man. He only has about three things to do in the morning before leaving for work, and he can fly out the door in 10 to 15 minutes. Before I leave in the morning, it seems I do at least 100 things: I wash myself, I dry my hair, I get dressed, I eat breakfast, I brush my teeth, and so on. That's why I need an hour and 15 minutes between the time I wake up and the time I walk out the door.

When a reflexive verb is used in Spanish, it's understood that the subject is performing the action for or upon itself because the reflexive pronoun says so. It then becomes unnecessary to use the possessive adjectives "my" (*mi, mis*), "your" (*tu, tus*), and so on, because it is obvious upon whom the action is being performed. The definite article is used instead:

Yo me cepillo los dientes.
yoh meh seh-pee-yoh lohs dee-yehn-tehs
I brush my teeth.

Ella se pinta las uñas.
eh-yah seh peen-tah lahs oo-nyahs
She polishes her nails.

¡Atención!

When using reflexive verbs, use the definite article that agrees with the part of the body being discussed.

The Position of the Reflexive Pronoun

By now, you know word order in Spanish differs greatly from what we are accustomed to in English. To us, word order seems to be backward in Spanish. In English, we tend to put reflexive pronouns after verbs. You might tell a friend, "I always look at myself in the mirror before I go out." In Spanish, this may or may not be the case. Fortunately, the rules for placement of pronouns in Spanish are quite consistent. Reflexive pronouns are placed in the same position as the direct and indirect object pronouns you already studied in Chapter 15:

Yo me divierto.   Yo no me divierto.
I have fun.   *I don't have fun.*

| Voy a divertirme. | *or* | Me voy a divertir. |

I'm going to have fun.

| Estoy divirtiéndome. | *or* | Me estoy divirtiendo. |

I'm having fun.

In an affirmative command, reflexive pronouns change position. They are placed immediately after and joined to the verb:

| ¡Levántese! | *but* | ¡No se levante! |
| Get up! | | Don't get up! |

| ¡Apúrense! | *but* | ¡No se apuren! |
| Hurry up! | | Don't hurry! |

When using the present progressive (the -*ing* form) and attaching the pronoun to the present participle (*estar* + present participle + pronoun), or when forming an affirmative command, remember to count back three vowels from the end and add an accent:

Estamos peinándonos.	¡Quédese aquí!
ehs-tah-mohs peh-yee-nahn-doh-nos	*keh-deh-seh ah-kee*
We're combing our hair. Stay here!	

Están cepillándose el pelo.	¡Siéntese, por favor!
ehs-tahn seh-pee-yahn-doh-seh ehl peh-loh	*see-yehn-teh-seh pohr fah-bohr*
They're brushing their hair.	Please sit!

Practicing Reflexive Verbs

Use what you've learned so far to describe five things you do before leaving the house in the morning.

Example: Yo me despierto.

Answer Key

It Hurts Right Here

Sample responses:

Flu: Tengo dolor de cabeza. Me duele todo el cuerpo. Yo toso y estoy agotado. Me siento mal.

Allergy: Yo toso y estornudo. Yo no puedo dormir.

Sprained ankle: Me duele el tobillo. Tengo una torcedura y una inflamación. No puedo caminar.

Migraine: Tengo dolor de cabeza. Tengo náuseas. Me siento mal.

Practicing Reflexive Verbs

Sample responses:

1. Yo me levanto.
2. Yo me cepillo los dientes.
3. Yo me desvisto.
4. Yo me baño.
5. Yo me visto.

Chapter 21

"Did I Pack the Toothpaste?"

In This Chapter

- ◆ Health-care items large and small
- ◆ The verb *venir* (to come)
- ◆ Tips on speaking in the past

In Chapter 20, you learned how to talk about any medical problems you might encounter. Perhaps you're experiencing some minor aches and pains or signs and symptoms that are bothersome but don't require a visit to the doctor. Whether you want to simply purchase a box of cough drops or you need a prescription filled, you'll want to make a quick stop at *una farmacia* (*oo-nah fahr-mah-see-yah;* a drugstore).

On our last trip, I inadvertently left our toiletry case at home. My husband, who always remains undaunted by life's small unpleasantries, gently reminded me that toothbrushes, toothpaste, razors, shaving cream, hairbrushes, combs, and so on are rather universal items. My blunder was only a minor inconvenience and certainly was not a reason to spoil a delightful vacation. This chapter can help you replenish your supplies and shows you how to talk about the past using the preterit (past) tense.

Finding What You Need

You've run out of an essential item. If you need medicine, look for a green cross, the universal symbol for pharmacies (*farmacias*). If you're looking for a tube of lipstick or a bottle of your favorite perfume, you must go to *una perfumería* (*oo-nah pehr-foo-meh-ree-yah*), which specializes in toiletries. When you need to have a prescription filled, you can use the following question to ask for the nearest pharmacy:

> ¿Dónde está la farmacia (de guardia) más cercana?
> *dohn-deh ehs-tah lah fahr-mah-see-yah (deh gwahr-dee-yah) mahs sehr-kah-nah*
> Where's the nearest (all-night) pharmacy?

You can then speak to the druggist:

> Necesito medicina.
> *neh-seh-see-toh meh-dee-see-nah*
> I need medication.

In a Flash

Put Spanish labels on all the items in your medicine cabinet. Learn their names by heart; then, remove the labels and try to name everything you see.

¿Podría preparar esta receta
(en seguida)?
*poh-dree-yah preh-pah-rahr ehs-tah rreh-seh-tah
(ehn seh-gee-dah)*
Could you please fill this prescription (immediately)?

¿Cuánto tiempo tardará?
kwahn-toh tee-yehm-poh tahr-dah-rah
How long will it take?

If you're simply looking for something over-the-counter, the following table can help you find it in the *farmacia*, the *perfumería*, or even the *supermercado*. Begin by saying to a clerk, "*Busco* ..." (*boos-koh*; "I'm looking for ...") or "*Necesito* ..." (*neh-seh-see-toh*; "I need ...").

Drugstore Items

Item	Spanish	Pronunciation
alcohol	el alcohol	*ehl ahl-koh-ohl*
antacid	un antiácido	*oon ahn-tee-yah-see-doh*
antihistamine	un antistamínico	*oon ahn-tee-stah-mee-nee-koh*
antiseptic	un antiséptico	*oon ahn-tee-sehp-tee-koh*
aspirin	la aspirina	*lah ahs-pee-ree-nah*

Item	Spanish	Pronunciation
Band-Aids	las curitas	*lahs koo-ree-tahs*
brush	un cepillo	*oon seh-pee-yoh*
condoms	los condones	*lohs kohn-doh-nehs*
cough drops	las pastillas para la tos	*lahs pahs-tee-yahs pah-rah lah tohs*
cough syrup	el jarabe para la tos	*ehl hah-rah-beh pah-rah lah tohs*
deodorant	un desodorante	*oon deh-soh-doh-rahn-teh*
eye drops	las gotas para los ojos	*lahs goh-tahs pah-rah lohs oh-hohs*
first-aid kit	el botiquín de primeros auxilios	*ehl boh-tee-keen deh pree-meh-rohs owk-see-lee-yohs*
heating pad	la almohadilla de calefacción	*lah ahl-moh-ah-dee-yah deh kah-leh-fahk-see-yohn*
ice pack	la bolsa de hielo	*lah bohl-sah deh ee-yeh-loh*
laxative	un laxante	*oon lahk-sahn-teh*
mouthwash	el enjuagador bucal	*ehl ehn-hwah-gah-dohr boo-kahl*
nail file	una lima	*oo-nah lee-mah*
nose drops	las gotas para la nariz	*lahs goh-tahs pah-rah lah nah-rees*
razor electric	una rasuradora eléctrica	*oo-nah rrah-soo-rah-doh-rah eh-lehk-tree-kah*
razor blade	las hojas de afeitar	*lash oh-hash deh ah-feh-yee-tahr*
safety pin	los seguros, los imperdibles	*lohs seh-goo-rohs, lohs eem-pehr-dee-blehs*
shampoo (anti-dandruff)	el champú (anti-caspa)	*ehl chahm-poo (ahn-tee kahs-pah)*
shaving cream	la crema de afeitar	*lah kreh-mah deh ah-feh-yee-tahr*
talcum powder	el polvo de talco	*ehl pohl-boh deh tahl-koh*
tissues	los pañuelos de papel	*lohs pah-nyoo-weh-lohs deh pah-pehl*
toothbrush	un cepillo de dientes	*oom seh-pee-yoh deh dee-yehn-tehs*
toothpaste	la pasta dentífrica	*lah pahs-tah dehn-tee-free-kah*
tweezers	las pinzas	*lahs peen-sahs*

For Babies

bottle	un biberón	*oon bee-beh-rohn*
diapers (disposable)	los pañales (desechables)	*lohs pah-nyah-lehs (deh-seh-chah-blehs)*
pacifier	un chupete	*oon choo-peh-teh*

Special Needs

The items in the following table could be bought from or located by special organizations that cater to the needs of the physically challenged or pharmacies that specialize in *el alquiler de aparatos médicos* (*ehl ahl-kee-lehr deh ah-pah-rah-tohs meh-dee-kohs*; the rental of medical appliances). The following might be helpful:

> ¿Dónde puedo obtener …?
> *dohn-deh pweh-doh ohb-teh-nehr*
> Where can I get…?

Special Needs

Medical Appliance	Spanish	Pronunciation
cane	un bastón	*oon bahs-tohn*
crutches	las muletas	*lahs moo-leh-tahs*
hearing aid	un aparato para sordos	*oon ah-pah-rah-toh pah-rah sohr-dohs*
walker	un andador	*oon ahn-dah-dohr*
wheelchair	una silla de ruedas	*oo-nah see-yah deh rroo-weh-dahs*

Come Along with Me

You've decided to call the pharmacy ahead of time to order or locate a certain product. If you want to tell the pharmacist when you'll be coming by to pick it up, use the verb *venir* (to come). Note that *venir* is a go-go verb because its *yo* form ends in *-go*. *Venir* is also similar to a shoe verb in that the *nosotros* and *vosotros* forms look like the infinitive, while the forms for the other subject pronouns do not.

To tell the phramacist when you'll be stopping by, say:

> Yo vengo a las dos.
> *yoh behn-goh ah lahs dohs*
> I'm coming at 2 o'clock.

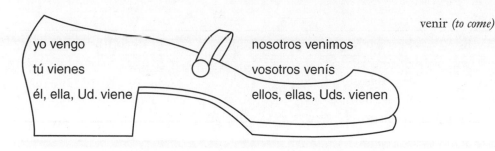

venir *(to come)*

yo vengo   nosotros venimos

tú vienes   vosotros venís

él, ella, Ud. viene   ellos, ellas, Uds. vienen

Living in the Past

No matter how much time I put aside to pack or how many times I run to add items to my packing list, I invariably forget something important. This year, it was the special shampoo and conditioner I need to achieve my unique look. The hotel brand was a generic disaster. I also left my hair dryer at home because the hotel brochure promised one in every room. It didn't lie, but it was the slowest hair dryer I've ever used, and I was sorry I didn't pack my own.

To discuss what you did or did not do, you must use the past tense. In Spanish, this tense is called the *pretérito*, the preterit.

The Preterit of Regular Verbs

Forming the preterit of regular verbs is quite easy because all the verbs follow their family's rules. Verbs that have spelling and stem changes and verbs that are totally irregular require a little more attention.

To form the preterit of regular verbs, drop the infinitive ending (*-ar*, *-er*, or *-ir*), and add the endings listed in the following tables.

-ar Verbs	Preterit Stem	Pronoun(s)	Preterit Endings
hablar	habl-	yo	-é
		tú	-aste
		él, ella, Ud.	-ó

continues

continued

-*ar* Verbs	Preterit Stem	Pronoun(s)	Preterit Endings
		nosotros	-amos
		vosotros	-asteis
		ellos, ellas, Uds.	-aron

-*er* and -*ir* Verbs	Preterit Stem	Pronoun(s)	Preterit Endings
vend**er**	vend-	yo	-í
abr**ir**	abr-	tú	-iste
		él, ella, Ud.	-ió
		nosotros	-imos
		vosotros	-isteis
		ellos, ellas, Uds.	-ieron

Verbs ending in -*car*, -*gar*, and -*zar* drop the -*ar* infinitive ending to form the preterit and have a spelling change only in the *yo* form. All other forms are regular.

-*car* Verbs	Change	Yo Form	Other Forms
bus**car**	c changes to qu	yo busqué	buscaste, buscó, buscamos, buscasteis, buscaron

You might find the common -*car* verbs in the following table useful.

Verb	Pronunciation	Meaning
aplicar	*ah-plee-kahr*	to apply
buscar	*boos-kahr*	to look for
colocar	*koh-loh-kahr*	to place, to put
comunicar	*koh-moo-nee-kahr*	to communicate
equivocarse	*eh-kee-boh-kahr-seh*	to be mistaken
explicar	*ehks-plee-kahr*	to explain
fabricar	*fah-bree-kahr*	to manufacture, to make

Verb	Pronunciation	Meaning
indicar	*een-dee-kahr*	to indicate
marcar	*mahr-kahr*	to mark, to designate
pescar	*pehs-kahr*	to fish
sacar	*sah-kahr*	to take out
significar	*seeg-nee-fee-kahr*	to mean
tocar	*toh-kahr*	to touch, to play (musical instrument)

-gar Verbs	Change	Yo Form	Other Forms
pa**gar**	g changes to gu	yo pagué	pagaste, pagó, pagamos, pagasteis, pagaron

You might find the common *-gar* verbs in the following table useful.

Verb	Pronunciation	Meaning
apagar	*ah-pah-gahr*	to put out, to turn off, to extinguish
colgar (ue)	*kohl-gahr*	to hang
encargar	*ehn-kahr-gahr*	to put in charge, to entrust
entregar (ie)	*ehn-treh-gahr*	to deliver
jugar (ue)	*hoo-gahr*	to play (sports, games)
llegar	*yeh-gahr*	to arrive
negar (ie)	*neh-gahr*	to deny
pagar	*pah-gahr*	to pay

-zar Verbs	Change	Yo Form	Other Forms
go**zar**	z changes to c	yo gocé	gozaste, gozó, gozamos, gozasteis, gozaron

You might find the common -*zar* verbs in the following table useful.

Verb	Pronunciation	Meaning
abrazar	*ah-brah-sahr*	to hug, to embrace
almorzar (ue)	*ahl-mohr-sahr*	to eat lunch
avanzar	*ah-bahn-sahr*	to advance, to hurry
comenzar (ie)	*koh-mehn-sahr*	to begin, to commence
cruzar	*kroo-sahr*	to cross
empezar (ie)	*ehm-peh-sahr*	to begin
gozar	*goh-sahr*	to enjoy
lanzar	*lahn-sahr*	to throw

Any -*ir* verbs that have a stem change in the present tense also have a stem change in the preterit. In the present, an *e* in the stem could change to *ie* or *i*. In the preterit, *e* only changes to *i* and *o* only changes to *u* in the third-person singular (*él, ella, Ud.*) and third-person plural forms (*ellos, ellas, Uds.*). (For a list of common verbs with these changes, refer to Chapter 12.) For all -*ir* verbs in which the endings are regular in the present, the endings are also regular in the past.

The following table lists some -*ir* verbs that are irregular in the past tense.

> **Memory Master**
>
> The verbs *reír* (to laugh) and *son-reír* (to smile) form the preterit as follows: *(son) reí, (son) reíste, (son) rió, (son) reísteis, (son) rieron.*

Infinitive	*Yo, Tú, Nosotros, Vosotros*	*Él, Ella, Ud.*	*Ellos, Ellas, Uds.*
preferir (to prefer)	preferí, preferiste, preferimos, preferisteis	prefirió	prefirieron
pedir (to ask)	pedí, pediste, pedimos, pedisteis	pidió	pidieron
dormir (to sleep)	dormí, dormiste, dormimos, dormisteis	durmió	durmieron

Verbs that end in -*er* or -*ir* with a vowel immediately preceding the infinitive ending (except *traer*, to bring, and *atraer*, to attract, which are irregular and are explained later in the chapter) change *i* to *y* in the third-person singular (*él, ella, Ud.*) and third-person plural (*ellos, ellas, Uds.*) forms in the preterit. In all other forms, the *i* has an accent mark, as shown in the following table.

Infinitive	Yo, Tú, Nosotros, Vosotros	Él, Ella, Ud.	Ellos, Ellas, Uds.
caer (to fall)	caí, caíste, caímos, caísteis	cayó	cayeron
creer (to believe)	creí, creíste, creímos, creísteis	creyó	creyeron
leer (to read)	leí, leíste, leímos, leísteis	leyó	leyeron
oír (to hear)	oí, oíste, oímos, oísteis	oyó	oyeron
poseer (to possess)	poseí, poseíste, poseímos, poseísteis	poseyó	poseyeron

Verbs ending in *-uir* also follow this rule, except an accent appears on the *i* only in the *yo* form. (See Chapter 12 for other verbs that fit this category.)

Infinitive	Yo, Tú, Nosotros, Vosotros	Él, Ella, Ud.	Ellos, Ellas, Uds.
incluir (to include)	incluí, incluiste, incluimos, incluisteis	incluyó	incluyeron

The Preterit of Irregular Verbs

Some verbs are irregular in the preterit, so you must memorize their stems. That's the bad news. The good news is that all irregular verbs in the preterit have the same endings, regardless of their infinitive endings. The endings are as shown in the following table.

Pronoun	Verb Ending	Pronoun	Verb Ending
yo	-e	nosotros	-imos
tú	-iste	vosotros	-isteis
él, ella, Ud.	-o	ellos, ellas, Uds.	-ieron

The following table lists the most common irregular verbs.

Irregular Verbs in the Preterit

Infinitive	Preterit Stem	Preterit Forms
andar (to walk)	anduv-	anduve, anduviste, anduvo, anduvimos, anduvisteis, anduvieron
cabcr (to fit)	cup-	cupe, cupiste, cupo, cupimos, cupisteis, cupieron
estar (to be)	estuv-	estuve, estuviste, estuvo, estuvimos, estuvisteis, estuvieron
hacer (to make, to do)	hic-, hiz-	hice, hiciste, hizo, hicimos, hicisteis, hicieron
poder (to be able to)	pud-	pude, pudiste, pudo, pudimos, pudisteis, pudieron
poner (to put)	pus-	puse, pusiste, puso, pusimos, pusisteis, pusieron
querer (to want)	quiss-	quise, quisiste, quiso, quisimos, quisisteis, quisieron
saber (to know)	sup-	supe, supiste, supo, supimos, supisteis, supieron
tener (to have)	tuv-	tuve, tuviste, tuvo, tuvimos, tuvisteis, tuvieron
venir (to come)	vin-	vine, viniste, vino, vinimos, vinisteis, vinieron

Of course, there's an exception to every rule. For the following verbs that are irregular in the preterit, the *-ieron* ending for the third-person plural forms (*ellos, ellas, Uds.*) becomes *-eron* before the letter *j*.

Infinitive	Preterit Stem	Preterit Forms
decir (to say)	dij-	dije, dijiste, dijo, dijimos, dijisteis, dijeron
producir (to produce)	produj-	produje, produjiste, produjo, produjimos, produjisteis, produjeron
traer (to bring)	traj-	traje, trajiste, trajo, trajimos, trajisteis, trajeron

Three high-frequency irregular verbs are *dar* (to give), *ir* (to go), and *ser* (to be). In the following preterit conjugations, note that accent marks are not used with these verbs, or with the irregular verb *ver* (to see).

Dar, although an *-ar* verb, uses the preterit endings for *-er* and *-ir* verbs:

yo di	nosotros dimos
tú diste	vosotros disteis
él, ella, Ud. dio	ellos, ellas, Uds. dieron

The preterit of *ver* resembles the preterit of *dar:*

yo vi	nosotros vimos
tú viste	vosotros visteis
él, ella, Ud. vio	ellos, ellas, Uds. vieron

Ir and *ser* have the same preterit forms, so you have to follow the conversation to know which one is being used. Use these conjugations for both verbs:

yo fui	nosotros fuimos
tú fuiste	vosotros fuisteis
él, ella, Ud. fue	ellos, ellas, Uds. fueron

> **Memory Master**
>
> When using reflexive verbs in the preterit, remember to include the reflexive pronoun:
>
> Nos levantamos temprano.
> We got up early.
>
> Me equivoqué.
> I made a mistake.

Talking About Your Past

You're sitting in a café with some friends, and the conversation turns to what you each did yesterday. Express what each person did in the past by giving the correct preterit form for the infinitive in parentheses.

1. Ud. (trabajar) _____ mucho.

2. Carlota (comer) _____ en el café.

3. Tú (escribir) _____ un poema.

4. Yo (leer) _____ un libro.

5. Nosotros (andar) _____ por el parque.

6. Yo (jugar) _____ al tenis.

continues

continued

7. Ellos (tener) _____ una cita.

8. Yo (equivocarse) _____.

9. Uds. (oír) _____ las noticias.

10. Vosotros (decir) _____ la verdad.

11. Ellas (dormir) _____ hasta la una.

12. Yo (pagar) _____ todas mis cuentas.

Questions in the Past

A yes-or-no question about the past can be formed using intonation, the tags *¿verdad?* or *¿no?*, or inversion. This is exactly the same way you would ask a question about the present:

> ¿Tú fuiste al cine?
> *too fwees-teh ahl see-neh*
> Did you go to the movies?

> Tú fuiste al cine, ¿verdad? (¿no?)
> *too fwees-teh ahl see-neh behr-dahd (noh)*
> You went to the movies, didn't you?

> ¿Fuiste tú al cine?
> *fwees-teh too ahl see-neh*
> Did you go to the movies?

To ask for information, simply put the question word at the beginning of the sentence:

> ¿Cuándo fuiste (tú) al cine?
> *kwahn-doh fwees-teh ahl see-neh*
> When did you go to the movies?

> ¿Con quién fuiste al cine?
> *kohn kee-yehn fwees-teh ahl see-neh*
> With whom did you go to the movies?

> ¿Cómo fuiste al cine?
> *koh-moh fwees-teh ahl see-neh*
> How did you go to the movies?

In a Flash _____

Practice asking a friend questions in the past. Vary them by asking for yes-or-no answers and for specific information.

To answer "yes" or "no" or to give more information, follow the pattern used for the present tense:

Sí, fui al cine.
see fwee ahl see-neh
Yes, I went to the movies.

No, no fui al cine.
noh, noh fwee ahl see-neh
No, I didn't go to the movies.

Fui al cine con Ana.
fwee ahl see-neh kohn ah-nah
I went to the movies with Ana.

Fui al cine en coche.
fwee ahl see-neh ehn koh-cheh
I went to the movies by car.

Answer Key

Talking About Your Past

1. trabajó
2. comió
3. escribiste
4. leí
5. anduvimos
6. jugué
7. tuvieron
8. me equivoqué
9. oyeron
10. dijisteis
11. durmieron
12. pagué

Making a Phone Call

In This Chapter

- Tips on making a phone call
- Correct phone etiquette
- What to say when you're having trouble
- The imperfect tense
- Preterit vs. imperfect

You're feeling rather chipper now that you've taken care of all your personal and medical needs. Chapter 21 really helped you put yourself back on course. Now you'd like to let the friends you left behind know how great everything is going. It's time to phone home.

To truly appreciate our excellent American telecommunications network, a person needs only to make a phone call in a foreign country. In many instances, a simple local call creates quite a challenge, and long-distance calls can be a nightmare. Operator assistance often is necessary for even the most mundane tasks.

To make things worse, imagine how difficult it can be to communicate with a foreign speaker when you cannot read lips or observe body language for clues. This chapter can help you in this situation. You'll learn how to place a local or international call from a foreign country and how to deal with wrong numbers and other calling problems. You'll also learn how to describe a continuous action in the past using the imperfect tense.

Placing the Call

Making a long-distance call from afar usually requires a complicated explanation of the phone system, some operator assistance, and a lot of patience—there can be an awful lot of numbers to punch in. In some countries, you might have to use special tokens and push certain buttons just to complete a local call. When learning how to use the phone, consult the following table so you can correctly describe the type of call you want to make.

Types of Phone Calls

Type of Phone Call	Spanish	Pronunciation
collect call	la llamada por cobrar, la llamada con cargo	*lah yah-mah-dah pohr koh-brahr, lah yah-mah-dah kohn kahr-goh*
credit-card call	la llamada con tarjeta de crédito	*lah yah-mah-dah kohn tahr-heh-tah deh kreh-dee-toh*
local call	la llamada local	*lah yah-mah-dah loh-kahl*
long-distance call	la llamada de larga distancia	*lah yah-mah-dah deh lahr-gah dees-tahn-see-yah*
out-of-the-country call	la llamada internacional	*lah yah-mah-dah een-tehr-nah-see-yoh-nahl*
person-to-person call	la llamada de persona a persona	*lah yah-mah-dah deh pehr-soh-nah ah pehr-soh-nah*

The following table lists different parts of the telephone.

The Telephone

Telephone Parts	Spanish	Pronunciation
booth	la cabina (casilla) telefónica	*lah kah-bee-nah (kah-see-yah) teh-leh-foh-nee-kah*
button	el botón	*ehl boh-tohn*

Telephone Parts	Spanish	Pronunciation
coin-return button	el botón de recobrar	*ehl boh-tohn deh rreh-koh-brahr*
cordless phone (portable phone)	el teléfono inalámbrico	*ehl teh-leh-foh-noh een-ah-lahm-bree-koh*
dial	el disco	*ehl dees-koh*
keypad	las teclas	*lahs teh-klahs*
phone card	la tarjeta telefónica	*lah tahr-heh-tah teh-leh-foh-nee-kah*
public phone	el teléfono público	*ehl teh-leh-foh-noh poo-blee-koh*
receiver	el auricular	*ehl ow-ree-koo-lahr*
slot	la ranura	*lah rrah-noo-rah*
speaker telephone	el teléfono altavoz	*ehl teh-leh-foh-noh ahl-tah-bohs*
telephone	el teléfono	*ehl teh-leh-foh-noh*
telephone book	la guía telefónica	*lah gee-yah teh-leh-foh-nee-kah*
telephone number	el número de teléfono	*ehl noo-meh-roh deh teh-leh-foh-noh*
token	la ficha	*lah fee-chah*
touch-tone phone	el teléfono de botones	*ehl teh-leh-foh-noh deh boh-toh-nehs*

Now you're ready to phone home. The following table provides the words you'll need to understand the Spanish directions for placing a phone call.

How to Make a Phone Call

Telephone Term	Spanish	Pronunciation
to call back	volver* a llamar	*bohl-behr ah yah-mahr*
to dial	marcar	*mahr-kahr*
to hang up (the receiver)	colgar*	*kohl-gahr*
to insert the card	introducir la tarjeta	*een-troh-doo-seer lah tahr-heh-tah*
to know the area code	saber la clave de área	*sah-behr lah klah-beh deh ah-reh-yah*
to leave a message	dejar un mensaje	*deh-hahr oon mehn-sah-heh*
to pick up (the receiver)	descolgar*	*dehs-kohl-gahr*
to telephone	telefonear	*teh-leh-foh-neh-yahr*
to wait for the dial tone	esperar el tono, la señal	*ehs-peh-rahr ehl toh-noh, lah seh-nyahl*

*These verbs are stem-changing shoe verbs. The o will change to ue in the present tense for all forms except nosotros and vosotros.

Who Is It?

Did you ever notice that it's more difficult to understand people over the telephone than it is in person? This is especially true if they're speaking a different language. Body language, facial expressions, and gestures can help us understand the message a speaker is conveying. Without those clues, your best bet is to become familiar with the Spanish expressions used for making and answering a phone call. The following table shows you how to begin a typical telephone conversation.

Making a Phone Call

Expression	Meaning
Expressions Used When Making a Call	
Diga. Oiga. Bueno.	Hello.
… por favor	… please
Soy … Habla …	It's …
¿Está …?	Is … in (there)?
Quisiera hablar con …	I would like to speak to …
¿Cuándo regresará?	When will he (she) be back?
Volveré a llamar más tarde.	I'll call back later.
Expressions Used When Answering a Call	
Diga. Oiga. Bueno.	Hello.
¿De parte de quién? ¿Quién habla?	Who's calling?
Soy …	This is …
No cuelgue, por favor.	Hold on.
Un momento.	Just a moment.
Él/Ella no está.	He/She is not in.
¿Quiere dejar un mensaje?	Do you want to leave a message?

Sorry, Wrong Number

You can run into many problems when making a phone call: a wrong number, a busy signal, a hang up, and so on. Here are some examples of phrases you might say or hear if you run into any difficulties:

¿Qué número está llamando?
keh noo-meh-roh ehs-tah yah-mahn-doh
What number are you calling?

Se nos cortó la línea.
seh nohs kohr-toh lah lee-neh-yah
We got cut off (disconnected).

No puedo oír nada.
noh pweh-doh oh-yeer nah-dah
I can't hear you.

Vuelva a llamarme más tarde.
bwehl-bah ah yah-mahr-meh mahs tahr-deh
Call me back later.

La línea está ocupada.
la lee-neh-yah ehs-tah oh-koo-pah-dah
The line is busy.

Remarque Ud. el número, por favor.
rreh-mahr-keh oo-stehd ehl noo-meh-roh pohr fah-bohr
Please redial the number.

El teléfono está descompuesto (dañado,
fuera de servicio).
*ehl teh-leh-foh-noh ehs-tah dehs-kohm-pwehs-toh (dah-nyah-doh,
fweh-rah deh sehr-bee-see-yoh)*
The telephone is out of order.

Es un error. (Yo tengo) Ud. tiene un número equivocado.
ehs oon eh-rrohr. (yoh tehn-goh) oo-stehd tee-yeh-neh oon noo-meh-roh eh-kee-boh-kah-doh
It's a mistake. (I have) You have the wrong number.

Memory Master

In English, when we want to express that someone is going to do something again, we generally use the prefix *re-*, as in *retry*, *recall*, *recycle*, or *redo*. In Spanish, the idiomatic expression *volver* (*ue*) + *a* + infinitive gets this meaning across. The verb *volver* must be conjugated:

Vuelva a llamar más tarde.
Call back later.

The Imperfect

We *shopped* till we *dropped.* When we *returned* to our cozy hotel room, my husband *decided* to take a nap. I **was sitting** in a chair reading a book when all of a sudden the lights *went out.* I *wondered* what *happened.* I *looked* out the window, and I *saw* that everything **was** dark. I didn't **know** what to do. Night **was falling** and I **was getting** hungry. I *woke* my husband, and we *decided* to find our way out in the darkness. It **was** so hard to walk. We **couldn't** see two feet in front of us. When we *got* to the stairs, we **were** relieved to see that someone from the hotel **was guiding** the guests with flashlights from the fifth floor to the lobby. We *made* the best of it and *ate* at a charming restaurant nearby. (This really happened to us, in the not-so-distant past in a luxury hotel in Puerto Rico.)

In English, we speak or write easily in the past without giving much thought to what we're saying. In Spanish, however, it's not that simple. There are two different simple past tenses: the *preterit* (*italicized in the preceding paragraph*) and the **imperfect** (**shown in bold**). This tends to make speaking in the past a bit confusing for a non-native speaker.

Just remember that, even if you mistake one for the other, you'll still be understood. Sometimes either tense is correct. What's the difference? The preterit expresses specific actions or events that were completed in the past; the imperfect expresses continuous or repeated actions, events, situations, or states in the past.

Memory Master

Use the imperfect for times in the past when you would record the continuous events on a video camera. Use the preterit when you would point and shoot an event that occurred at a specific moment in time. In the imperfect, regular -er and -ir verbs have the same endings.

Formation of the Imperfect

Before going into a more detailed explanation, let's see how the imperfect is formed. There are only three irregular verbs in the imperfect tense, and no changes are necessary for verbs with spelling and stem changes:

Memory Master

The imperfect is a past tense that tells what the subject *was* doing or *used to* do.

◆ To form the imperfect of regular verbs, drop the infinitive ending (*-ar, -er,* or *-ir*) and add the proper endings.

-ar Verbs	Imperfect Stem	Conjugation
hablar	habl-	yo habl**aba**
		tú habl**abas**
		él, ella, Ud. habl**aba**
		nosotros habl**ábamos**
		vosotros habl**abais**
		ellos, ellas, Uds. habl**aban**

-er and *-ir* Verbs	Imperfect Stem	Conjugation
vender	vend-	yo vend**ía**
		tú vend**ías**
		él, ella, Ud. vend**ía**
		nosotros vend**íamos**
		vosotros vend**íais**
		ellos, ellas, Uds. vend**ían**
abrir	abr-	yo abr**ía**
		tú abr**ías**
		él, ella, Ud. abr**ía**
		nosotros abr**íamos**
		vosotros abr**íais**
		ellos, ellas, Uds. abr**ían**

◆ The following are the three irregular verbs in the imperfect.

Infinitive	Meaning	Imperfect Endings
ir	to go	iba, ibas, iba, íbamos, ibais, iban
ser	to be	era, eras, era, éramos, erais, eran
ver	to see	veía, veías, veía, veíamos, veíais, veían

The Preterit vs. the Imperfect

Which tense should you use? And when? The preterit expresses an action that was completed at a specific time in the past. Thinking of a camera might help you understand this concept. The preterit represents an action that could be captured by a snapshot—the action happened and was completed:

> Yo fui al cine ayer.
> *yoh fwee ahl see-neh ah-yehr*
> I went to the movies yesterday.

Memory Master

Think of the imperfect as a continuous wavy line traveling through the past. The preterit is simply a dot, one moment in past time.

The imperfect expresses an action that continued in the past over an indefinite period of time. Think again of a camera. The imperfect represents an action that could be captured—the action continued to flow. It *was* happening, *used to* happen, or *would* (meaning *used to*) happen. The imperfect is also a descriptive tense:

> Yo iba al cine con mi abuelo.
> *yoh ee-bah ahl see-neh kohn mee ah-bweh-loh*
> I used to go to the movies with my grandfather.

The following two lists provide a more in-depth look at the differences between the two tenses:

Preterit:

◆ Expresses specific actions or events that were started and completed at a definite time in the past (even if the time isn't mentioned):

> Viajé con mi amigo.
> *bee-yah-heh kohn mee ah-mee-goh*
> I traveled with my friend.

◆ Expresses a specific action or event that occurred at a specific point in time:

> Ayer yo salí a la una.
> *ah-yehr yoh sah-lee ah lah oo-nah*
> Yesterday I went out at 1 o'clock.

◆ Expresses a specific action or event that was repeated a stated number of times:

> Fuimos al cine tres veces.
> *fwee-mohs ahl see-neh trehs beh-sehs*
> We went to the movies three times.

Imperfect:

◆ Describes ongoing or continuous actions in the past (which might or might not have been completed):

Yo viajaba con mi amigo.
yoh bee-yah-hah-bah kohn mee ah-mee-goh
I was traveling with my friend.

◆ Describes repeated or habitual actions that took place in the past:

Generalmente yo salía a la una.
heh-neh-rahl-mehn-teh yoh sah-lee-yah ah lah oo-nah
I usually went out at 1 o'clock.

◆ Describes a person, place, thing, or state of mind:

Estábamos contentos.	El mar estaba peligroso.
ehs-tah-bah-mohs kohn-tehn-tohs	*ehl mahr ehs-tah-bah peh-lee-groh-soh*
We were happy.	The sea was dangerous.
Quería salir.	La puerta estaba abierta.
keh-ree-yah sah-leer	*lah pwehr-tah ehs-tah-bah ah-bee-yehr-tah*
I wanted to go out.	The door was open.

What Happened?

It was a day like any other, or so I thought. Little did I know what was in store for me. Complete my story with the correct form of the verbs provided, using either the preterit or imperfect tense:

(1. Ser) _____ las cinco de la tarde. (2. Estar) _____ lloviendo cuando yo (3. salir) _____ de mi oficina para regresar a casa. (4. Tomar) _____ el autobús. (5. Llegar) _____ delante de mi casa media hora más tarde. (6. Entrar) _____ y (7. subir) _____ a mi apartamento. (8. Sacar) _____ mis llaves pero no las (9. necesitar) _____. (10. Observar) _____ que mi puerta (11. estar) _____ abierta. Yo no (12. saber) _____ por qué. (13. Tener) _____ mucho miedo. (14. Estar) ____ convencido de que alguien me (15. robar) _____. (16. Empujar) _____ la puerta con cuidado y (17. entrar) _____ lentamente. No (18. oír) _____ nada. (19. Marchar) _____ hacia el teléfono, cuando de repente todos mis amigos (20. gritar) _____ en voz alta: ¡Feliz cumpleaños! ¡Qué sorpresa!

Answer Key

What Happened?

1. Eran	6. Entré	11. estaba	16. Empujé
2. Estaba	7. subí	12. sabía	17. entré
3. salí	8. Saqué	13. Tenía	18. oí
4. Tomé	9. necesité	14. Estaba	19. Marchaba
5. Llegué	10. observé	15. robó	20. gritaron

"Where's the Nearest Post Office?"

In This Chapter

◆ Mail: sending and receiving

◆ The difference between *saber* and *conocer*

◆ The present perfect tense

In Chapter 22, you learned how to successfully complete a phone call; how to carry on a polite conversation using proper phone etiquette; and how to deal with typical, everyday telephone problems. You've looked at your hotel telephone bill and have decided it's too costly to phone home as often as you'd like. Writing letters is the simplest solution, so now you're off to the local post office.

Your friends will be deeply offended if you don't send them postcards, and you don't want to see the look in your mom's eyes if she doesn't receive a letter from you while you're on your trip. Let's say you bought a great souvenir, but it's too heavy to lug on the plane. Shipping it sounds like a great idea. If you follow directions, fill out the proper forms, and apply the correct postage, you can rest assured your mail will get to its destination.

This chapter shows you how to send air, registered, and special-delivery mail. You'll also learn how to write letters that describe your past and present activities and acquaintances.

"Please, Mr. Postman!"

There's so much to write about, you hardly know where to begin. You've seen the Prado, run with the bulls in Pamplona, and basked in the sun on the Costa del Sol. You can't wait for your family and friends to read about your wonderful adventures. You don't want your postcards and letters to arrive home after you do. You want speedy delivery, and you're prepared to pay the extra price for airmail service. Naturally, you'll want to keep a few essentials on hand such as envelopes and stamps. The following table provides the vocabulary you need to send your mail.

Mail and Post Office Terms

Postal Terms	Spanish	Pronunciation
address	la dirección	*lah dee-rehk-see-yohn*
addressee	el destinatario	*ehl dehs-tee-nah-tah-ree-yoh*
airmail	el correo aéreo	*ehl koh-rreh-yoh ah-yee-reh-yoh*
customes declaration	la declaración aduanera	*la deh-klah-rah-see-yohn ah-doo-ah-neh-rah*
envelope	el sobre	*ehl soh-breh*
letter	la carta	*lah kahr-tah*
mailbox	el buzón	*ehl boo-sohn*
package	el paquete	*ehl pah-keh-teh*
postcard	la tarjeta postal	*lah tahr-heh-tah pohs-tahl*
postage	el franqueo	*ehl frahn-keh-yoh*
postal code	el código postal	*ehl koh-dee-goh pohs-tahl*
postal meter	la franqueadora postal	*lah frahn-keh-yah-doh-rah pohs-tahl*
postal worker	el cartero (la cartera)	*ehl kahr-teh-roh (lah kahr-teh-rah)*
rate	la tarifa de franqueo	*lah tah-ree-fah deh frahn-keh-yoh*

Postal Terms	Spanish	Pronunciation
sender	el remitente	*ehl rreh-mee-tehn-teh*
slot	la ranura	*lah rrah-noo-rah*
stamp	el sello	*ehl seh-yoh*
surface mail	la vía terrestre	*lah bee-yah teh-rehs-treh*
window	la ventanilla	*lah behn-tah-nee-yah*

The services provided by the Spanish Postal Service are twofold in nature:

◆ Services pertaining strictly to different types of correspondence such as letters, postcards, and packages.

◆ Services dealing with postal banking services such as postal and telegraphic money orders. Unlike in other European cities, post offices in Spain do not normally handle telephone calls.

Getting Postal Service

You've written some postcards to your friends, dashed off a letter to your closest relatives, and even managed some business correspondence. If you need directions to the nearest post office or mailbox, simply ask the following question:

¿Dónde está el correo (buzón) más próximo?
dohn-deh ehs-tah ehl koh-rreh-yoh (boo-sohn) mahs prohk-see-moh
Where is the nearest post office (mailbox)?

You'll find that, just like back home, you might have to fill out special forms and paperwork depending on the types of letters and packages you've decided to send. Postage rates depend on how quickly you want your mail delivered. It's important to be able to correctly identify the type of service you need:

¿Cuál es la tarifa de franqueo de …?
kwahl ehs lah tah-ree-fah deh frahn-keh-yoh deh
What is the postage rate for …?

Type of Delivery	Spanish	Pronunciation
an insured letter	una carta asegurada	*oo-nah kahr-tah ah-seh-goo-rah-dah*
a letter to the United States	una carta a los Estados Unidos	*oo-nah kahr-tah ah lohs ehs-tah-dohs oo-nee-dohs*
an airmail letter	una carta por correo aéreo	*oo-nah kahr-tah pohr koh-rreh-yoh ah-yee-reh-yoh*

Here are some other useful phrases:

Quisiera mandar esta carta (este paquete) por correo
regular (aéreo, urgente).
kee-see-yeh-rah mahn-dahr ehs-tah kahr-tah (ehs-teh pah-keh-teh) pohr koh-rreh-yoh
rreh-goo-lahr (ah-yee-reh-yoh, oor-hehn-teh)
I would like to send this letter (this package) by regular mail (by airmail, by
special delivery).

Quisiera mandar este paquete contra reembolso.
kee-see-yeh-rah mahn-dahr ehs-teh pah-keh-teh kohn-trah rreh-ehm-bohl-soh
I would like to send this package C.O.D.

¿Cuándo llegará (llegarán)?
kwahn-doh yeh-gah-rah (yeh-gah-rahn)
When will it arrive?

Sending a Telegram

People generally send telegrams when there's important news to announce or to
acknowledge: your oldest son is finally getting married, the birth of a child or grand-
child, a fabulous business deal, or your best friend got an exciting promotion. When
you want to send a telegram, the following phrases will prove helpful:

Quisiera mandar un telegrama (a cobro revertido).
kee-see-yeh-rah mahn-dahr oon teh-leh-grah-mah (ah koh-broh rreh-behr-tee-doh)
I would like to send a telegram (collect).

¿Cuánto cuesta por palabra?
kwahn-toh kwehs-tah pohr pah-lah-brah
How much is it per word?

¿Puede darme un formulario (un impreso), por favor?
pweh-deh dahr-meh oon fohr-moo-lah-ree-yoh (oon eem-preh-soh) pohr fah-bohr
May I please have a form?

¿Dónde están los formularios?
dohn-deh ehs-tahn lohs fohr-moo-lah-ree-yohs
Where are the forms?

Can You Read This?

Looking for something to read while you wait in line at the post office? Perhaps you're interested in the local news and your hotel provides a complimentary newspaper each morning. Wherever you go, there might be important signs you need to read. If you see the word *aviso* (*ah-bee-soh*), you know there is some kind of warning such as *agua no potable* (undrinkable water). The following table features items you might read while visiting a Spanish-speaking country.

Things to Read

Item to Be Read	Spanish	Pronunciation
ad	un anuncio	*oon ah-noon-see-yoh*
book	un libro	*oon lee-broh*
magazine	una revista	*oo-nah rreh-bees-tah*
menu	una carta, un menú	*oo-nah kahr-tah, oon meh-noo*
newspaper	un periódico	*oon peh-ree-yoh-dee-koh*
novel	una novela	*oo-nah noh-beh-lah*
pamphlet	un folleto	*oon foh-yeh-toh*
receipt	un recibo	*oon rreh-see-boh*
sign	un letrero	*oon leh-treh-roh*
warning	un aviso	*oon ah-bee-soh*

Did You Know That ...?

Do you know the name of a great Spanish restaurant? You do? What is its address? How about its phone number? You know the owner? She's your second cousin and really knows how to prepare a mean *paella?* That's great. To express certain facts, information, relationships, and abilities, you need the two Spanish verbs that express "to know": *saber* and *conocer.* Study the verbs first and then read the paragraphs that follow for an explanation of how to use each verb properly.

saber (to know)		conocer (to know)	
yo sé	nosotros sabemos	yo conozco	nosotros conocemos
tú sabes	vosotros sabéis	tú conoces	vosotros conocéis
él, ella, Ud. sabe	ellos, ellas, Uds. saben	él, ella, Ud. conoce	ellos, ellas, Uds. conoce

If there are two ways to express "to know," how are you supposed to know when to use each one? It is important to remember that the Spanish differentiate between knowing facts and how to do things (*saber*) and knowing (being acquainted with) people, places, things, and ideas (*conocer*).

The verb *saber* shows knowledge gained through learning or experience. It expresses that someone knows a fact or has memorized something. *Saber* means "to know how" when it is followed by an infinitive:

¿Sabe la dirección?　　　　　¿Él sabe nadar?
sah-beh lah dee-rehk-see-yohn　*ehl sah-beh nah-dahr*
Do you know the address?　　Does he know how to swim?

Yo sé donde está.
yoh seh dohn-deh ehs-tah
I know where it is.

The verb *conocer* shows familiarity with a person, a place, or a thing. If you can replace "to know" with "to be acquainted with," you know to use the verb *conocer:*

¿Conoce a Marta?
koh-noh-seh ah mahr-tah
Do you know Martha? (Are you acquainted with her?)

In a Flash

Make a list of people you know and things you know how to do.

¿Conoces este poema?
koh-noh-sehs ehs-teh poh-eh-mah
Do you know that poem? (Have you heard it but you don't know the words?)

Notice the difference between the following sentences:

Yo sé la canción.   Yo conozco la canción.

I know the song (by heart).   I know the song (I'm familiar with it).

Using Saber **and** Conocer

If you keep the differences between the two verbs in mind, you will quickly learn to use them properly. Show that you've gotten the hang of it by filling in the blanks with the correct form of *saber* or *conocer*:

1. Ellos _____ donde está el correo.

2. Yo no _____ su número de teléfono.

3. ¿_____ Ud. al señor Castro?

4. Nosotros _____ esquiar.

5. ¿_____ tú a esa mujer?

6. Ella _____ Madrid.

7. ¿_____ Uds. que yo soy cubana?

8. Vosotros _____ este monumento.

What Have You Done?

"Good grief!" you exclaim as you realize you've forgotten to call your loved ones to tell them you've arrived safely. To express what you have or have not done, you must use the present perfect tense in Spanish. This tense refers to an action that has already happened, either in the general past or quite recently in relation to now. ("I've started to study Spanish.") It can also be used to speak about past events that carry over into the present. ("I've always wanted to study that language [and I still want to now].")

The present perfect is a compound tense, which means it is made up of more than one part. Two elements are needed to form the present perfect—the helping verb *haber* (*ah-behr*; to have), which expresses that something has taken place, and a past participle, which expresses exactly what the action was.

The present perfect tense is formed as follows:

subject noun or pronoun + helping verb + past participle

The Helping Verb *Haber*

Because *haber* generally follows the subject of a declarative sentence, it must be conjugated. The following table gives the present tense of this helping verb.

The Helping Verb *Haber* (to Have)

Conjugation of *Haber*	Pronunciation	Meaning
yo he	*yoh eh*	I have
tú has	*too ahs*	you have
él, ella, Ud. ha	*ehl, eh-yah, oo-stehd ah*	he, she, it has; you have
nosotros hemos	*nohs-oh-trohs eh-mohs*	we have
vosotros habéis	*bohs-oh-trohs ah-beh-yees*	you have
ellos, ellas, Uds. han	*eh-yohs, eh-yahs, oo-steh-dehs ahn*	they, you have

¡Atención!

Don't confuse the verb *tener* (to have), which is used to express "have" in a general sense, with *haber* (to have), which is only used as a helping verb in compound tenses:

Yo tengo muchos amigos.   Yo he telefoneado a mis amigos.
I have many friends.   I have called my friends.

Forming Past Participles

To this helping verb, you must now add a past participle. The helping verb is always conjugated because it is the first verb. The past participle remains the same, no matter what the subject might be:

◆ To form the past participles of regular verbs, drop the infinitive ending (-*ar*, -*er*, or -*ir*) and add the endings shown in the following table.

-*ar* Verb	Past Participle Stem	Past Participle Ending
hablar	habl-	-ado

-*er* and -*ir* Verbs	Past Participle Stem	Past Participle Ending
vender	vend-	-ido
decidir	decid-	-ido

◆ For verbs ending in -*er* or -*ir* in which a vowel immediately precedes the infinitive ending, add an accent mark on the *i* as follows:

Infinitive	Past Participle Stem	Past Participle
caer (to fall)	ca-	caído
creer (to believe)	cre-	creído
leer (to read)	le-	leído
oír (to hear)	o-	oído
reír (to laugh)	re-	reído
traer (to bring)	tra-	traído

You probably will use the irregular past participles in the following table often.

Infinitive	Past Participle	Past Infinitive	Participle
abrir (to open)	abierto	poner (to put)	puesto
cubrir (to cover)	cubierto	resolver (to resolve)	resuelto
decir (to say, to tell)	dicho	romper (to break)	roto
escribir (to write)	escrito	ver (to see)	visto
hacer (to do, to make)	hecho	volver (to return)	vuelto
morir (to die)	muerto		

Presently Perfect

Now let's take this formula and put the present perfect to use:

Yo he hablado con mi familia.
yoh heh ah-blah-doh kohn mee fah-meel-yah
I have spoken with my family.

Tú has recibido una carta.
too ahs rreh-see-bee-doh oo-nah kahr-tah
You have received a letter.

Él ha hecho el trabajo.
ehl ah eh-choh ehl trah-bah-hoh
He has done the work.

Nosotros hemos comido demasiado.
noh-soh-trohs eh-mohs koh-mee-doh deh-mah-see-yah-doh
We've eaten too much.

Ellos han visto El Prado.
eh-yohs ahn bees-toh ehl prah-doh
They have seen El Prado.

Memory Master

The present perfect tense is used to express an action that began in the past and continues to the present, or is some way connected to the present: *I have eaten here often.*

The preterit is used to express an action that was completed in the past: *I ate here once.*

The imperfect is used to express a continuous action in the past: *I used to eat here.*

The past participle cannot be separated from the helping verb. This is the case even when using the word *no*, an adverb, or a subject noun or pronoun in a question:

Jaime no ha dicho la verdad.
James didn't tell the truth.

Nosotros siempre hemos llegado puntualmente.
We've always arrived on time.

¿Han llamado los muchachos?
Have the boys called?

¿No ha comprendido ella?
Didn't she understand?

Using the Present Perfect

It's a holiday weekend, and most people have some spare time to themselves. Describe what each person has or has not done to make the most of this opportunity. Use the correct forms of the helping verb *haber* and the past participle of the indicated infinitive.

Example: (yo/mirar) la television
Yo he mirado la televisión.

(Ud./no poner) la mesa
Ud. no ha puesto la mesa.

1. (nosotros/ir) al cine _____

2. (ellos/jugar) al fútbol _____

3. (tú/no) trabajar _____

4. (yo/leer) una novela _____

5. (Ud./no escribir) cartas _____

6. (vosotros/no correr) al centro _____

7. (Uds./no traer) su ropa a la lavandería _____

8. (ella/volver) a casa temprano _____

Answer Key

Using Saber and Conocer

1. saben	3. conoce	5. conoces	7. saben
2. sé	4. sabemos	6. conoce	8. conocéis

Using the Present Perfect

1. Nosotros hemos ido …

2. Ellos han jugado …

3. Tú no has trabajado …

4. Yo he leído …

5. Ud. no ha escrito …

6. Vosotros no habéis corrido …

7. Uds. no han traído …

8. Ella ha vuelto …

Part 5

Taking Care of Business

It's a small world after all, especially where business today is concerned. Knowledge of a foreign language is becoming increasingly important in all walks of life in an ever-expanding, multicultural world.

Part 5 is dedicated to readers whose jobs and businesses require more than a cursory knowledge of Spanish. In our high-tech society, all the modern and essential computer terms and phrases—as well as the vocabulary necessary to fax and to photocopy—are a must. Banking and business expressions will also certainly come in handy. For people who must travel extensively or who would like to combine business with pleasure, alternatives to the traditional hotel stay are presented.

By the time you've finished Part 5, if you've worked seriously, steadfastly, and conscientiously, you'll be well equipped and ready to handle just about any situation that might arise—in Spanish. Good luck! I feel confident that you can do it on your own.

Chapter 24

Doing Business

In This Chapter

- ◆ Stationery store supplies
- ◆ Faxes, photocopies, and computers
- ◆ The language of business
- ◆ The future tense

Chapter 23 ensured that your family and friends would be able to read all about your exploits. What if you need to do business in a Spanish-speaking country? Writing an intelligent, well-worded letter is a valuable skill. You should also be able to talk about the faxes, photocopies, and computers that are so important in business today. This chapter presents key phrases used in business and teaches you how to describe your plans for your company's future.

"I Need Supplies"

To successfully conduct any type of business, you need to keep certain basic supplies on hand. No doubt, you'll want to stop at *la papelería* (*lah pah-pehl-eh-ree-yah;* the stationery store), to stock up on the business items listed in the following table. You can start by saying the following:

> Quisiera comprar …
> *kee-see-yeh-rah kohm-prahr*
> I would like to buy …

At the Stationery Store

Business Supply	Spanish	Pronunciation
ballpoint pen	el bolígrafo	*ehl boh-lee-grah-foh*
calculator (solar)	la calculadora (solar)	*lah kahl-koo-lah-doh-rah (soh-lahr)*
envelopes	los sobres	*lohs soh-brehs*
eraser	la goma de borrar	*lah goh-mah deh boh-rrahr*
notebook	el cuaderno	*ehl kwah-dehr-noh*
paper	el papel	*ehl pah-pehl*
paper clips	los sujetapapeles	*lohs soo-heh-tah-pah-peh-lehs*
pencils	los lápices	*lohs lah-pee-sehs*
pencil sharpener	el sacapuntas	*ehl sah-kah-poon-tahs*
ruler	la regla	*lah rreh-glah*
scotch tape	la cinta adhesiva	*lah seen-tah ahd-eh-see-bah*
stapler	la grapadora	*lah grah-pah-doh-rah*
stationery	los objetos de escritorio	*lohs ohb-heh-tohs deh ehs-kree-toh-ree-yoh*
wrapping paper	el papel del envoltorio	*ehl pah-pehl dehl ehn-bol-toh-ree-yoh*
writing pad	el bloc	*ehl blohk*

Photocopies, Faxes, and Computers

If you want your business to run smoothly, you can't do without three items: faxes, photocopies, and computers. Use the following sections to help you keep them running smoothly.

Making Photocopies

I recently left the country to get some materials for this book. I pestered a lot of people, but I got just about everything I needed. As luck would have it, when I went to the business center to have photocopies made, all the machines were out of order. Off I trudged to the nearest photocopy store, where I used the following phrases:

Quisiera hacer una fotocopia de este papel
(este documento).
kee-see-yeh-rah ah-sehr oo-nah foh-toh-koh-pee-yah deh ehs-teh pah-pehl
(ehs-teh doh-koo-mehn-toh)
I would like to make a photocopy of this paper (this document).

Quisiera mandar hacer una fotocopia de este
documento.
kee-see-yeh-rah mahn-dahr ah-sehr oo-nah foh-toh-koh-pee-yah deh ehs-teh
doh-koo-mehn-toh
I would like to have a photocopy made of this document.

¿Cuánto cuesta por página?
kwahn-toh kwehs-tah pohr pah-hee-nah
What is the cost per page?

¿Puede Ud. agrandarlo (cincuenta por ciento)?
pweh-deh oo-stehd ah-grahn-dahr-loh (seen-kwehn-tah pohr see-yehn-toh)
Can you enlarge it (by 50 percent)?

¿Puede Ud. reducirlo (veinticinco por ciento)?
pweh-deh oo-stehd rreh-doo-seer-loh (behn-tee-seen-koh pohr see-yehn-toh)
Can you reduce it (by 25 percent)?

¿Puede Ud. hacer una copia en color?
pweh-deh oo-stehd ah-sehr oo-nah koh-pee-yah ehn koh-lohr
Can you make a color copy?

Let Me Take Care of That

Mandar (conjugated) + *hacer* (the infinitive form) describes having something done for
someone. Use the indirect object (*le* or *les*, meaning "for him," "for her," or "for
them") + *mandar* + *hacer* + noun. You also can use *mandar* + *hacer* + noun + the preposition *para* + the name of the person (or the prepositional pronoun referring to the
person) for whom the work is being done, as in the following examples:

Yo les mando hacer una fotocopia.
yoh lehs mahn-doh ah-sehr oo-nah foh-toh-koh-pee-yah
I'm having a photocopy made for them.

Yo mando hacer una fotocopia para mi jefe (él).
yoh mahn-doh ah-sehr oo-nah foh-toh-koh-pee-yah pah-rah mee heh-feh (ehl)
I'm having a photocopy made for my boss.

Fax It

Let's face it: a fax machine has become almost as important as a telephone in many households. My son went to visit a college in Pittsburgh, and we gave him cash to pay for his hotel room. Imagine our surprise when he called and informed us that they wouldn't accept his money. They threatened to cancel his room unless he could provide a credit card (which he didn't have at the time). So off we went at 10 P.M. to find a fax machine and send a photocopy of our credit card.

When you're able to transmit and receive messages and information in a matter of minutes, you can speed up the time it takes to transact business. That translates into extra cash. If you're conducting business in a Spanish-speaking country, it's a must to be fax-literate. The following phrases will definitely help you with that:

¿Cuál es su número de fax?
kwahl ehs soo noo-meh-roh deh fahks
What is your fax number?

Quisiera mandar un fax.
kee-see-yeh-rah mahn-dahr oon fahks
I'd like to send a fax.

¿Puedo enviar por fax este documento, por favor?
pweh-doh ehn-bee-yahr pohr fahks ehs-teh doh-koo-mehn-toh pohr fah-bohr
May I fax this document, please?

Enviémelo por fax.
ehn-bee-yeh-meh-loh pohr fahks
Fax it to me.

Yo no recibí (Yo no he recibido) su fax.
yoh noh rreh-see-bee (yoh noh eh rreh-see-bee-doh) soo fahks
I didn't get your fax.

¿Recibió Ud. (¿Ha recibido Ud.) mi fax?
rreh-see-bee-yoh oo-stehd (ah rreh-see-bee-doh oo-stehd) mee fahks
Did you receive my fax?

Su fax es ilegible.
soo fahks ehs ee-leh-hee-bleh
Your fax is illegible.

¿Puede Ud. enviármelo otra vez?
pweh-deh oo-stehd ehn-bee-yahr-meh-loh oh-trah behs
Please send it again.

Favor de confirmar que Ud. recibió
(Ud. ha recibido) mi fax.
fah-bohr deh kohn-feer-mahr keh oo-stehd rreh-see-bee-yoh
(oo-stehd ah rreh-see-bee-doh) mee fahks
Please confirm that you've received my fax.

I Love My Computer

Today, a computer is an absolute necessity. Not only do you have to know how to operate one, you also must know about the industry standards and programs for your field and for the system you're using. The phrases and table that follow will help you conduct business using computers, even if you're not a computer geek:

> **Memory Master**
>
> Use the present progressive tense to express what you're doing now. Conjugate the verb *estar* and add the present participle: drop the infinitive ending and add *-ando* for *-ar* verbs and *-iendo* for *-er* and *-ir* verbs.

¿Qué sistema (tipo, género) de computadora tiene Ud.?
keh sees-teh-mah (tee-poh, heh-neh-roh) deh kohm-poo-tah-doh-rahh tee-yeh-neh oo-stehd
What kind of computer do you have?

¿Qué sistema operador usa Ud. (está Ud. usando)?
keh sees-teh-mah oh-peh-rah-dohr oo-sah oo-stehd (ehs-tah oo-stehd oo-sahn-doh)
What operating system are you using?

Mini-Dictionary for Computer Users

Computer Term	Spanish	Pronunciation
access (to access)	el acceso (accesar)	*ehl ahk-seh-soh (ahk-seh-sahr)*
bookmark	la marca	*lah mahr-kah*
boot	arrancar	*ah-rrahn-kahr*
brand name	la marca	*lah mahr-kah*
bug	el error	*ehl eh-rrohr*
byte	el byte, el octeto	*ehl bee-teh, ehl ohk-teh-toh*

continues

Mini-Dictionary for Computer Users (continued)

Computer Term	Spanish	Pronunciation
cartridge	el cartucho	*ehl kahr-too-choh*
laser	de laser	*deh lah-sehr*
ink jet	de tinta	*deh teen-tah*
CD-ROM	el disco optinúmerico	*ehl dees-koh ohp-tee-noo-meh-ree-koh*
click	hacer clic	*ah-sehr kleek*
clone	el clone	*ehl kloh-neh*
compatible	compatible	*kohm-pah-tee-bleh*
computer	la computadora, el ordenadar	*lah kohm-poo-tah-doh-rah, ehl ohr-deh-nah-dahr*
computer science	la informática	*lah een-fohr-mah-tee-kah*
connection	la conexión	*lah koh-nehk-see-yohn*
CPU	la unidad central	*lah oo-nee-dahd sehn-trahl*
cursor	el cursor	*ehl koor-sohr*
cyberspace	el ciberespacio	*ehl see-behr-ehs-pah-see-yoh*
DOS	el sistema disco operante	*ehl sees-teh-mah dees-koh oh-peh-rahn-teh*
database	la base de datos	*lah bah-seh deh dah-tohs*
disk drive	la disquetera	*lah dees-keh-teh-rah*
diskette	el disquete	*ehl dees-keh-teh*
download	bajar, descargar	*bah-hahr, dehs-kahr-gahr*
driver	el piloto	*ehl pee-loh-toh*
drop-down menu	el menúderrama	*ehl meh-noo-deh-rrah-mah*
e-mail	el correo electrónico	*ehl koh-rreh-yoh eh-lehk-troh-nee-koh*
e-mail address	la dirrección de correo electrónico	*lah dee-rehk-see-yohn deh koh-reeh-yoh eh-lehk-troh-nee-koh*
function key	la tecla de función	*lah tehk-lah deh foon-see-yohn*
hacker	el/la pirata	*ehl/lah pee-rah-tah*
hard disk	el disco duro	*ehl dees-koh doo-roh*
home page	la página inicial	*lah pah-hee-nah ee-nee-see-yahl*
icon	el icono	*ehl ee-koh-noh*
insert	insertar	*een-sehr-tahr*

Computer Term	Spanish	Pronunciation
interface	la interfaz	*lah een-tehr-fahs*
Internet	el internet	*ehl een-tehr-neht*
joystick	el joystick, el control	*ehl johy-steek, ehl kohn-trohl*
key	la tecla	*lah tehk-lah*
keyboard	el teclado	*ehl tehk-lah-doh*
laptop computer	la computadora portátil	*lah kohm-poo-tah-doh-rah pohr-tah-teel*
link (to link)	el enlace (enlazar)	*ehl ehn-lah-seh (ehn-lah-sahr)*
memory card	la carta de extensión de memoria	*lah kahr-tah deh ehks-tehn-see-yohn deh meh-moh-ree-yah*
merge	fusionar	*foo-see-yoh-nahr*
modem	el modem	*ehl moh-dehm*
monitor	el monitor	*ehl moh-nee-tohr*
mouse	el ratón	*ehl rrah-tohn*
network	la red	*lah rrehd*
peripherals	los periféricos	*lohs peh-ree-feh-ree-kohs*
public domain	el dominio público	*ehl doh-mee-nee-oh poo-blee-koh*
scan	barrer	*bah-rrehr*
scanner	el scanner	*ehl skah-nehr*
screen	la pantalla	*lah pahn-tah-yah*
search engine	el buscador	*ehl boos-kah-dohr*
server	el servidor	*ehl sehr-bee-dohr*
shareware	los programas compartidos	*lohs proh-grah-mahs kohm-pahr-tee-dohs*
software	el software	*ehl sohft-wehr*
spell checker	el verificador de ortografía	*ehl beh-ree-fee-kah-dohr deh ohr-toh-grah-fee-yah*
spreadsheet	la hoja de cálculo electrónica	*lah oh-hah deh kahl-koo-loh eh-lehk-troh-nee-kah*
word processor	el procesador de textos	*ehl proh-seh-sah-dohr deh tehks-tohs*

Surfing the Net

Whenever I can't seem to find my husband, I just go down to the den. Chances are excellent that he's right there, face glued to the computer screen, eyes glued to the monitor, fingers poised on the keyboard. Although his first love is golf, his newest passion is surfing the net. He spends hours traveling to different countries and collecting information about every subject imaginable. If you care to join him, you can do so in Spanish!

Send Your Business This Way

If you're planning to import or export merchandise to a firm that uses Spanish as its primary language, knowledge of the key words in the following table ought to provide what the average businessperson might need.

Mini-Dictionary for Business People

Business Term	Spanish	Pronunciation
accountant	el contador	*ehl kohn-tah-dohr*
amount	el importe	*ehl eem-pohr-teh*
assets	el activo, los bienes	*ehl ahk-tee-boh, lohs bee-yeh-nehs*
authorize	autorizar	*ow-toh-ree-sahr*
bill	la factura	*lah fahk-too-rah*
bill of sale	el contrato de venta, la escritura de venta	*ehl kohn-trah-toh deh behn-tah, lah ehs-kree-too-rah deh behn-tah*
bookkeeping	la contabilidad	*lah kohn-tah-bee-lee-dahd*
business	los negocios	*lohs neh-goh-see-yohs*
buy	comprar	*kohm-prahr*
buy for cash	pagar al contado	*pah-gahr ahl kohn-tah-doh*
cash a check	cobrar un cheque	*koh-brahr oon cheh-keh*
competitive price	el precio competidor	*ehl preh-see-yoh kohm-peh-tee-dohr*
consumer	el consumidor	*ehl kohn-soo-mee-dohr*
contract	el contrato	*ehl kohn-trah-toh*
credit	el crédito	*ehl kreh-dee-toh*

Business Term	Spanish	Pronunciation
debit	el débito	*ehl deh-bee-toh*
deliver	entregar	*ehn-treh-gahr*
discount	el descuento, la rebaja	*ehl dehs-kwehn-toh, lah rreh-bah-hah*
due	vencido	*ben-see-doh*
expenses	los gastos	*lohs gahs-tohs*
export	exportar	*ehks-pohr-tahr*
foreign trade	el comercio exterior	*ehl koh-mehr-see-yoh ehks-teh-ree-yohr*
goods	los productos	*lohs proh-dook-tohs*
import	importar	*eem-pohr-tahr*
interest rates	los tipos de interés	*lohs tee-pohs deh een-teh-rehs*
invoice	la factura	*lah fahk-too-rah*
management	la gestión	*lah hehs-tee-yohn*
manager	el gerente	*ehl heh-rehn-teh*
merchandise	la mercancía	*lah mehr-kahn-see-yah*
money	el dinero	*ehl dee-neh-roh*
office	la oficina	*lah oh-fee-see-nah*
overhead expenses	los gastos generales	*lohs gahs-tohs heh-neh-rah-lehs*
owner	el propietario	*ehl proh-pee-yeh-tah-ree-yoh*
package	el paquete	*ehl pah-keh-teh*
partner	el socio	*ehl soh-see-yoh*
payment	el pago	*ehl pah-goh*
percent	por ciento	*pohr see-yehn-toh*
producer	el productor	*ehl proh-dook-tohr*
property	la propiedad	*lah pro-pee-yeh-dahd*
purchase	la compra	*lah kohm-prah*
retailer	el minorista	*ehl mee-noh-rees-tah*
sale	la venta	*lah behn-tah*
sample	la muestra	*lah mwehs-trah*
selling price	el precio de venta	*ehl preh-see-yoh deh behn-tah*
send	mandar	*mahn-dahr*

continues

Mini-Dictionary for Business People (continued)

Business Term	Spanish	Pronunciation
send back	devolver	*deh-bohl-behr*
send C.O.D.	mandar contra reembolso	*mahn-dahr kohn-trah rreh-yehm-bohl-soh*
settle	arreglar	*ah-rreh-glahr*
shipment	el envío	*ehl ehn-bee-yoh*
tax	el impuesto	*ehl eem-pwehs-toh*
tax-exempt	libre de impuestos	*lee-breh deh eem-pwehs-tohs*
trade	el comercio	*ehl koh-mehr-see-yoh*
transact business	hacer negocios	*ah-sehr neh-goh-see-yohs*
value-added tax	el impuesto sobre el valor añadido	*ehl eem-pwehs-toh soh-breh ehl bah-lohr ah-nyah-dee-doh*
wholesaler	el mayorista	*ehl mah-yoh-rees-tah*

What's in Store for the Future

A successful businessperson looks toward the future and prepares for it wisely. In Spanish, the future can be expressed in one of these three ways:

◆ Use a present tense form of the verb, usually in conjunction with other words that show the future is implied:

¿Qué vuelo llega esta noche?
keh bweh-loh yeh-gah ehs-tah noh-cheh
What flight is arriving tonight?

◆ Use the irregular verb *ir* + *a* + infinitive. Because the verb *ir* means "to go," it is understandable that it is used to express what the speaker is going to do. Because "to go" is the first verb, it must be conjugated. The action that the speaker is going to perform is expressed by the infinitive of the verb:

Memory Master

To refresh your memory, here's the present tense conjugation of *ir:*

yo voy	nosotros vamos
tú vas	vosotros vaís
él, ella, Ud. va	ellos, ellas, Uds. van

Voy a ir al centro.
boy ah eer ahl sehn-troh
I'm going to go to the city.

Ellos van a echar (mandar) la carta al correo.
eh-yohs bahn ah eh-chahr (mahn-dahr) lah kahr-tah ahl koh-rreh-yoh
They are going to send the letter.

The Future Tense

The future also can be expressed by changing the verb to the future tense. The future tense tells what the subject will do or what action will take place in the future. The future tense of regular verbs can be formed by adding the future endings to the infinitive of the verb.

Verb	Future Stem	Verb Conjugation	Pronunciation
hablar	hablar	yo hablar**é**	*ah-blah-reh*
		tú hablar**ás**	*ah-blah-rahs*
		él, ella, Ud. hablar**á**	*ah-blah-rah*
		nosotros hablar**emos**	*ah-blah-reh-mohs*
		vosotros hablar**éis**	*ah-blah-rah-yees*
		ellos, ellas, Uds. hablar**án**	*ah-blah-rahn*
vender	vender	yo vender**é**	*behn-deh-reh*
		tú vender**ás**	*behn-deh-rahs*
		él, ella, Ud. vender**á**	*behn-deh-rah*
		nosotros vender**emos**	*behn-deh-reh-mohs*
		vosotros vender**éis**	*behn-deh-reh-yees*
		ellos, ellas, Uds. vender**án**	*behn-deh-rahn*
abrir	abrir	yo abrir**é**	*ah-bree-reh*
		tú abrir**ás**	*ah-bree-rahs*
		él, ella, Ud. abrir**á**	*ah-bree-rah*
		nosotros abrir**emos**	*ah-bree-reh-mohs*
		vosotros abrir**éis**	*ah-bree-reh-yees*
		ellos, ellas, Uds. abrir**án**	*ah-bree-rahn*

Yo hablaré con mis amigos mañana.
yoh ah-blah-reh kohn mees ah-mee-gohs mah-nyah-nah
I will speak with my friends tomorrow.

Nosotros no venderemos nuestra casa.
noh-soh-trohs noh behn-deh-reh-mohs nwehs-trah kah-sah
We will not sell our house.

¿Abrirán Uds. una cuenta?
ah-bree-rahn oo-steh-dehs oo-nah kwehn-tah
Will you open an account?

The Future Tense of Irregular Verbs

Some verbs form the future tense by dropping the *e* from the infinitive ending and adding the future endings previously mentioned.

Infinitive	Future Stem	Future Endings
caber (to fit)	cabr-	-é, -ás, -á, -emos, -éis, -án
poder (to be able)	podr-	
querer (to want)	querr-	
saber (to know)	sabr-	

For some verbs, the *e* or *i* is dropped from the infinitive ending and is replaced by a *d*. The future endings are then added.

Infinitive	Future Stem	Future Endings
poner (to put)	pondr-	-é, -ás, -á, -emos, -éis, -án
salir (to leave)	saldr-	
tener (to have)	tendr-	
valer (to be worth)	valdr-	
venir (to come)	vendr-	

The verbs *decir* and *hacer* also are irregular, as shown in the following table.

Infinitive	Future Stem	Future Endings
decir (to say)	dir-	-é, -ás, -á, -emos, -éis, -án
hacer (to make, to do)	har-	

In the Future

Express what will happen in the future:

1. (valer) Mi casa _____ un millón de dólares.

2. (tener) Tú _____ que ir en España.

3. (querer) Yo _____ aprender el italiano.

4. (hacer) Nosotros _____ un viaje en Europa.

5. (venir) Mis primos _____ a mi casa.

6. (poder) Vosotros _____ comprar un coche nuevo.

Answer Key

In the Future

1. valdrá

2. tendrás

3. querré

4. haremos

5. vendrán

6. podréis

Chapter 25

Renting a Villa

In This Chapter

- Apartments and houses
- Rooms, furnishings, amenities, and appliances
- Tips on using the conditional tense

Although you love the luxury of a well-appointed hotel, it might not prove to be cost effective for you in the long run. You might want to purchase or rent a place to stay instead. Why not consider an apartment, a house, a condominium, or even a piece of time-share property? Should you make this decision, this chapter will teach you how to get the furnishings, appliances, and amenities you want and need. You'll also learn how to express what you would do in certain circumstances by using the conditional.

I Want to Live in a Castle

Renting or buying a piece of real estate in a Spanish-speaking country is becoming more and more popular. If you've decided you're ready to escape the rat race and are looking for a change of scenery, you'll want to be able to pick up the real estate section of a Spanish newspaper and understand what the ads offer. You'll also want to be able to discuss the ad with the owner or real estate agent. Do you want cathedral ceilings? A two-car garage? A fireplace? What makes your home your castle? The following table, which lists the various features people look for in a home, will prepare you for your big move. Use the verb *necesito* (*neh-seh-see-toh;* I need) to express what you want.

The House, the Apartment, the Rooms

Stuff for Your Home	Spanish	Pronunciation
air conditioning (central)	el aire acondicionado (central)	*ehl ah-yee-reh ah-kohn-dee-see-yoh-nah-doh (sehn-trahl)*
apartment	el apartamento	*ehl ah-pahr-tah-mehn-toh*
appliances	los aparatos eléctricos	*lohs ah-pah-rah-tohs eh-lehk-tree-kohs*
attic	el ático, el entretecho	*ehl ah-tee-koh, ehl ehn-treh-teh-choh*
backyard	el jardín	*ehl hahr-deen*
balcony	el balcón	*ehl bahl-kohn*
basement	el sótano	*ehl soh-tah-noh*
bathroom	el cuarto de baño	*ehl kwahr-toh deh bah-nyoh*
bedroom	el dormitorio	*ehl dohr-mee-toh-ree-yoh*
cathedral ceiling	el vacío catedral	*ehl bah-see-yoh kah-teh-drahl*
ceiling	el techo	*ehl teh-choh*
closet	el armario	*ehl ahr-mah-ree-yoh*
courtyard	el patio	*ehl pah-tee-yoh*
den	el estudio	*ehl ehs-too-dee-yoh*
dining room	el comedor	*ehl koh-meh-dohr*
elevator	el ascensor	*ehl ah-sehn-sohr*
family room	la sala de estar	*lah sah-lah deh ehs-tahr*
fireplace	la chimenea	*lah chee-meh-neh-yah*
floor	el suelo	*ehl sweh-loh*
floor (story)	el piso	*ehl pee-soh*
garage	el garaje	*ehl gah-rah-heh*
ground floor	la planta baja	*lah plahn-tah bah-hah*

Stuff for Your Home	Spanish	Pronunciation
hallway	el pasillo	*ehl pah-see-yoh*
heating	la calefacción	*lah kah-leh-fahk-see-yohn*
electric	eléctrica	*eh-lehk-tree-kah*
gas	a gas	*ah gahs*
kitchen	la cocina	*lah koh-see-nah*
laundry room	la lavandería	*lah lah-bahn-deh-ree-yah*
lease	el contrato de arrendamiento	*ehl kohn-trah-toh deh ah-rrehn-dah-mee-yehn-toh*
living room	la sala	*lah sah-lah*
maintenance	el mantenimiento	*ehl mahn-teh-nee-mee-yehn-toh*
owner	el dueño	*ehl dweh-nyoh*
rent	el alquiler	*ehl ahl-kee-lehr*
roof	el techo	*ehl teh-choh*
room	el cuarto, la habitación	*ehl kwahr-toh, lah ah-bee-tah-see-yohn*
security deposit	la fianza, la garantía	*lah fee-yahn-sah, lah gah-rahn-tee-yah*
shower	la ducha	*lah doo-chah*
staircase	la escalera	*lah ehs-kah-leh-rah*
terrace	la terraza	*lah teh-rrah-sah*
window	la ventana	*lah behn-tah-nah*

Be It Ever So Humble

You don't cook, so a microwave is a must. How else will you be able to heat up leftovers? You're not in the habit of hanging laundry out on a line—a washer/dryer combination must be available to you. Can you live without a television? What furniture do you need? Before you rent or buy a piece of property, it's always wise to find out what is included. Consult the following table for the names of pieces of furniture you might want. Use *Hay ...?* (*ah-yee;* Is [Are] there ...?) to ask your questions.

Furniture and Accessories

Furniture and Accessories	Spanish	Pronunciation
armchair	el sillón	*ehl see-yohn*
bed	la cama	*lah kah-mah*
bookcase	la estantería	*lah ehs-tahn-teh-ree-yah*
carpet	la moqueta	*lah moh-keh-tah*
chair	la silla	*lah see-yah*
clock	el reloj	*ehl rreh-loh*
curtains	las cortinas	*lahs kohr-tee-nahs*
dishwasher	el lavaplatos	*ehl lah-bah-plah-tohs*
dresser	la cómoda	*lah koh-moh-dah*
dryer	la secadora	*lah seh-kah-doh-rah*
DVD player	el lector (de) DVD	*ehl lehk-tohr (deh) deh-beh-deh*
freezer	el congelador	*ehl kohn-heh-lah-dohr*
furniture	los muebles	*lohs mweh-blehs*
home appliances	los aparatos eléctricos	*lohs ah-pah-rah-tohs eh-lehk-tree-kohs*
lamp	la lámpara	*lah lahm-pah-rah*
mirror	el espejo	*ehl ehs-peh-hoh*
oven	el horno	*ehl ohr-noh*
refrigerator	el refrigerador	*ehl rreh-free-heh-rah-dohr*
rug	la alfombra	*lah ahl-fohm-brah*
sofa	el sofá	*ehl soh-fah*
stove	la estufa	*lah ehs-too-fah*
table	la mesa	*lah meh-sah*
television (large screen)	el televisor (con pantalla grande)	*ehl teh-leh-bee-sohr (kohn pahn-tah-yah grahn-deh)*
VCR	el VCR la video casete de grabadora	*ehl bee-cee-ahr lah bee-deh-yoh kah-seht-teh deh grah-bah-doh-rah*
washing machine	la lavadora	*lah lah-bah-doh-rah*

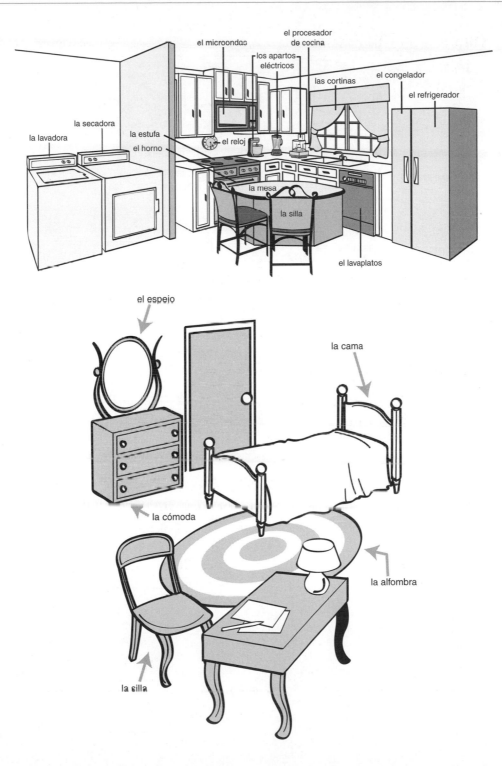

Are You Buying or Renting?

Do you have any questions? Of course you do. That's normal when you rent or buy a piece of property. To express your preferences or questions, use the following phrases to help you get exactly what you want:

Busco …
boos-koh
I'm looking for …

los anuncios clasificados
lohs ah-noon-see-yohs klah-see-fee-kah-dohs
the classified ads

los bienes raíces
lohs bee-yeh-nehs rrah-yee-sehs
the real estate section (of the newspaper) section

una agencia inmobiliaria
oo-nah ah-hehn-see-ya heen-moh-bee-lee-yah-ree-yah
a real estate agency

Quisiera alquilar (comprar) …
kee-see-yeh-rah ahl-kee-lahr (kohm-prahr)
I would like to rent (buy) …

un apartamento
oon ah-pahr-tah-mehn-toh
an apartment

una casa
oo-nah kah-sah
a house

un condominio
oon kohn-doh-mee-nee-yoh
a condominium

¿Cuánto es el alquiler?
kwahn-toh ehs ehl ahl-kee-lehr
What is the rent?

¿Cuántos son los gastos de mantenimiento del
apartamento (de la casa)?
kwahn-tohs sohn lohs gahs-tohs deh mahn-teh-nee-mee-yehn-toh dehl
ah-pahr-tah-mehn-toh (deh lah kah-sah)
How much is the maintenance of the apartment (house)?

¿Está incluído(a) el gas (la calefacción,
la electricidad)?
ehs-tah een-kloo-wee-doh(dah) ehl gahs (lah kah-leh-fahk-see-yohn,
lah eh-lehk-tree-see-dahd)
Is the gas (heat, electricity) included?

¿De cuántos son las mensualidades?
deh kwahn-tohs sohn lahs mehn-soo-wah-lee-dah-dehs
How much are the monthly payments?

Quisiera pedir una hipoteca.
kee-see-yeh-rah peh-deer oo-nah ee-poh-teh-kah
I'd like to apply for a mortgage.

¿Tengo que dejar un depósito?
tehn-goh keh deh-hahr oon deh-poh-see-toh
Do I have to leave a deposit?

What Are Your Needs?

Suppose you're looking for a permanent place to stay in a Spanish-speaking country. Are the number of bathrooms and bedrooms important to you? Do you plan to cook and require a modern kitchen? Do you need a two-car garage? Tell the real estate agent exactly what would make you happy.

These Are the Conditions

Would you prefer to live in the city or on the beach? Would you rather take possession of a furnished or unfurnished property? How about a swimming pool? The conditional is a mood in Spanish that expresses what the speaker would do or what would happen under certain circumstances. The subjunctive of the verb *querer* (see Chapter 26) or the conditional of the verb *gustar* are frequently used to express what the speaker would like.

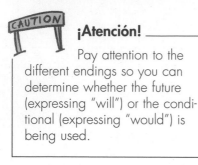

¡Atención!

Pay attention to the different endings so you can determine whether the future (expressing "will") or the conditional (expressing "would") is being used.

Quisiera (Me gustaría) alquilar
una casa.
kee-see-yeh-rah (meh goos-tah-ree-yah) ahl-kee-lahr
oo-nah kah-sah
I would like to rent a house.

Forming the Conditional

The conditional is formed with the same stem used to form the future tense, whether you're using a regular or irregular verb. The endings for the conditional, however, are different. They are exactly the same as the *-er* and *-ir* verb endings for the imperfect tense. To form the conditional, start with the future stem and add the imperfect endings shown in the following table.

Verb	Conditional Stem	Conditional Endings	Pronunciation
hablar	hablar	-ía	*ee-yah*
vender	vender	-ías	*ee-yahs*
abrir	abrir	-ía	*ee-yah*
		-íamos	*ee-yah-mohs*
		-íais	*ee-ah-yees*
		-ían	*ee-yahn*

Yo le hablaría.
yoh leh ah-blah-ree-yah
I would speak to him (her).

Nosotros no venderíamos
nuestro coche a ningún precio.
noh-soh-trohs noh behn-deh-ree-yah-mohs
nwehs-troh koh-cheh ah neen-goon preh-see-yoh
We would not sell our car at any price.

¿Abrirían Uds. una cuenta
conjunta?
ah-bree-ree-yahn oo-steh-dehs oo-nah kwehn-tah
kohn-hoon-tah
Would you open a joint account?

<table>
<tr><th colspan="2">Memory Master</th></tr>
<tr><td colspan="2">The conditional endings are the same for all verbs whether they belong to the -ar, -er, or -ir family or are irregular. You will also notice that all the conditional endings have accents.</td></tr>
</table>

The Conditional of Irregular Verbs

Some verbs form the conditional by dropping the *e* from the infinitive ending and adding the conditional endings shown in the following table.

Infinitive	Conditional Stem	Conditional Endings
caber (to fit)	cabr-	-ía
poder (to be able)	podr-	-ías
querer (to want)	querr-	-ía
saber (to know)	sabr-	-íamos
		-íais
		-ían

For some verbs, the *e* or *i* is dropped from the infinitive ending and is replaced with a *d*. The conditional endings are then added.

Infinitive	Conditional Stem	Conditional Endings
poner (to put)	pondr-	-ía
salir (to leave)	saldr-	-ías
tener (to have)	tendr-	-ía
valer (to be worth)	valdr-	-íamos
venir (to come)	vendr-	-íais
		-ían

The verbs *decir* and *hacer* are irregular, as shown in the following table.

Infinitive	Conditional Stem	Conditional Endings
decir (to say)	dir-	-ía
hacer (to make, to do)	har-	-ías
		-ía
		-íamos
		-íais
		-ían

What Would You Do?

I think everyone dreams of winning the lottery, especially when the stakes are high. What would you do with $25 million? I bet you can rattle off a list of things immediately. Do you have visions of a fancy sports car, luxurious world-wide travel, and a beautiful home with every possible amenity? Make a list of everything you would do if you won *la lotería* (*lah loh-teh-ree-yah*) tomorrow.

Answer Key

What Are Your Needs?

Sample responses:

> Quisiera una casa grande amueblada con tres habitaciones, una terraza, un garaje, y una piscina. ¿Qué aparatos elécticos hay? Necesitamos un refrigerador, un microondas, una lavadora y una secadora.

What Would You Do?

Sample responses:

> Yo me compraría un nuevo coche deportivo y una casa muy grande. Yo daría mucho dinero a los pobres. Yo viajaría por todo el mundo. Yo iría a España con toda mi familia. Yo no trabajaría.

Chapter 26

It's a Question of Money

In This Chapter

- ◆ Learn banking terms
- ◆ The subjunctive

You're now prepared for an extended stay in a Spanish-speaking country. In Chapter 25, you learned the necessary words to buy or rent new living quarters and to get the facilities you want to live the good life. This could mean a dining area to accommodate all your business staff or a backyard with an in-ground pool.

This chapter should be helpful to anyone who has to make a trip to the bank: tourists who want to change money, a businessperson seeking financial assistance, an investor in foreign affairs, or a potential home buyer. Here you will also learn how to use the subjunctive to express your special wants, needs, and desires.

Remember to bring along your passport; it's the only acceptable form of identification in banks.

At the Bank

People visiting a foreign country might stop in a bank for many reasons. Because banks reputedly give good exchange rates, they often attract tourists who want to change their money to local currency. People with more far-reaching goals might want to establish credit and set up savings and checking accounts. Others might seek to purchase land, real estate, or a business. If you fit into any of these categories, you'll find the phrases in the following table quite useful.

Mini-Dictionary of Banking Terms

Banking Term	Spanish	Pronunciation
advance payment	el pago adelantado	*ehl pah-goh ah-deh-lahn-tah-doh*
automatic teller machine	el cajero automático	*ehl kah-heh-roh ow-toh-mah-tee-koh*
balance	el saldo	*ehl sahl-doh*
bank	el banco	*ehl bahn-koh*
bank account	la cuenta bancaria	*lah kwehn-tah bahn-kah-ree-yah*
bankbook	la cartilla de ahorros, la libreta de ahorros	*lah kahr-tee-yah deh ah-oh-rrohs, lah lee-breh-tah deh ah-oh-rrohs*
bill	la factura	*lah fahk-too-rah*
borrow	pedir prestado	*peh-deer prehs-tah-doh*
branch	la sucursal	*lah soo-koor-sahl*
cash	el dinero en efectivo	*ehl dee-neh-roh ehn eh-fehk-tee-boh*
to cash	cobrar	*koh-brahr*
cashier	el cajero	*ehl kah-heh-roh*
change (transaction)	el cambio	*ehl kahm-bee-yoh*
check	el cheque	*ehl cheh-keh*
checkbook	la chequera	*lah cheh-keh-rah*
checking account	la cuenta corriente	*lah kwehn-tah koh-rree-yehn-teh*
coin	la moneda	*lah moh-neh-dah*
deposit	el depósito, el ingreso	*ehl deh-poh-see-toh, ehl een-greh-soh*
endorse	endosar	*ehn-doh-sahr*
exchange rate	el tipo de cambio	*ehl tee-poh deh kahm-bee-yoh*

Banking Term	Spanish	Pronunciation
fill out	llenar	*yeh-nahr*
interest	el interés	*ehl een-teh-rehs*
simple	simple	*seem-pleh*
compound	compuesto	*kohm-pwehs-toh*
interest rate	la tasa (el tipo) de interés	*lah tah-sah (ehl tee-poh) deh een-teh-rehs*
invest	invertir	*een-behr-teer*
investment	la inversión	*lah een-behr-see-yohn*
loan	el préstamo	*ehl preh-stah-moh*
manage	administrar, manejar	*ahd-mee-nees-trahr, mah-neh-hahr*
money exchange bureau	el departamento de intercambio	*ehl deh-pahr-tah-mehn-toh deh een-tehr-kahm-bee-yoh*
monthly statement	el extracto de cuenta	*ehl ehks-trahk-toh deh kwehn-tah*
mortgage	la hipoteca	*lah ee-poh-teh-kah*
pay cash	pagar en efectivo	*pah-gahr ehn eh-fehk-tee-boh*
payment	el pago	*ehl pah-goh*
percentage	el porcentaje	*ehl pohr-sehn-tah-heh*
receipt	el recibo	*ehl rreh-see-boh*
safe	la caja fuerte	*lah kah-hah fwehr-teh*
save	ahorrar	*ah-oh-rrahr*
savings account	la cuenta de ahorros	*lah kwehn-tah deh ah-oh-rrohs*
sign (to)	firmar	*feer-mahr*
signature	la firma	*lah feer-mah*
teller	el cajero	*ehl kah-heh-roh*
traveler's check	el cheque de viajero	*ehl cheh-keh deh bee-yah-heh-roh*
window	la ventanilla	*lah behn-tah-nee-yah*
withdraw	sacar, retirar	*sah-kahr, rreh-tee-rahr*

Things I Need to Do

If you're planning a trip to the bank, the phrases in this section will be helpful in common, everyday banking situations: making deposits and withdrawals, opening a checking account, or taking out a loan.

¿Cuál es el horario de trabajo?
kwahl ehs ehl oh-rah-ree-yoh deh trah-bah-hoh
What are the banking hours?

Express your wishes by using "*Quisiera …*" with any of the following phrases:

Quisiera …
kee-see-yeh-rah
I would like …

hacer un depósito
ah-sehr oon deh-poh-see-toh
to make a deposit

cobrar un cheque
koh-brahr oon cheh-keh
to cash a check

hacer un retiro
ah-sehr oon rreh-tee-roh
to make a withdrawal

abrir una cuenta
ah-breer oo-nah kwehn-tah
to open an account

hacer un pago
ah-sehr oon pah-goh
to make a payment

liquidar una cuenta
lee-kee-dahr oo-nah kwehn-tah
to close an account

pedir un préstamo
peh-deer oon prehs-tah-moh
to apply for a loan

cambiar divisas
kahm-bee-yahr dee-bee-sahs
to change some foreign money

Other helpful phrases you can use at a bank include the following:

¿Cuál es la tasa (el tipo) de cambio del dólar hoy?
kwahl ehs lah tah-sah (ehl tee-poh) deh kahm-bee-yoh dehl doh-lahr oh-yee
What is today's exchange rate for the dollar?

¿Tiene un cajero automático?
tee-yeh-neh oon kah-heh-roh ow-toh-mah-tee-koh
Do you have an automatic teller machine?

Quisiera hacer un préstamo personal.
kee-see-yeh-rah ah-sehr oon prehs-tah-moh pehr-soh-nahl
I'd like to take out a personal loan.

¿Cuál es el plazo del préstamo?
kwahl ehs ehl plah-soh dehl prehs-tah-moh
What is the time period of the loan?

¿De cuánto son las mensualidades?
Deh kwahn-toh sohn lahs mehn-soo-wah-lee-dah-dehs
How much are the monthly payments?

¿Cuál es la tasa (el tipo) de interés?
kwahl ehs lah tah-sah (ehl tee-poh) deh een-teh-rehs
What is the interest rate?

What Are Your Needs?

If you're like me, no matter how much money you have, you always need just a little bit more to tide you over. In Spanish, you can express need in two ways.

Need can be expressed using *tener* (conjugated) + *que* + verb (infinitive):

Yo tengo que ir al centro.   Nosotros tenemos que partir.
I have to go downtown.   We have to leave.

You can also express need using the expression *Es necesario que* … (*ehs neh-seh-sah-ree-yoh keh*; It is necessary that …"). This and other expressions showing necessity are followed by a special verb form called the subjunctive.

The Moody Subjunctive

The subjunctive is a mood, not a tense, and it expresses wishing, wanting, emotion, and doubt. It is used after many expressions showing uncertainty. Because the subjunctive is not a tense (a verb form indicating time), the present subjunctive can be used to refer to actions in the present or in the future.

To use the subjunctive, the following conditions must be met:

- Two different clauses must exist with two different subjects.

- The two clauses must be joined by *que*.

- One of the clauses must show need, necessity, emotion, or doubt:

    Es necesario que yo hable con mi amigo.
    ehs neh-seh-sah-ree-yoh keh yoh ah-bleh kohn mee ah-mee-goh
    I (I'll) have to speak to my friend.

Es necesario que nosotros vendamos nuestra casa.
ehs neh-seh-sah-ree-yoh keh noh-soh-trohs behn-dah-mohs nwehs-trah kah-sah
We (We'll) have to sell our house.

Es necesario que Uds. abran una cuenta de ahorros.
ehs neh-seh-sah-ree-yoh keh oo-steh-dehs ah-brahn oo-nah kwehn-tah deh ah-oh-rrohs
You (You'll) have to open a savings account.

Forming the Regular Subjunctive

To form the present subjunctive of regular verbs, drop the *-o* ending from the *yo* form in the present tense and add the opposite endings. All *-ar* verbs change present tense *a* to *e*, and *-er* and *-ir* verbs change present tense *e* or *i* to *a*, as shown in the following table. (This is just like the command form you learned in Chapter 10.)

The Present Subjunctive of Regular Verbs

-*ar* **Verbs**	
Hablar	
que yo habl**e**	que nosotros habl**emos**
que tú habl**es**	que vosotros habl**éis**
que él (ella, Ud.) habl**e**	que ellos (ellas, Uds.) habl**en**

-*er* **Verbs**	
Vender	
que yo vend**a**	que nosotros vend**amos**
que tú vend**as**	que vosotros vend**áis**
que él (ella, Ud.) vend**a**	que ellos (ellas, Uds.) vend**an**

-*ir* **Verbs**	
Abrir	
que yo abr**a**	que nosotros abr**amos**
que tú abr**as**	que vosotros abr**áis**
que él (ella, Ud.) abr**a**	que ellos (ellas, Uds.) abr**an**

Irregular Verbs in the Subjunctive

Because the subjunctive is formed by dropping the *–o* ending from the *yo* form of the verb, verbs whose *yo* form is irregular will also have irregular subjunctive forms, to which the proper subjunctive endings are then added, as shown in the following table.

The Infinitive	*Yo* Form	Subjunctive Stem	Subjunctive Endings (The Same for All)
conocer (to know)	conozco	conozc-	-a, -as, -a, -amos, -áis, -an
decir (to say)	digo	dig-	
hacer (to make, to do)	hago	hag-	
oír (to hear)	oigo	oig-	
poner (to put)	pongo	pong-	
salir (to go out)	salgo	salg-	
traer (to bring)	traigo	traig-	
venir (to come)	vengo	veng-	

Spelling Change Verbs in the Present Subjunctive

Verbs ending in *-car*, *-gar*, and *-zar* have the following changes in the present subjunctive to maintain the proper pronunciation:

♦ For *-car* verbs, *c* changes to *qu* in all forms of the subjunctive and *a* changes to *e* in the ending:

Buscar (to look for)	
que yo busque	que nosotros busquemos
que tú busques	que vosotros busquéis
que él (ella, Ud.) busque	que ellos (ellas, Uds.) busquen

♦ For *-gar* verbs, *g* changes to *gu* in all forms of the subjunctive and *a* changes to *e* in the ending:

Pagar (to pay)	
que yo pague	que nosotros paguemos
que tú pagues	que vosotros paguéis
que él (ella, Ud.) pague	que ellos (ellas, Uds.) paguen

◆ For *-zar* verbs, *z* changes to *c* in all forms of the subjunctive and *a* changes to *e* in the ending:

Cruzar (to cross)	
que yo cruce	que nosotros crucemos
que tú cruces	que vosotros crucéis
que él (ella, Ud.) cruce	que ellos (ellas, Uds.) crucen

Stem-Changing Verbs in the Present Subjunctive

For verbs ending in *-ar* and *-er*, the same change occurs in the stem vowel in the subjunctive that occurs in the stem vowel in the present tense (see Chapter 12). The stem vowel does not change in the *nosotros* and *vosotros* forms. To form the present subjunctive of regular verbs, drop *o* from the *yo* form of the present and add opposite verb endings: *-ar* verbs change present tense *a* to *e*; *-er* and *-ir* verbs change present tense *e* or *i* to *a*.

pensar *(to think)*

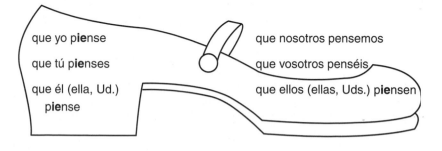

que yo p**ie**nse — que nosotros pensemos

que tú p**ie**nses — que vosotros penséis

que él (ella, Ud.) p**ie**nse — que ellos (ellas, Uds.) p**ie**nsen

volver *(to turn)*

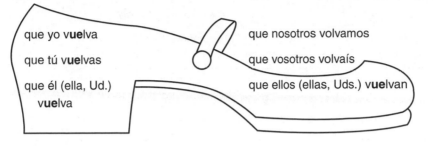

que yo **vue**lva   que nosotros vol**vamos**

que tú **vue**lvas   que vosotros vol**váis**

que él (ella, Ud.)   que ellos (ellas, Uds.) **vue**lvan
  vuelva

For verbs ending in *-ir*, the same change occurs in the stem vowel in the subjunctive that occurs in the stem vowel in the present tense (again, see Chapter 12). Additionally, the stem vowel changes from *e* to *i* or from *o* to *u* in the *nosotros* and *vosotros* forms. Remember to change to the opposite vowel in the ending for the subjunctive (*-ir* verbs change *e* or *i* to *a*):

sentir *(to feel)*

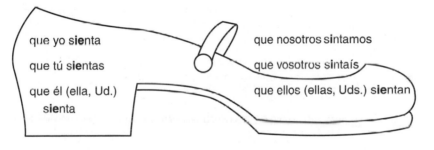

que yo **sie**nta   que nosotros sin**tamos**

que tú **sie**ntas   que vosotros sin**táis**

que él (ella, Ud.)   que ellos (ellas, Uds.) **sie**ntan
  sienta

dormir *(to sleep)*

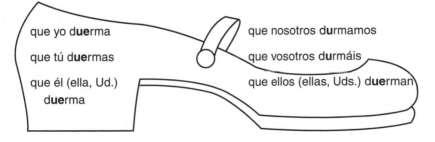

que yo **due**rma   que nosotros dur**mamos**

que tú **due**rmas   que vosotros dur**máis**

que él (ella, Ud.)   que ellos (ellas, Uds.) **due**rman
  duerma

pedir *(to ask)*

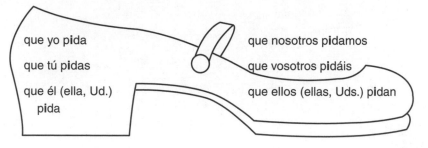

que yo pida	que nosotros pidamos
que tú pidas	que vosotros pidáis
que él (ella, Ud.) pida	que ellos (ellas, Uds.) pidan

Some verbs ending in *-iar* and *-uar* (see Chapter 12) require an accent on the *i* (*í*) and the *u* (*ú*) in all forms of the subjunctive except *nosotros* and *vosotros*. In the *vosotros* form, the *e* of the subjunctive ending takes the accent.

Guiar (to guide)	
que yo guíe	que nosotros guiemos
que tú guíes	que vosotros guiéis
que él (ella, Ud.) guíe	que ellos (ellas, Uds.) guíen

Continuar (to continue)	
que yo continúe	que nosotros continuemos
que tú continúes	que vosotros continuéis
que él (ella, Ud.) continúe	que ellos (ellas, Uds.) continúen

Highly Irregular Verbs

Some verbs follow no rules and must be memorized. The most useful of such verbs are listed in the following tables.

Dar (to give)	
que yo dé	que nosotros demos
que tú des	que vosotros deis
que él (ella, Ud.) dé	que ellos (ellas, Uds.) den

Estar (to be)

que yo esté	que nosotros estemos
que tú estés	que vosotros estéis
que él (ella, Ud.) esté	que ellos (ellas, Uds.) estén

_Ir_ (to go)

que yo vaya	que nosotros vayamos
que tú vayas	que vosotros vayáis
que él (ella, Ud.) vaya	que ellos (ellas, Uds.) vayan

Saber (to know)

que yo sepa	que nosotros sepamos
que tú sepas	que vosotros sepáis
que él (ella, Ud.) sepa	que ellos (ellas, Uds.) sepan

Ser (to be)

que yo sea	que nosotros seamos
que tú seas	que vosotros seáis
que él (ella, Ud.) sea	que ellos (ellas, Uds.) sean

So Much to Do, So Little Time

I have a million things to do today; I bet you do, too. A great way to escape the hassles and obligations of your daily routine is to go on vacation. When you return, however, it's back to the grind. Describe what the following people have to do using _tener que_ + infinitive and then _es necesario que_ + subjunctive:

Example: él/trabajar
Él tiene que trabajar.
Es necesario que él trabaje.

1. nosotros/preparar la cena
2. ella/aprender el español
3. ellos/vivir en Puerto Rico
4. yo/cerrar esa cuenta
5. vosotros/no perder su cartera
6. tú/no mentir
7. Ud./no dormir tarde
8. él/pedir la cuenta

Impersonal Expressions

Es necesario que is a common expression used with the subjunctive. The following table lists some other common impersonal expressions that require the subjunctive.

Phrase	Pronunciation	Meaning
Es aconsejable que	*ehs ah-kohn-seh-hah-bleh keh*	It is advisable that
Es bueno que	*ehs bweh-noh keh*	It is good that
Es difícil que	*ehs dee-fee-seel keh*	It is difficult that
Es dudoso que	*ehs doo-doh-soh keh*	It is doubtful that
Es fácil que	*ehs fah-seel keh*	It is easy that
Es importante que	*ehs eem-pohr-tahn-teh keh*	It is important that
Es imposible que	*ehs eem-poh-see-bleh keh*	It is impossible that
Es increíble que	*ehs een-kreh-yee-bleh keh*	It is incredible that
Es indispensable que	*ehs een-dees-pehn-sah-bleh keh*	It is indispensable that
Es malo que	*ehs mah-loh keh*	It is bad that
Es mejor que	*ehs meh-hohr keh*	It is better that
Es posible que	*ehs poh-see-bleh keh*	It is possible that
Es preciso que	*ehs preh-see-soh keh*	It is essential that
Es probable que	*ehs proh-bah-bleh keh*	It is probable that
Es una lástima que	*ehs oo-nah lahs-tee-mah keh*	It is a pity that
Más vale que	*mahs bah-leh keh*	It is better that

Answer Key

So Much to Do, So Little Time

1. Nosotros tenemos que preparar …
   Es necesario que preparemos …

2. Ella tiene que aprender …
   Es necesario que aprenda …

3. Ellos tienen que vivir …
   Es necesario que vivan …

4. Yo tengo que cerrar …
   Es necesario que cierre …

5. Vosotros no tenéis que perder …
   Es necesario que no perdáis …

6. Tú no tienes que mentir.
   Es necesario que no mientas.

7. Ud. no tiene que dormir …
   Es necesario que no duerma …

8. El tiene que pedir …
   Es necesario que no pida …

Verb Charts

Regular Verbs

-*ar* Verbs

USAR **to use** Gerund: usando Past participle: usado Commands: ¡Use Ud.! ¡Usen Uds.! ¡Usemos!

Present (do)	Preterit (did)	Imperfect (was)	Future (will)	Conditional (would)
uso	usé	usaba	usaré	usaría
usas	usaste	usabas	usarás	usarías
usa	usó	usaba	usará	usaría
usamos	usamos	usábamos	usaremos	usaríamos
usáis	usasteis	usabais	usaréis	usaríais
usan	usaron	usaban	usarán	usarían

-er Verbs

COMER to eat Gerund: comiendo Past participle: comido Commands: ¡Coma Ud.! ¡Coman Uds.! ¡Comamos!

Present	Preterit	Imperfect	Future	Conditional
como	comí	comía	comeré	comería
comes	comiste	comías	comerás	comerías
come	comió	comía	comerá	comería
comemos	comimos	comíamos	comeremos	comeríamos
coméis	comisteis	comíais	comeréis	comeríais
comen	comieron	comían	comerán	comerían

-ir Verbs

VIVIR to live Gerund: viviendo Past participle: vivido Commands: ¡Viva Ud.! ¡Vivan Uds.! ¡Vivamos!

Present	Preterit	Imperfect	Future	Conditional
vivo	viví	vivía	viviré	viviría
vives	viviste	vivías	vivirás	vivirías
vive	vivió	vivía	vivirá	viviría
vivimos	vivimos	vivíamos	viviremos	viviríamos
vivís	vivisteis	vivíais	viviréis	viviríais
viven	vivieron	vivían	vivirán	vivirían

Stem-Changing Verbs

-ar Verbs

PENSAR (e to ie)   to think
Present: pienso, piensas, piensa, pensamos, pensáis, piensan
Other verbs like pensar include cerrar (to close), comenzar (to begin), and empezar (to begin).

MOSTRAR (o to ue)   to show
Present: m**ue**stro, m**ue**stras, m**ue**stra, mostramos, mostráis, m**ue**stran
Other verbs like mostrar include almorzar (to eat lunch), contar (to tell), costar (to cost), encontrar (to find), recordar (to remember), and volver (to return).

JUGAR   to play (a sport or game)
Present: j**ue**go, j**ue**gas, j**ue**ga, **jugamos, jugáis,** j**ue**gan
Preterit: jug**ué**, jugaste, jugó, jugamos, jugasteis, jugaron

-er Verbs

DEFENDER (e to ie)   to defend
Present: defi**e**ndo, defi**e**ndes, defi**e**nde, defendemos, defendéis, defi**e**nden
Other verbs like defender include descender (to descend), entender (to understand, to hear), perder (to lose), and querer (to want).

VOLVER (o to ue)   to return
Present: v**ue**lvo, v**ue**lves, v**ue**lve, volvemos, volvéis, v**ue**lven
Another verb like volver is poder (to be able to, can).

-ir Verbs

PEDIR (e to i)   to ask for   Gerund: pidiendo

Present: p**i**do, p**i**des, p**i**de, pedimos, pedís, p**i**den
Preterit: pedí, pediste, pidió, pedimos, pedisteis, p**i**dieron
Other verbs like pedir include impedir (to prevent), medir (to measure), repetir (to repeat), and servir (to serve).

SENTIR (e to ie, i)   to feel   Gerund: sintiendo

Present: s**ie**nto, s**ie**ntes, s**ie**nte, sentimos, sentís, s**ie**nten
Preterit: sentí, sentiste, sintió, sentimos, sentisteis, sintieron
Other verbs like sentir include advertir (to warn, to notify), consentir (to consent), mentir (to lie), preferir (to prefer), and referir (to refer).

DORMIR (o to ue, u)   to sleep   Gerund: d**u**rmiendo

Present: d**ue**rmo, d**ue**rmes, d**ue**rme, dormimos, dormís, d**ue**rmen
Preterit: dormí, dormiste, d**u**rmió, dormimos, dormisteis, d**u**rmieron
Another verb like dormir is morir (to die).

-uir Verbs (except *-guir*)

INCLUIR (i to y) **to include** Gerund: incluyendo

Present: incluyo, incluyes, incluye, incluimos, incluís, incluyen
Preterit: incluí, incluiste, incluyó, incluimos, incluisteis, incluyeron
Other verbs like incluir include concluir (to conclude, to end), construir (to construct), contribuir (to contribute), destruir (to destroy), and sustituir (to substitue).

-eer Verbs

LEER (i to y) **to read**
Preterit: leí, leíste, leyó, leímos, leísteis, leyeron

-iar Verbs

ENVIAR (i to í) **to send**
Present: envío, envías, envía, enviamos, enviáis, envían
Other verbs like enviar include confiar + en (to confide in), guiar (to guide), and variar (to vary).

-uar Verbs

ACTUAR (u to ú) **to act**
Present: actúo, actúas, actúa, actuamos, actuáis, actúan
Another verb like actuar is continuar (to continue).

Spelling-Change Verbs

-cer or *-cir* Verbs

CONVENCER (c to z) **to convince**
Present: convenzo, convences, convence, convencemos, convencéis, convencen

CONOCER (c to zc) **to know**
Present: conozco, conoces, conoce, conocemos, conocéis, conocen

-ger or *-gir* Verbs

EXIGIR (g to j) **to demand**
Present: exijo, exiges, exige, exigimos, exigís, exigen

-guir **Verbs**

DISTINGUIR (gu to g)   to distinguish
Present: distingo, distingues, distingue, distinguimos, distinguís, distinguen

-car **Verbs**

BUSCAR (c to qu)   to look for
Preterit: busqué, buscaste, buscó, buscamos, buscasteis, buscaron

-gar **Verbs**

PAGAR (g to gu)   to pay
Preterit: pagué, pagaste, pagó, pagamos, pagasteis, pagaron

-zar **Verbs**

GOZAR (z to c)   to enjoy
Preterit: gocé, gozaste, gozó, gozamos, gozasteis, gozaron

Irregular Verbs

DAR   to give

Present: doy, das, da, damos, dáis, dan
Preterit: di, diste, dio, dimos, disteis, dieron

DECIR   to say   Gerund: diciendo

Past participle: dicho
Present: digo, dices, dice, decimos, decís, dicen
Preterit: dije, dijiste, dijo, dijimos, dijisteis, dijeron
Future: diré, dirás, dirá, diremos, diréis, dirán
Conditional: diría, dirías, diría, diríamos, diríais, dirían

ESTAR   to be

Present: estoy, estás, está, estamos, estáis, **están**
Preterit: estuve, estuviste, estuvo, estuvimos, estuvisteis, estuvieron

HACER   to make, to do   Past participle: hecho

Present: hago, haces, hace, hacemos, hacéis, hacen
Preterit: hice, hiciste, hizo, hicimos, hicisteis, hicieron
Future: haré, harás, hará, haremos, haréis, harán
Conditional: haría, harías, haría, haríamos, haríais, harían

IR   **to go**   **Gerund:** yendo

Present: voy, vas, va, vamos, vais, van
Preterit: fui, fuiste, fue, fuimos, fuisteis, fueron
Imperfect: iba, ibas, iba, íbamos, ibais, iban

OÍR   **to hear**   **Gerund:** oyendo

Present: oigo, oyes, oye, oímos, oís, oyen
Preterit: oí, oíste, oyó, oímos, oísteis, oyeron

PODER (o to ue)   **to be able to, can**   **Gerund:** pudiendo

Present: puedo, puedes, puede, podemos, podéis, pueden
Preterit: pude, pudiste, pudo, pudimos, pudisteis, pudieron
Future: podré, podrás, podrá, podremos, podréis, podrán
Conditional: podría, podrías, podría, podríamos, podríais, podrían

PONER   **to put**   **Past participle:** puesto

Present: pongo, pones, pone, ponemos, ponéis, ponen
Preterit: puse, pusiste, puso, pusimos, pusisteis, pusieron
Future: pondré, pondrás, pondrá, pondremos, pondréis, pondrán
Conditional: pondría, pondrías, pondría, pondríamos, pondríais, pondrían

QUERER   **to want**

Present: quiero, quieres, quiere, queremos, queréis, quieren
Preterit: quise, quisiste, quiso, quisimos, quisisteis, quisieron
Future: querré, querrás, querrá, querremos, querréis, querrán
Conditional: querría, querrías, querría, querríamos, querríais, querrían

SABER   **to know**

Present: sé, sabes, sabe, sabemos, sabéis, saben
Preterit: supe, supiste, supo, supimos, supisteis, supieron
Future: sabré, sabrás, sabrá, sabremos, sabréis, sabrán
Conditional: sabría, sabrías, sabría, sabríamos, sabríais, sabrían

SALIR   **to go out, to leave**

Present: salgo, sales, sale, salimos, saléis, salen
Future: saldré, saldrás, saldrá, saldremos, saldréis, saldrán
Conditional: saldría, saldrías, saldría, saldríamos, saldríais, saldrían

SER to be

Present: soy, eres, es, somos, sois, son
Preterit: fui, fuiste, fue, fuimos, fuisteis, fueron
Imperfect: era, eras, era, éramos, erais, eran

TENER to have

Present: tengo, tienes, tiene, tenemos, tenéis, tienen
Preterit: tuve, tuviste, tuvo, tuvimos, tuvisteis, tuvieron
Future: tendré, tendrás, tendrá, tendremos, tendréis, tendrán
Conditional: tendría, tendrías, tendría, tendríamos, tendríais, tendrían

TRAER to bring   Past participle: traído

Present: traigo, traes, trae, traemos, traéis, traen
Preterit: traje, trajiste, trajo, trajimos, trajisteis, trajeron

VENIR to come   Gerund: viniendo

Present: vengo, vienes, viene, venimos, venís, vienen
Preterit: vine, viniste, vino, vinimos, vinisteis, vinieron
Future: vendré, vendrás, vendrá, vendremos, vendréis, vendrán
Conditional: vendría, vendrías, vendría, vendríamos, vendríais, vendrían

VER to see   Past participle: visto

Present: veo, ves, ve, vemos, veis, ven
Preterit: vi, viste, vio, vimos, visteis, vieron
Imperfect: veía, veías, veía, veíamos, veíais, veían

Appendix B

Dictionaries

Spanish to English

This dictionary follows international alphabetic order. The Spanish letter combination *ch* and *ll* are not treated as separate letters; therefore, *ch* will follow *cg* instead of being at the end of *c*, and *ll* will appear after *lk* and not at the end of *l*. Note that *ñ* is treated as a separate letter and follows *n* in alphabetical order.

a at, to

abogado (*m.*) lawyer

abordar to board

abrazar to embrace, to hug

abrigo (*m.*) overcoat

abril April

abrir to open

aceite (*m.*) oil

acompañar to accompany

aconsejable advisable

adiós good-bye

aduana (*f.*) customs

advertir (ie) warn

aeromozo(a) steward(ess)

aeropuerto (*m.*) airport

agosto August

agua (*f.*) water

ahora now

ahorrar to save

ajo (*m.*) garlic

al to the

al centro downtown

alegre happy

Alemania Germany

algodón (*m.*) cotton

allá there

almacén (*m.*) department store

alquilar to rent

alrededor de around

alto tall

amarillo yellow

anaranjado orange

andar to walk

antes (de) before

aprender to learn

aquí here

arreglar to adjust, to fix

arroz (*m.*) rice

asado baked, roasted

ascensor (*m.*) elevator

asegurar to guarantee

así so, thus

asiento (*m.*) seat

aterrizar to land

avión (*m.*) airplane

aviso warning

ayer yesterday

ayudar to help

azúcar (*m.*) sugar

azul blue

bajar to go down

bajo short

banco bank

baño bathroom

barbero hairdresser

bastante enough, quite, rather

beber to drink

bien well

bienvenido welcome

bistec (*m.*) beef steak

bizcocho biscuit, sponge cake

blanco white

boca mouth

boleto ticket

bolígrafo ballpoint pen

bolsa pocketbook

bonito pretty

botella bottle

brazo arm

bueno good

buscar to look for

buzón (*m.*) mailbox

caja box

caja fuerte safe, safe-deposit box

cajero automático automatic teller machine

cama bed

camarero (a) waiter(ress)

cambiar to change

cambio de dinero money exchange

camisa shirt, tailored

carne (*f.*) meat

carta letter, menu, card

cartera briefcase, wallet

casa house

casi almost

centro comercial mall

cerca (de) near

cerrar (ie) to close

cerveza beer

césped (*m.*) lawn

chaleco salvavidas life vest

champiñon (*m.*) mushroom

champú (*m.*) shampoo

cheque (*m.*) check

cheque de viajero (*m.*) traveler's check

ciento hundred

cinco five

cincuenta fifty

cine (*m.*) movies

cinturón (*m.*) belt

cinturón de seguridad (*m.*) seat belt

claro light, of course

cobrar to cash

coche (*m.*) car

comenzar (ie) to begin

comer to eat

comisaría de policía police station

cómo how

comprar to buy, to purchase

comprender to understand

con with

contestar to answer

contra against

correo electrónico e-mail

corto short

creer to believe

cruzar to cross

cuál which

cuándo when

cuánto how much, many

cuarenta forty

cuarto room, quarter

cuarto de baño bathroom

cuatro four

cucharita teaspoon

cuchillo knife

dar to give

de about, from, of

de nada you're welcome

de nuevo again

debajo de below, beneath, under

deber to owe

deber + infinitive to have to + infinitive

decir to say, to tell

dejar to allow, to leave

delante de in front of

demasiado too much

descuento discount

desde from, since

después (de) after

detrás de behind

día (*m.*) day

diciembre December

diente (*m.*) tooth

diez ten

dinero currency, money

doce twelve

dolor (*m.*) pain

domingo Sunday

dónde where

dos two

durante during

durar to last

empezar (ie) to begin

en in

encontrar (ue) to find, to meet

enero January

enfermo sick

enfrente de in front of

entre among, between

escala stop-over

escribir to write

escuchar to listen to

esperar to hope, to wait

Estados Unidos United States

estar to be

este (*m.*) East

estudiar to study

evitar to avoid

fácil easy

factura bill, invoice

faltar to lack, to miss

febrero February

feo ugly

firmar to sign

flaco thin

folleto pamphlet

fresa strawberry

frito fried

fumar to smoke

gerente (*m.*) manager

gobernanta maid service

grande big

gustar to like

habitación (*f.*) room

hablar to speak, to talk

hacer to do, to make

hacia toward

hasta until

helado ice cream

hijo(a) child, son (daughter)

hora hour, time

hoy today

huevo egg

iglesia church

impermeable (*m.*) raincoat

ir to go

joven young

joya jewel

jueves (*m.*) Thursday

jugar to play

jugo juice

juguete (*m.*) toy

julio July

junio June

lápiz (*m.*) pencil

lavandería laundry

lavar (se) to wash (oneself)

leche (*f.*) milk

leer to read

librería bookstore

libro book

llave (*f.*) key

llegar to arrive

llevar to carry, to wear

lugar (*m.*) place

lunes (*m.*) Monday

madre (*f.*) mother

mandar to order, to send

mano (*f.*) hand

mantequilla butter

manzana apple

mañana tomorrow, morning

marroquinería leather goods store

martes (*m.*) Tuesday

marzo March

más more

mayo May

mejor better

menos less

mensaje (*m.*) message

mercado market

mes (*m.*) month

mesa table

metro subway

mezclar to mix

miércoles (*m.*) Wednesday

mil thousand

mirar to look at, to watch

montar to go up, to ride

monto sum, total

mostrar (**ue**) to show

mucho much, many

muebles (*m. pl.*) furniture

museo museum

muy very

nadie nobody

naipe (*m.*) card

negro black

noche (*f.*) evening

norte (*m.*) north

noventa ninety

noviembre November

nueve nine

nuevo new

nuez (*f.*) nut, walnut

ochenta eighty

ocho eight

octeto byte

octubre October

oeste (*m.*) west

oír to hear

once eleven

otoño autumn

padre (*m.*) father

pagar to pay

país (*m.*) country

pan (*m.*) bread

panadería bakery

pantalones (*m. pl.*) pants

papa potato

papel (*m.*) paper

para for

parada stop

partir to divide

pasado last

pasar to pass, to spend time

pastel (*m.*) cake, pie

pastilla pill

pato duck

pavo turkey

película film, movie, roll (film)

pelo hair

pensar to think

pequeño small

perder (**ie**) to lose, to miss

periódico newspaper

pez (*m.*) fish

piscina swimming pool

piso floor (story)

planta baja ground floor

playa beach

poco little, few

poder (**ue**) to be able

pollo chicken

poner to put

por along, by, per, through

por favor please

por qué why

portero bellman

postre (*m.*) dessert

precio price

preguntar to ask

prestar to lend

primavera spring

primero first

pronóstico weather forecast

pronto soon

próximo next

qué what

querer (**ie**) to want

queso cheese

quién who, whom

quince   fifteen

quitar   to leave

recibir   to receive

recibo   receipt

recordar (ue)   to remember

regresar   to return

reloj (*m.*)   clock, watch

revista   magazine

rojo   red

ropa   clothing

roto   broken

sábado   Saturday

sacar   to take out

sal (*f.*)   salt

sala   living room

salida   departure, exit, gate

salir   to go out, to leave, to de-board, to exit

seguir (i)   to follow, continue

seis   six

sello   stamp

semana   week

señor (*m.*)   sir, Mr.

señora   Mrs., lady

señorita   Miss, young lady

septiembre   September

ser   to be

sesenta   sixty

setenta   seventy

siempre   always

siete   seven

sin   without

sobre   on, upon

subir   to climb, to go up

sucio   dirty

sucursal (*f.*)   branch

sur (*m.*)   South

tabaquería   tobacco store

también   also, too

tan   as, so

tarde   late

tarde (*f.*)   afternoon

tarifa   rate

tasa   rate

temprano   early

tenedor (*m.*)   fork, holder

tener   to have

tener que + infinitive   to have to + infinitive

tiempo   time, weather

tienda   store

tirar   to pull, to shoot, to throw

toalla   towel

tocar   to touch

todavía   still, yet

todo   all

tomar   to take

traer   to bring

traje (*m.*)   suit

trece   thirteen

treinta   thirty

tren (*m.*)   train

tres   three

último   last

uno   one

valer   to be worth

vaso   glass

veinte   twenty

vender   to sell

venir   to come

venta   sale

ventana   window

ver   to see

verano   summer

verde   green

viaje (*m.*)   trip

viernes (*m.*)   Friday

vivir   to live

volver(ue)   to return

vuelo   flight

ya   already

zapato   shoe

English to Spanish

able (to be)   poder (ue)

about   de

above   encima de

to accompany   acompañar

ad   anuncio (*m.*)

address   dirección (*f.*)

to adjust   arreglar

advisable aconsejable

afraid (to be afraid [of]) tener miedo [de]

after después (de)

afternoon tarde (*f.*)

again de nuevo

against contra

ago hace

to agree with estar de acuerdo con

air conditioning aire acondicionado (*m.*)

airline aerolínea

airport aeropuerto

all todo

almost casi

already ya

also también

always siempre

American consulate consulado americano

American embassy embajada americana

to answer contestar

April abril

around alrededor (de)

to arrive llegar

ashtray cenicero

to ask preguntar, pedir

August agosto

automatic teller machine cajero automático

autumn otoño

to avoid evitar

bad malo

bag saco

baggage claim area reclamo de equipage

bakery panadería

ballpoint pen bolígrafo

Band-Aid curita

bank banco

bathing suit traje de baño (*m.*)

bathrooms baño

to be estar, ser

beach playa

beer cerveza

before antes (de)

to begin comenzar, empezar (ie)

behind detrás (de)

to believe creer

bellman portero

below debajo de

beneath debajo de

better mejor

between entre

big grande

bill factura

black negro

blanket manta

blue azul

to board abordar

book libro

bookstore librería

booth (phone) cabina telefónica

to borrow prestar

bottle botella

box caja

boyfriend novio

branch (office) sucursal (*f.*)

brand name marca

bread pan (*m.*)

briefcase cartera (*f.*)

to bring traer

broiled a la parrilla

brown pardo, marrón

butter mantequilla

to buy comprar

by por

to call telefonear

can lata (*f.*)

candy dulces (*m. pl.*)

candy store confitería

cane bastón (*m.*)

car coche (*m.*), automóvil (*m.*), carro

cart carrito

to cash a check cobrar un cheque

cashier cajero

chair silla

to change cambiar

change (coins) moneda

check cheque (*m.*)

checkbook chequera

cheese queso

chicken pollo

child hijo

church iglesia

to close cerrar (ie)

clothing ropa

coffee café (*m.*)

comb peine (*m.*)

to come venir

to continue continuar, seguir (i)

corner rincón (*m.*)

to cost costar (ue)

cup taza, copa

customer cliente (*m.*)

customs aduana

daughter hija

day día (*m.*)

December diciembre

to decide decidir

to declare declarar

delicatessen tienda de ultramarinos

to deliver entregar

dentist dentista (*m.*)

department store almacén (*m.*)

departure salida

dessert postre (*m.*)

to dial marcar

diaper (disposable) pañal desechable (*m.*)

difficult difícil

dirty sucio

discount descuento, rebaja

to do hacer

doctor doctor (*m.*), médico

door puerta

doorman portero

dozen docena

to drink beber

duck pato

during durante

e-mail correo electrónico

early temprano

to earn ganar

East este (*m.*)

easy fácil

to eat comer

egg huevo

eight ocho

eighteen dieciocho

eighty ochenta

elevator ascensor (*m.*)

eleven once

employee empleado

to end terminar

to enjoy gozar

enough bastante

entrance entrada

envelope sobre (*m.*)

exchange rate tasa de cambio

exit salida

to explain explicar

to express expresar

facing frente a

far (from) lejos (de)

father padre (*m.*)

February febrero

to feel sentirse (ie)

fifteen quince

fifty cincuenta

to fill (out) llenar

film película

to find hallar, encontrar (ue)

fish pez (*m.*), pescado

five cinco

to fix arreglar

flight vuelo

to follow seguir (i)

for para, por

to forget olvidarse (de)

fork tenedor (*m.*)

forty cuarenta

four cuatro

fourteen catorce

Friday viernes (*m.*)

from de, desde

front, in front (of) delante (de)

front desk recepción (*f.*)

fruit fruta

gasoline gasolina

gate salida, puerta

girlfriend novia

to give dar

glass vaso

to go ir

to go down   bajar

to go out   salir

gold   oro

good   bueno

good-bye   adiós

gray   gris

green   verde

grocery store   abacería

hair   pelo

ham   jamón (*m.*)

hamburger   hamburguesa

hanger   percha

happy   alegre

hat   sombrero

to have   tener

to have to …   tener que + infinitive, deber + infinitive

to hear   oír

hello   buenos días

to help   ayudar

here   aquí

holiday   fiesta

to hope   esperar

hour   hora

house   casa

how   cómo

how much, many   cuánto

hundred   cien, ciento

hungry (to be hungry) tener hambre

hurry (to be in a hurry) tener prisa

ice cream   helado

ice cubes   cubitos de hielo

immediately   en seguida

in   en

instead of   en vez de

jacket   chaqueta

jam   mermelada

January   enero

jar   pomo

jelly   mermelada

jewelry store   joyería

juice   jugo

July   julio

June   junio

to keep   guardar

ketchup   salsa de tomate

key   llave (*f.*), tecla

knife   cuchillo

to land   aterrizar

to last   durar

last   pasado, último

late   tarde

late in arriving   en retraso

laundry   lavandería

to learn   aprender

leather   cuero

to leave   dejar, salir

to lend   prestar

less   menos

letter   carta

life vest   chaleco salvavidas

to like   gustar

liquor store   tienda de licores

to listen to   escuchar

little   poco

to live   vivir

lobster   langosta

to look at   mirar

to look for   buscar

to lose   perder (ie)

magazine   revista

maid   criada

maid service   gobernanta

mailbox   buzón (*m.*)

to make   hacer

mall   centro comercial

management   gestión (*f.*)

manager   gerente (*m.*)

March   marzo

May   mayo

to mean   significar

mechanic   mecánico

to meet   encontrar (ue)

menu   carta, menú (*m.*)

message   mensaje (*m.*)

milk   leche (*f.*)

to miss   perder (ie)

Monday   lunes (*m.*)

money   dinero

money exchange   cambio de dinero

month   mes (*m.*)

more   más

morning   mañana

mother   madre (*f.*)

movie   película

movies   cine (*m.*)

Mrs.   señora

museum   museo

mustard   mostaza

napkin   servilleta

near   cerca (de)

necessary   necesario

to need   necesitar

new   nuevo

news   noticias

newspaper   periódico

next   próximo

next to   al lado de

nice   simpático

nine   nueve

nineteen   diecinueve

ninety   noventa

nobody   nadie

north   norte (*m.*)

to notify, to warn   advertir (ie)

November   noviembre

now   ahora

October   octubre

of   de

of course   por supuesto, claro

often   a menudo

okay   de acuerdo

on   sobre

one   uno

onion   cebolla

to open   abrir

opposite   frente a

orange   anaranjado

orange   naranja

to order   mandar

out of order   fuera de servicio

to owe   deber

owner   propietario

package   paquete (*m.*)

pain   dolor (*m.*)

pamphlet   folleto

pants   pantalones (*m. pl.*)

paper   papel (*m.*)

parents   padres (*m. pl.*)

park   parque (*m.*)

passport   pasaporte (*m.*)

to pay   pagar

pencil   lápiz (*m.*)

pepper   pimienta

percent   por ciento

phone (public)   teléfono público

phone card   tarjeta telefónica

pie   pastel (*m.*)

piece   pedazo

pill   pastilla

pillow   almohada

pineapple   piña

place   lugar (*m.*)

plate   plato

to play (games)   jugar

to play (an instrument)   tocar

please   por favor

pocketbook   bolsa

police officer   agente de policía (*m.*)

police station   comisaría de policía (*f.*)

pool   piscina

porter   portero

postage   franqueo

postcard   tarjeta postal

potato   papa, patata

pound   libra

pretty   bonito

price   precio

problem   problema (*m.*)

to put   poner, colocar

quickly   rápidamente

raincoat   impermeable (*m.*)

rate   tarifa

rather   bastante

to read   leer

ready   listo

receipt   recibo

to receive   recibir

red   rojo

relatives   parientes (*m. pl.*)

to remember   recordar (ue)

to rent   alquilar

to **repair** reparar

to **repeat** repetir (i)

to **return** regresar, volver (ue)

rice arroz (*m.*)

roll (film) película

room cuarto

safe caja fuerte

safety pin seguro, imperdible (*m.*)

sale venta

salesperson vendedor (*m.*)

salt sal (*f.*)

salt shaker salero

Saturday sábado

to **say** decir

scissors tijeras

seafood mariscos

seat asiento

seat belt cinturón de seguridad (*m.*)

to **see** ver

to **sell** vender

to **send** mandar, enviar

to **send back** devolver (ue)

September septiembre

to **serve** servir (i)

to **settle** arreglar

seven siete

seventeen diecisiete

seventy setenta

shampoo champú (*m.*)

shirt camisa

shoe zapato

short bajo, corto

to **show** enseñar

sick enfermo

since desde

sir señor (*m.*)

sister hermana

six seis

sixteen dieciséis

sixty sesenta

skirt falda

slice trozo

small pequeño

to **smoke** fumar

sneakers tenis (*m. pl.*)

soap jabón (*m.*)

soap opera telenovela

soda gaseosa, soda

son hijo

soon pronto

South sur (*m.*)

South America Sud América (*f.*), América del Sur

Spain España

to **speak** hablar

to **spend money** gastar

to **spend time** pasar

spicy picante

spoon cuchara

spring primavera

stadium estadio

stain mancha

staircase escalera

stamp sello

stapler grapadora

still todavía

stop parada

stop-over escala

store tienda

string cuerda

student estudiante (*m. f.*)

to **study** estudiar

to **substitute** sustituir

subway metro

suddenly de repente

sugar azúcar (*m.*)

suit traje (*m.*), sastre (*m.*)

suitcase maleta

summer verano

Sunday domingo

sunglasses gafas de sol

suntan lotion loción de sol (*f.*)

supermarket supermercado

sweater suéter (*m.*)

to **swim** nadar

swimming pool piscina

T-shirt camiseta

table mesa

tailor sastre (*m.*)

to **take** tomar

take off despegue (*m.*)

to **take out** sacar

to **take place** tener lugar

to talk   hablar

tall   alto

tax   impuesto

tea   té (*m.*)

to teach   enseñar

teacher   profesor (*m.*)

telephone   teléfono

telephone book   guía telefónica

telephone number   número de teléfono

television   televisíon (*f.*)

television set   televisor (*m.*)

to tell   decir, contar (ue)

ten   diez

thank you   muchas gracias

theater   teatro

then   pues

there   allá

to think   pensar (ie)

thirsty (to be thirsty)   tener sed

thirteen   trece

thirty   treinta

thousand   mil

three   tres

through   por

Thursday   jueves (*m.*)

ticket   boleto

tie   corbata

time   tiempo, hora

time (at the same time)   al mismo tiempo

time (at what time?)   ¿a qué hora?

time (on time)   a tiempo

tip   propina

tire   goma, llanta

tissue   pañuelo de papel

to   a

tobacco store   tabaquería

today   hoy

tomorrow   mañana

too   también

too much   demasiado

tooth   diente (*m.*)

toothbrush   cepillo de los dientes

toothpaste   pasta dentífrica

toward   hacia

towel   toalla

toy   juguete (*m.*)

train   tren (*m.*)

to travel   viajar

traveler's check   cheque de viajero (*m.*)

trip   viaje (*m.*)

to turn   doblar

to turn off   apagar

to turn on   encender (ie)

twelve   doce

twenty   veinte

two   dos

umbrella   paraguas (*m.*)

under   debajo de

to understand   comprender, entender (ie)

United States   Estados Unidos

until   hasta

upon   sobre

value   valor (*m.*)

vegetable   legumbre (*f.*)

very   muy

to visit   visitar

to wait for   esperar

waiter   camarero

wallet   cartera

to want   querer (ie)

warning   aviso

to watch   mirar, guardar

to wear   llevar, usar

weather   tiempo

Wednesday   miércoles (*m.*)

week   semana

welcome   bienvenido

well   bien

west   oeste (*m.*)

what   qué

wheelchair   silla de ruedas

when   cuándo

where   dónde

which   cuál

white   blanco

who(m)   quién

why   por qué
window   ventana
window (ticket)   ventanilla
wine   vino
winter   invierno
without   sin
wool   lana
to work   funcionar, trabajar
worth (to be)   valer
to wrap   envolver (ue)
to write   escribir

yellow   amarillo
yesterday   ayer
yet   todavía
young   joven
you're welcome   de nada

zero   cero

Index

W–X–Y–Z